JOURNEY OF A DAYSMAN

THE LIFE AND LEGACY OF KELLY MILLER

IDA E. JONES

Seymour Press

Journey of a Daysman: The Life and Legacy of Kelly Miller

©Ida E. Jones 2024

© Seymour Press 2024
Lanham, MD

Cover Design by KINGLOPE

ISBN: 978-1-938373-78-7
LCCN: 2024950469

All Rights Reserved. No part of the book may be reproduced in any form without written permission from Seymour Press.

Table of Contents

List of Illustrations i

Acknowledgements v

Foreword vii

Preface xii

Introduction 1

One: Entry to a Land Made Sick by Strife: 1863-1879 21

Two: A Vastly Different Life: 1880-1889 60

Three: A New World: 1890-1916 92

Four: The Negro is Scarcely Considered: 1917-1925 161

Five: Yardstick of Progress: 1926-1939 232

Epilogue 285

Chronology of Miller's Life 290

Bibliography 298

Notes 309

Index 311

List of Illustrations

1. Kelly Miller 1880, Kelly Miller family papers, Stuart A. Rose Manuscript, Archives, and Rare Book Library Repository Emory University - pg. 33.
2. James Monroe Gregory, frontispiece image, *Frederick Douglass the Orator*, Springfield, MA, Willey Company, 1893 - pg. 77.
3. Francis Lewis Cardozo, Photo from Congress documents on Francis Lewis Cardozo. Public Domain image. - pg. 86.
4. Francis Grimke, Schomburg Center for Research in Black Culture, Photographs and Prints Division, The New York Public Library. "F. J. Grimké, a preacher of the New Democracy" New York Public Library Digital Collections. Accessed November 27, 2024 - pg. 102.
5. Alexander Crummell Schomburg Center for Research in Black Culture, Manuscripts, Archives and Rare Books Division, The New York Public Library. "Alexander Crummell, clergyman, teacher and missionary" New York Public Library Digital Collections. Accessed November 27, 2024 - pg. 109.
6. https://digitalcollections.nypl.org/items/a7d0e925-f893-eff6-e040-e00a18060357 - pg. 109.
7. JW Cromwell Schomburg Center for Research in Black Culture, Manuscripts, Archives and Rare Books Division, The New York Public Library. "J. W. Cromwell" New York Public Library Digital Collections. Accessed November 27, 2024 - pg. 109.
8. Dunbar Schomburg Center for Research in Black Culture, Jean Blackwell Hutson Research and Reference Division, The New York Public Library.

"Paul Lawrence Dunbar." New York Public Library Digital Collections. - pg. 109.
9. American Negro Academy tearsheet, Schomburg Center for Research in Black Culture Accessed August 29, 2024
10. Young Kelly Miller, Scurlock Collection, Archives Center, National Museum of American History, Smithsonian Institution. - pg. 114.
11. Miller Sheet Music, Jesse Moorland Music Collection, JEM 25.393 Moorland Spingarn Research Center, Howard University - pg. 120.
12. Miller Sigma Pi Phi, Epsilon Boule, Mary Church Terrell papers Box 149-5 folder 7, Moorland Spingarn Research Center, Howard University - pg. 129.
13. Mary Church Terrell Schomburg Center for Research in Black Culture, Jean Blackwell Hutson Research and Reference Division, The New York Public Library. "Mrs. Mary Church Terrell, President of the National Association of Colored Women" New York Public Library Digital Collections. Accessed November 27, 2024 - pg. 135.
14. Nannie Helen Burroughs Schomburg Center for Research in Black Culture, Jean Blackwell Hutson Research and Reference Division, The New York Public Library. "Miss Nannie H. Burroughs." New York Public Library Digital Collections. Accessed November 27, 2024 - pg. 138.
15. Charlotte Hawkins Brown Schomburg Center for Research in Black Culture, Jean Blackwell Hutson Research and Reference Division, The New York Public Library. "Charlotte Hawkins Brown." New York Public Library Digital Collections. Accessed

November 27, 2024. Kelly Miller and Annie May Butler, in Atlantic City, New Jersey - pg. 140.
16. Miller with a founder of the West Virginia Colored Institute Byrd Prillerman (seated) and Tuskegee Institute founder Booker T. Washington in West Virginia. West Virginia - pg. 149.
17. Schomburg Center for Research in Black Culture, Jean Blackwell Hutson Research and Reference Division, The New York Public Library. "Kelly Miller, LL.D.; Professor of Mathematics, Howard University, Washington, D.C.; Corresponding Secretary, National Sociological Society; Member of the Commission on the Race Problem, Sociological Society." New York Public Library Digital Collections. Accessed August 29, 2024.
18. Colored Yeowomen Schomburg Center for Research in Black Culture, Jean Blackwell Hutson Research and Reference Division, The New York Public Library. "Colored Yeowomen; Employees of Navy Department, Washington, D.C." New York Public Library Digital Collections. Accessed August 29, 2024 - pg. 171.
19. "A Big Job for Anybody's Mule," depicts the obstacles to forming a viable Negro Sanhedrin, *Washington Tribune*, January 24, 1924. - pg. 207.
20. Alain Locke Schomburg Center for Research in Black Culture, Photographs and Prints Division, The New York Public Library. "Alain Locke " New York Public Library Digital Collections. Accessed November 27, 2024 - pg. 215.
21. Kelly Miller standing, Scurlock Collection, Archives Center, National Museum of American History, Smithsonian Institution - pg. 226.
22. HU Alumni Association of Los Angeles, 1918 - pg. 230.

23. Miller, Johnson, Left to right Mrs. Annie Butler Miller, President Mordecai Johnson, Mrs. Emmett J. Scott and Miller HUA-1537 Moorland Spingarn Research Center, Howard University. - pg. 250.
24. Miller garden 2225 4th Street, NW circa 1930, Scurlock Collection, Archives Center, National Museum of American History, Smithsonian Institution. - pg. 269.
25. Kelly Miller with dog on front porch, August 15, 1936. Possibly from Kelly Miller family papers, Stuart A. Rose Manuscript, Archives, and Rare Book Library Repository Emory University. - pg. 270.

Acknowledgments

First, I give honor to God for the opportunity to discover the work and legacy of Kelly Miller, Jr. during my tenure at Howard University's Moorland-Spingarn Research Center. Since the initial encounter with Miller in 2004, the providential hand of God provided me with a deeper understanding of the purpose and potential of biography and blessed me with the ability to share the life of this remarkable human being.

Dr. Estrelda Alexander, Vanderlyn Hampton, and Alexander Stewart assisted me in reimaging Kelly Miller. Scholars of the African American Christian tradition through the Apostolic-Pentecostal-Charismatic tradition heard another voice speaking through the pen of Miller. Thank you for amplifying that voice and allowing me to reimagine Miller in a Black-centered, ecumenical agency of self-help throughout his life.

Thank you, Dr. Tommy J. Curry, for your willingness to write a forward for the book. I greatly appreciate how you situate Miller in a fashion that others of his ilk moved. I plan to employ and build upon this new paradigm regarding my historical heroes and sheroes.

Archival colleagues, historians and memory workers Matthew Miller West Virginia History and Archives; David Haberstich and Kay Peterson of the National Museum of American History Smithsonian Institution; Sonja N. Woods Moorland Spingarn Research Center; Elizabeth Clark-Lewis and C.R. Gibbs; Annie B. Luke and Sam Perryman wealth of professional and personal encouragement made this volume a reality.

Since my first encounter with Kelly Miller, character and integrity surfaced as essential attributes for leadership. His sober outlook on the condition and potential of African Americans is mirrored in our contemporary times.

The Miller clan rounded out the picture of this little-known daysman. His great-granddaughter, the late Reverend Stephanie Patrice Newman connected me to her cousin, Hank MacIntosh, son of, the late Gloria Miller Clark. Mrs. Gloria Miller Clark lived with her grandfather Kelly Miller when her father Isaac Newman Miller died unexpectedly, leaving a wife and two daughters in 1928. May Miller Sullivan lovingly shared her father with the ages by donating the unfinished autobiography of this self-proclaimed iconoclast and independent thinker. She attempted to finish his biography, but did not live to finish her father's work.

Lastly, my family has shown unflagging support, as have my parents, the late Enos Adolphus Jones and the late Iris Elizabeth Greenidge Jones, who were attentive ears, financial backers, prayer warriors, and confidants. The support and kind words of uncle Ralph Greenidge, late uncle Arthur Greenidge, aunt the late Elfreda Jones Solomon, and cousins Wendy House, the late Gwen Foster Allen, and the late Carol Greenidge House.

Foreword

From the inherent sense of self-respect and in vindication of the essential claims of humanity, the Negro must insist that his blood is as good as any which courses through human veins.

The Everlasting Stain
Kelly Miller, 1924

The polarized 21st century, in which political ideology and the declaration of one's racial identity are the ground of *politics itself*, makes it difficult to appreciate—much less conceptualize—the philosophical radicality of a historical figure like Kelly Miller. By contemporary standards, he would be considered conservative, for he emphasized political strategy and the calculated use of the ballot rather than Pan-Africanism or black nationalism. He understood the seemingly insurmountable obstacles while steadfastly opposing the growing tide of black pessimism. Miller believed the foundation of racial uplift and improvement was the moral elevation and the reclamation of Black civilization found throughout history.

These methods dedicated to shaping the evolving spiritual qualities of black people are unrecognizable to many 21st-century scholars. In his time, Miller was universally recognized as a race man dedicated to the improvement, education, and political power of Black people. Yet, he is rarely engaged by contemporary scholars of black intellectual history. Miller is viewed as a historical relic, out of touch with contemporary black political sentiment and irrelevant to current theories of black progress. However, it is exactly this anachronistic impulse and diametrically opposite perspective on seemingly irreconcilable differences that black scholars should attend to.

Kelly Miller was a renowned early 20th-century thinker who his peers of his day saw as a formidable theorist of America's race problem. He systematically engaged the work of W. E. B. DuBois and Booker T. Washington and often suggested a middle ground between their positions. As a reconciler and a harmonizer of two opposing movements among black people, Miller was a remarkable anomaly in an "age of impatience" that "cared little for philosophical analysis" or any philosophical discussion" for want of a creed.

Miller remains an ignored intellectual figure despite his impact on black philosophy, history, and social science throughout the 19th and early 20th centuries. For years, black academics have devoted their attention to exploring the thoughts of W. E. B. DuBois, Frederick Douglass, and Anna Julia Cooper because these figures seem more compatible with American post-civil rights ideology. Despite DuBois's Pan-Africanism, Douglass's dedication to the Haitian Revolution, and Cooper's emphasis on black homes and families, these thinkers have been interpreted as proponents of American liberalism, integration, and feminism.

Any movement does not encapsulate Miller easily, for he believed the assimilation of black people into American society had to be based on acknowledging the real irreverence the white race had for equality. He understood the role of political power and the need to manipulate the values and economic interests of the white race. His works did not appeal to the better sentiments of whites, yet he cherished the humility of black people and the lessons it offered American democracy. Because of this, his complexities resist being easily incorporated into pre-existing academic canons despite his moderate political stance.

Miller's realism burdened his mind, just as pessimism weighed upon his heart. He did not believe that faith in the moral conscience of American or European whites would ever arrest their greed or thirst for blood, but he believed in the birthright and strength of the black race. Not one for mincing words concerning white racism, he understood that claims of white supremacy were fed by the delusions about an exclusive right to civilization. "Civilization," penned Miller, "is not a spontaneous generation with any race or nation known to history, but the torch is handed down from race to race and from age to age, [that] gains in brilliance as it goes," and the white race was no more responsible for civilization than the races preceding them. For him, racism was the only reason that the development of the American Negro's brilliance through education and specialized work would be resented by whites. As Miller explained *in An Appeal to Conscience*, "[t] he more progressive and ambitious the Negro becomes, the less tolerable he seems to be to his white lord and master. The good old Negro slave who was ever faithful and loyal to the welfare of his lord and master was always acceptable to him. But his more ambitious son, with a college diploma in his knapsack, is *persona non grata*".

Throughout the 1920s, Miller articulated an account of racism as a consequence of the imperial aspirations of Europe and the United States that made equality of black Americans and the darker races the world over an insurmountable challenge. In *The Everlasting Stain*, he explains that though its malignity may be modified, its intensity could be mitigated by wise and sensible procedure "the Negro did not create or control prejudice and mournful lamentations were of no avail. For him, white people's attempt to create history and spread civilization made racial equality a struggle against white hatred, nationalism, and capitalist greed. However, he sought to refute the growing pessimism of leading race men and women through social-scientific and philosophical reflection. For example, In a scathing response to Felton Johnson's poem "Tired," Miller asserted that a "pessimist is apt to be a moral and intellectual dyspeptic"... which causes mental indigestion." Instead, Miller demanded faith in the strength of the demand by the Negro to realize his humanity.

For over a decade, Dr. Jones' *work has* inspired historians and has been the authoritative text on Miller's life and career. The republication of her work is long overdue and shows there is still much to be learned from research on this important figure. Jones's appreciation for Miller's painstakingly arduous service to black Americans is seen on every page and line of this book. She perfectly captures the multi-dimensionality of Miller's brilliance as a mathematician and social theorist. She carefully explains how his expertise developed across numerous fields and prepared him to comment on statistical methodology, moral education, and theories of racial evolution and American race relations.

Jones choice of the Biblical figure of the daysman as a type of Christ whose position between humanity and divinity is sacrificial and empathic" communicates the importance of Miller's work and life. She explains that the role of the daysman, as found in the book of Job Chapter 9, is to serve as an arbiter, umpire, or mediator. Jones explores how Miller placed himself between two opposing theories of racial development and uplift. The discord between manual labor advocated by Booker T. Washington and the liberal arts or spiritual program of DuBois created a niche for Miller's thinking about the socio-political program of Black folks. Jones describes how, through university battles, personal struggles, and world wars, Miller's public proclamations and writings championed black integrity and manhood as he contextualized arguments concerning black womanhood against charges of misogyny that became a common slander against 19th-century black male intellectuals.

In her interpretation of Miller's life, Jones insists upon historical rigor and nuance, offering us an opportunity to understand Miller as human—not a pristine figure nor an idol. Though Miller was dedicated to racial progress and bound to his Americanism and unfailing hope in the strength of Black folk's souls., Jones' work narrates his life through triumph and turmoil and presents him as perfectly flawed and emergent. She must be commended and praised for this sterling contribution to black intellectual history and thought. We are all indebted to her historical acumen and passion for Kelly Miller.

Dr. Tommy J. Curry
University of Edinburgh

Preface

This work is more than a tribute to the creation of the Moorland-Spingarn Research Center or the recounting of the politics at Howard University during Kelly Miller's tenure first as a student, then professor, then dean. Rather, it attempts to situate the private, public, and polemic life of a man who exemplifies

My work, born of my intellectual fascination with all things Miller, borrows heavily from his unpublished autobiography and the unpublished biographical work of his eldest daughter, May Miller Sullivan, and his published and unpublished Newspaper articles. It attempts to present Miller in objective fullness: a life of family, friends, love, loss, hope, despair, awareness, and ambivalence. Miller experienced all these things and weathered those emotional storms with sobriety and an argus-eyed focus on locating the truth. Hopefully, readers will learn and appreciate the sacrifice, heart, and desire of a man whose simplicity and selflessness are worthy of exploring and emulating.

His autobiography interlaced American history from Emancipation to Reconstruction to World War I and the Great Depression throughout its pages. His was an authentic African American story of a contented childhood that incorporated grief of loss. He believed his divinely orchestrated life was a median between slavery and freedom, despair and hope. And that placed him and his contemporaries between the chasm of a dark past and a bright future in which their successes, failures, drive, and depth would indelibly mark future generations into the next century. Like the daysman he modeled, Miller strove to harmonize the past and present, thus striking a balance and mediating opposing perspectives through a life dedicated to learning, sharing, and increasing the knowledge of blacks and all Americans.

Miller engendered several eponymous titles. Some of these, including "World's Greatest Unknown Negro," "Belated Rationalist," "Sage of the Potomac," and "Lighting Calculator" were complimentary. Others, such as "Contemptible Cur," and "Old Turk" were less so; yet, regardless of the labels, Miller was not swayed by flattery or derision but plotted a life path, that sought to locate and communicate truth through service. His head and hand were guided by the heart to live a life grounded in understanding the eternal consequences of moral accountability. Miller believed that education made men and women wiser and more efficient but that the intellect should not exert sovereignty over morality. There had to be a synergy since education alone could not make a whole person.

Miller preached this unique doctrine of education and morality in every hill and dale where African American children could be inspired. Whether he reached one or one hundred he strived to remain true to his principles throughout his life.

Lately, Miller's life has piqued the interest of the academy as new paradigms are formed. Unfortunately, though Miller left a wealth of writings about race, education, gender, politics, and contemporary issues of his day, he left no institution or school of thought.

I have attempted to faithfully present the private, public, and polemic dimensions of a life dedicated to racial uplift through mediating and harmonizing disparate ideas. Hopefully, readers of this volume will become acquainted with the man I have come to respect and appreciate as one who wrote and recited poetry, adored his family, found humor in witty jokes, and loved and promoted his race and will learn to appreciate the sacrifice, heart, and desire of a man whose simplicity and selflessness is worthy of exploring and at least in part emulating. This kind of life is worthy of recognition and mining for techniques of how to weather national popularity, mediocrity, and obscurity with grace.

Introduction

> I am anxious about many things concerning the Negro race. I am anxious about its political rights, its civil privileges, industrial outlook, educational opportunity, but my chief anxiety is that it will persevere in the eternal moral and spiritual verities...If it will but persevere in these things all things will be added in the fulness (sic) of time.
>
> "The Heart of the Race Problem,"
> Kelly Miller, 1909.

In 1909, Kelly Miller penned an article entitled "The Heart of the Race Problem," to explain the global problem of race and the uniqueness of the American situation. Though he understood that imperialism, colonialism, and tribal wars had reduced black people across the globe to culturally, socially, and ideologically inferior positions, he saw the American example differently. For him, the social, geographical, and political interactions between this country's white and black people afforded an opportunity for racial reconciliation. Most black people were not leaving for Africa or other colonies. America's destiny rested on creating equal terms for all its citizens. Thus, Miller believed the heart of the race problem lies in devising means for accomplishing social equality through education. For him, the four tenets of education—morality, character, patriotism, and virtue—could "enable us to understand, not only the nature around [us], but the far more intricate problems of the relation of man to man."[1] He saw that exposure of Americans of all strata to education and human contact without stereotypes and prejudice could overcome narrow-mindedness.

In the pseudoscientific era of the early 1900s, Charles Darwin's evolutionary theory of the "survival of the fittest" was appropriated by academic, legal, and government agencies to circumscribe the boundaries of African American achievement. Popular culture feasted on a bevy of minstrel shows where white men depicted contrived antebellum southern plantation life. These primarily Irish and Jewish actors entertained mostly northern white audiences by donning burned cork make-up affecting the sooty complexion of blackness and speaking in broken English to convey the childlike simplicity many attributed to black Americans. Concurrently, silent films such as Thomas Alva Edison's *Watermelon Contest* and *Chicken Thieves* and D.W. Griffith's *The Birth of a Nation* employed a new medium for African Americans' denigration by portraying black people as simple-minded, violent, criminals, or sexually wanton creatures. These acceptable forms of entertainment expressed what was considered a "believable" account of black life, so much so that President Woodrow Wilson remarked that Griffith's incendiary *film* was history written in light.[2]

---

[1] Kelly Miller, The Heart of the Race Problem, American Missionary Association.

[2] There is great debate over the impetus and veracity of President Woodrow Wilsons scathing comment in the wake of screening Birth of a Nation at the White House. On February 11, 2020, Dr. Jonathan Holloway, delivered the Hubert H. Humphrey Lecture. His paper titled: History Written in Lightning: Racial Memory, Woodrow Wilson, and the Making of the Nation. His lecture sought to assess the damage President Wilson's administration and genteel racism wreak on racial progress and equality in the United States. "The assault on Black Americans and their status did not stop at policy. One of the key racial flashpoints of Wilson's presidency was his decision to screen The Birth of a Nation at the White House on February 18, 1915. The showing of D.W. Griffiths' slanderous propaganda

The tensions these stereotypes fueled led to race riots and negated images of any positive and constructive contributions of working-class African Americans who sharecropped, operated beauty and barber shops, and were grocers and craftsmen during post-enslavement and Reconstruction.

He often referred to African Americans as a backward race, alluding to the idea that enslavement dulled our innate abilities. However, he saw that given an opportunity for education, cultivation and nurture, any evidence of social retardation would be reversed, and black men and women would experience their full human potential.

In 1910, the Howard University cum laude alumnus and dean, sought to establish a National Negro Library and Museum to provide the entire world access to primary source materials by black Americans and Africans. Unfortunately, the museum idea languished at the upper level of university leadership. Still, Miller persuaded Howard alumnus and trustee, Jesse Moorland to donate his collection of over 3,000 printed items to the university as the core of what became the Moorland-Spingarn Research Center. The 1946 donation by

---

film, which celebrated the violent dismantling of Reconstruction, elicited furious denunciations from all corners of Black America. (Wilson's reported observation that the film was "like writing history with lightning," provided the title for Holloway's lecture.) Holloway sketched out the personal and professional relationship between Wilson and Thomas Dixon, Jr., the author of the book (The Clansman) upon which the film was based. "It's worth noting that Dixon had remained in touch with Wilson after their time in graduate school," he said, "and admired the segregationist policies being deployed in Washington. He wrote to Wilson directly on the matter, saying that 'the establishment of Negro men over white women employees of the Treasury Department has, in the minds of many thoughtful men and women, long been a serious offense against the cleanness of our social life." Lighting Writing Jonathan Holloway and Richard Bryne Fall 2020 Wilson Quarterly https://www.wilsonquarterly.com/ quarterly /the-ends-of-history/lightning-writing

Jewish-American historian, lawyer, and civil rights activist, Arthur Spingarn provided a second anchor collection, culminating in the formation of the Center in 1973.

Though Miller was the driving force behind the Center's creation, nothing about him was included in the university's popularly known history, architecture, or ceremony, except his unlabeled eight-by-ten portrait by an exit door near the Center's reading room.

Miller did not foresee the outcome of World War I, nor did he discount the rising violence and lynch mobs throughout the South. He continued to promulgate education, morality, and patriotism. He was not blindly optimistic about racial equality to counter rising postwar racial animosity; thus, in 1923, he crafted the Negro Sanhedrin as a clearinghouse to harmonize their efforts of racial uplift groups, pool their strengths, and establish an agenda to attack racial hatred, instead of stumbling and squabbling over methods and means.

Between 1890 and 1925, Miller's name filled the newspaper columns and correspondences by leading African American notables such as Booker T. Washington, W. E. B. DuBois, Mary McLeod Bethune, Nannie Helen Burroughs, Mary Church Terrell, Carter G. Woodson, and others who engaged him, consulted with him, and shared a platform with him.

Miller sought to navigate a moderate position within the explosive terrain of the early twentieth-century American race issue that was an urgent matter for his generation. As a daysman—exemplified in the biblical character, Job, the opinionated educator expressed his ideas through writings as he sought to mediate common ground and harmonize divergent opinions.

From childhood, his Christian ethos colored his optimistic outlook on racial strife. And though, unlike Washington and DuBois, Miller did not create a lasting institution such as the Tuskegee Institute or an ideology such as Pan-Africanism, his contributions to raising the national conversation on race matters cannot be ignored. Miller's former student, W.A.C. Hughes, noted that there was a special "something" about him that,

> ... made his heart sensitive to the cry of suffering. Something enlarged his contempt for pettiness. Something softened his prejudices. Something made him patient with the erring. Something exalted his vision, broadened his outlook, and stimulated his enthusiasm for that which was good and righteous. Something nerved him to face opposition and stand for justice without counting the cost.[3]

That was something that was his solution to the heart of the race problem through education. Miller believed industrial, classical, cultural, and historical education, tempered with morality and virtue, would contribute to a rational dialogue about human differences among Northern and Southern people and their leaders of both races. Miller did not personally encounter animosity in his relationships with white people, such as his early teacher, Reverend Willard Richardson. He knew that bigoted white people wore white robes in the night and three-piece suits in university classrooms. He believed, however, that new generations

---

[3] Kelly Miller Papers, Box 71-7 scrapbook, Moorland Spingarn Research Center, Howard University, Washington, DC. This scrapbook contains a wealth of material pertaining to Miller's funeral and reflections from colleagues, friends, former students, and the Black Press.

would cross previously taboo barriers and create their own language about race. Miller held that if educated African Americans could return to their communities, like leaven, they would elevate the race and demonstrate their worthiness as brothers, not servants at the table of humankind.

In April 1950, the *Negro Digest* published an article entitled "America's Greatest Unknown Negro." that explored the contributions of Kelly Miller, who died 11 years earlier, and questioned why Miller's legacy had been relegated to obscurity. It read in part:

> A new junior high school in Washington, D.C., was recently christened Kelly Miller in honor of one of the greatest unsung leaders of the Negro race... But few youngsters today have ever heard of this man who wielded one of the most potent pens in America.[4]

The article provides three possible explanations to the question: He left no lasting institution such as Booker T. Washington's Tuskegee Institute, or corpus of work like W. E. B. DuBois' *The Souls of Black Folk,* or organization like Marcus Garvey's Universal Negro Improvement Association. Instead, Miller limited his interest to the issues of his day. Others note that the rising generation of younger African American leaders saw Miller's formula of racial uplift through assimilation and philosophical debate as anachronistic. Yet, the fact that Miller did not create a university, organization, or ideology does not negate his contribution to the intellectual and educational history of African American people.

---

[4] C. Alvin Hughes "America's Greatest Unknown Negro," *Negro History Digest*, April 1950. 42.

Miller played the role of the daysman, as found in the biblical story of Job.[5] In Scripture, a daysman served as an arbiter, umpire, or mediator[6] and a type of Christ whose position between humanity and divinity is sacrificial and empathic. In Job, the daysman does four things. First, he acknowledges God's justice. Secondly, he realizes he is not able to contend with God. He decides men should not be judged by their outward condition, and fourth, he complains of his troubles. Miller keenly drew a parallel between the condition of black Americans and that of Job. The suffering inflicted upon Job was not of God but from Satan. God allowed it to happen because God knew his servant in character and fortitude, Satan did not.

Miller's theological foundation in the Presbyterian denomination an outgrowth of Calvinism rests on several beliefs among which predestination, total depravity of human beings, justification by faith and Christ as mediator. Toward this end, Miller added a sepia filter that Dr. James Cone would construct into Black liberation theology. Miller's indictment against whiteness and white supremacy is a contributing sociological precursor to Cone's endeavor to decenter academic, white male interpretation of holy scripture. Instead, Cone center's the gospel of Jesus Christ as central to liberation theology for all people not an exclusive segment of

---

[5] Job 9.

[6] In his Commentary, Matthew Henry states, "There is a Mediator, a Daysman, or Umpire, for us, even God's own beloved Son, who has purchased peace for us with the blood of his cross, who is able to save to the uttermost all who come unto God through him. If we trust in his name, our sins will be buried in the depths of the sea, we shall be washed from all our filthiness, and made whiter than snow, so that none can lay anything to our charge." Chapter 9:33-35 "Neither is there any daysman betwixt us that might lay his hand upon us both. Let him take his rod away from me, and let not his fear terrify me: Then would I speak, and not fear him; but it is not so with me." See, Henry, Matthew. *Matthew Henry Commentary on the Whole Bible (Complete).* 1706. http://www.biblestudytools.com/commentaries/matthew-henry-complete.

society. Both Cone and Miller share a displeasure for the abuses of whiteness and white supremacy in robbing black Americans of basic human rights and dignity. The deviation is Miller's insistence that enslavement dulled the innate abilities of black people. He often referred to black people as a backward race because of the tremendous psychological damage of enslavement. He used his life as a yardstick to gauge the heights where education and morality could move black people one generation removed from enslavement.[7]

Toward this end, as a daysman Miller acknowledged God's justice. He knew that the God of his mother and grandmother, was just. Their God would gather the wrongs done and render a final decision with eternal consequences. "He vehemently insisted that principles of justice and impartiality and fair dealing must be applied in all dealings

---

[7] Brief for the Higher Education of the Negro, "The Negro's Traditional Place in Society" and "The Relative Claims of Industrial and Higher Education" pp3-4 Washington, DC 1903] Ridicule and contempt have characterized the habitual attitude of the American mind toward the Negro's higher strivings. The African was brought to this country for the purpose of performing manual and menial labor. His bodily powers alone were required to accomplish this industrial mission. No more account was taken of his higher susceptibilities than of the mental and moral faculties of the lower animals…The Negro has sustained servile relation to the Caucasian for so long a time that it is easy as it is agreeable to Aryan pride to conclude that servitude is his ordained place in society. When it was first proposed to furnish means for the higher development of this race, some, who assumed the wisdom of their day and generation, entertained the proposition with a sneer, others, with a smile…Whenever the higher education of the Negro is broached, industrial training is always suggested as a counter irritant. Partisans of rival claims align themselves in hostile array and will not so much as respect a flag of truce. These one-eyed enthusiasts lack binocular vision. The futile discussion as to whether industrial or higher education is of greater importance to the Negro is suggestive of a subject of great renown in rural debating societies: which is of greater importance to man, air or water. We had as well attempt to decide whether the base or altitude is the more important element of a triangle. The two forms of training should be considered on the basis of their relative, not rival, claims. [The Project Gutenberg eBook of Brief For the Higher Education of the Negro, by Prof. Kelly Miller.]

of blacks as to other races."⁸ Miller infused his writings with a just God who left clear instructions and would render reward or judgement according to obedience.

> Our great national savior told us that this nation was conceived in liberty and dedicated to the proposition that all men are created equal. A nation that falls below the level of its fundamental ideals and foes in quest of false idols cannot hope to escape the date of all apostate people who history makes record. God has given America the moral opportunity to become the leader among the nations of the world along the line of national rectitude. Great will be its condemnation if, for any reason, it fails to live up to this great opportunity…God has chosen the humble things of life to confound the mighty.⁹

The second element of the daysman is realizing he is not able to content with God. Miller's scientific mind love history and sociology. The human condition was twofold, the result of a just God working in and through fallen humanity. The enslavement and residual condition of African Americans demonstrated greater avarice of white society and injustice than the stereotype of black intellectual inferiority. In an essay titled "Race Contact" Miller illustrates the history of human contact between the white and black citizens of the United States.

---

⁸ History Series: Kelly Miller: A Profile Courageous Freedom Fighter, Afro-American, October 4, 1975, p14A.
⁹ Kelly Miller, *An Appeal to Conscience; America's Code of Caste A Disgrace to Democracy*. New York, NY: MacMillan Company, 1918, 93-94.

The United States thus becomes the world's most interesting laboratory for working out the intricate issues of race adjustment. Well might the social philosopher observe with keenest interest this tremendous experiment, for if this experiment succeeds, it will furnish a sure criterion for the solution of the various race problems which are coterminous with the ends of the earth...The more progressive and ambitious the Negro becomes, the less tolerable he seems to be to [whites]...The attitude of the white race towards the Negro must be accounted for in the light of the origin of their relationship. The Negro was brought to this country for the purpose of performing manual and menial labor...His function was purely mechanical.[10]

In the case of Americans, Miller offered that the two races will continue to exist side by side. "They are linked to a common destiny of good or evil and their relations should be characterized by amity rather than by enmity." This entrenched realization reduced the European-ness of whites and the African-ness to an American people whose fraught collaboration in creating the country needed to be acknowledged and excised from tropes into viable forward thinking movement. "The brotherhood of man is more fundamental than the fellowship of race. A physical and spiritual identity of all peoples occupying common territory is a logical necessity of thought."[11]

---

[10] Kelly Miller, "Race Contacts" *An Appeal to Conscience; America's. Code of Caste a Disgrace to Democracy*, Berkeley, CA: University of California Libraries, 1920, 16.
[11] Ibid. 26.

The third element of a daysman acknowledges that men should not be judged by their outward condition. The former servitude of black people did not relegate their eternal progeny to servitude. Romantic and false nostalgia of the "the plantation" filled books, magazines, theaters and rituals of southern whites longing for the good old days. That reverie prohibited progressive movement in de jure and de facto ways for younger black Americans. In *The Everlasting Stain*, Miller's chapter on Christianity and Backward Races, indicts white/western Christianity of hypocrisy that utilized missionary activities to subjugate people of color into complicity in their own destruction:

> The white Christian say to his black co-religionist: "So far and no farther." It is a psychological impossibility for a self-thinking mind to accept the religious teaching of the overlord who denies him the right to vote, makes him ride in Jim Crow cards, shuts him out from hotels, deprives him a part in the government which he is taxed to support, and refuses him the right to work a level with his powers and preparation. A religion which stultifies the soul cannot save it.[12]

The failure to integrate black Americans into the fabric of American society could only be addressed by the solvent of religion. Miller writes, "I make no universal indictment of the white race. The apostasy of the white man gives the Negro the moral advantage of exemplifying the value of the Christian virtues and graces, at a time when such exemplification is a consummation devotedly to be wished."

---

[12] Kelly Miller, *"Christianity and Backward Races,"* Race Adjustment: *The Everlasting Stain,* New York: Neale Publishing Company, 1908, 291-292.

The fourth aspect of the daysman is that he complains of his trouble. There many areas for complaint, Miller did not rest in those spaces in pity but utilized the societal failings to amplify the moral burden white supremacy had on American democracy and Christian beliefs. In his first published book Race Adjustments, an essay titled Social Equality touts the accomplishments of black Americans. He dismisses the belief that educated black people desire to become affiliated or seek the approval of white people.

> The Negro and the white man in this country must live together for all time which we foresee. They must mingle in business and in public life. All their relations should be characterized by mutual respect, courtesy and good will.[13]

For Miller, "[t]he race problem in America casts a shadow of suspicion upon the claims of democracy as the ideal form of government."[14] President Warren G. Harding, October 1921 Birmingham speech by reinforced the "fundamental, inescapable and eternal differences of race" placing black Americans in a separate lesser class of citizenship. President Harding equated the Great Migration as a "draining away" leaving a vast reservoir of ignorance in its wake.[15] The south Harding implored needed to reconsider some inclusion of black Americans into the political landscape to aid in "solving our national issues, because of a division on race lines." Miller reasoned:

---

[13] Kelly Miller, "Social Equality" in *Race Adjustment*, 118.
[14] Ibid., 106-107.
[15] Warren G. Harding, "Address of the President of the United States at the Celebration of the Semi-centennial Founding of the City of Birmingham, Alabama" (26 October 1921) https://voicesofdemocracy.umd.edu/warren-g-harding-address-at-.

> The danger lurking in your platform, Mr. President, lies in its essential illogicality. You have attempted to derive a Northern conclusion from a Southern premise; and in doing so you have satisfied neither the North, the South nor the Negro. The South accepts your premise, but rejects your conclusion, the Negro accepts your conclusion, but rejects your premise; while the North maintains a hesitant and lukewarm attitude towards both...From the Negro's point of view you have attempted to build a superstructure of righteousness upon a fallacious foundation. [According your formula] the Negro would be degraded into an inferior caste which would render any form of equality impossible.[16]

Miller concluded that flawed foundation stripped black Americans of their inalienable right as human beings and American citizenship claim to political and civil equality codified in the Fourteenth Amendment. Miller continued publishing open letters to United States presidents Benjamin Harrison, Grover Cleveland, William McKinley, Theodore Roosevelt, William Howard Taft and Woodrow Wilson. He was critical of Franklin D. Roosevelt's New Deal as it pertained to black Americans in rural southern areas and women working in domestic service. In essence, Miller employed his scientific mind, filtered through a black Christian lens to move his people forward, as well as, well intentioned white people and American society. He denounced injustice, inequity and white supremacy in all

---

[16] Miller, "Social Equality," 113-114.

forms. He was equality critical of squabbles and unscrupulous black people on every strata of life.

Job's story portrays testing and trials. After a conversation between Satan and God, the once prosperous man's health, wealth, and family were touched by misfortune within one day. He was left sick, mourning the death of his children, and losing his wealth. The chapter presents the level of emotional turmoil Job encountered.

Miller exemplified the role of a daysman for his race in the heated debate over classical and industrial education as he described:

> Booker T. Washington became the monarch of all he surveyed; opposition was silenced all but to the point of inaudibility. Dubois persisted in cynical criticism; Trotter, alone, continued in his pronounced and stubborn opposition. The Association for the Advancement of Colored People was organized as a radical movement consisting of white and colored so-called radicals to offset what they considered a pernicious influence of the Tuskegee doctrine. During all these years I was ridiculed as a "straddler," because I refused partisan allegiance to either faction. Although I was a friend of Booker T. Washington, I had it understood that I was not his "fool friend" or "henchman," like the politicians who followed him as the ass to his master's crib for the provender which it contains. I followed the leading of my own light.[17]

---

[17] KMP, Box 71-2 folder chapter 24, Manuscript Division, MSRC, Howard University, Washington, DC. Two copies of his unpublished autobiography are the principle biographical background text. One has chapter titles while the other simply has standard chapter numbers. They are similar, yet the titled chapter

The astute thinker and self-proclaimed iconoclast sought to change the world one person at a time while simultaneously standing between the race and its critics. He believed that African American social justice was a lofty, but a future that he could vicariously witness by preparing the rising generations. Using Howard University as his field, Miller tilled the ground for over four decades and traversed the country, preaching the gospel of education and virtue. In a 1935 article, Miller wrote:

> I have an abiding faith that all human problems of which the race problem is but a troublesome incident, will finally be solved. This will not take place in my day, but I trusted that my past forty years of endeavor will neither hinder nor delay, this great consummation in God's fullness of time.[18]

His address entitled "The Heart of the Race Problem," was delivered on October 21, 1909. In it, Miller described the type of leadership he believed was needed:

> Jesus tells that" he who would be great among you, let him be your servant... It makes little difference what kind of service one is engaged in, but it is the amount of skill and system and character and energy, and enterprise injected into that service, that counts for honor and distinction. And so, I think of the Negro race – if it will but have its feet tendoned and mortised in the granite foundation of truth and righteousness, and will but adjust its life according to

---

version I refer throughout this work is more developed. The entire Miller papers at MSRC will be referenced as KMP.

[18] KMP, Box 71-3 folder 87 clippings 8/3/35.

the laws of God's moral gravitation, it will endure and overcome despite the wrath and rage of a frowning world... There is no body of workers in all this wide world upon whose shoulders devolve weightier tasks than upon the Negro men and women of light and leading, who must partake of the things of civilization and show them unto their brethren.[19]

In the spirit of a daysman, Miller relinquished the notion of having the largest, most popular, or most important solution to the race problem. Rather, he saw himself as a servant standing between the giver and the receiver as an integral part of a larger plan orchestrated by God.[20]

Outline of the Book

The five chapters of the book bring the story of the life and times of this largely forgotten daysman to light. Chapter one, "Entry into a Land Made Sick by Strife: 1863–1879," presents the America into which Kelly Miller was born. The Civil War era was a precarious period for African Americans. Relationships between white and black people, city and country dwellers, and southern residents and northern missionaries were characterized by violence and economic turmoil. Yet, Miller's sense of self was established in a

---

[19] Kelly Miller, "The Heart of the Race Problem" faculty writings, 3. MSRC, Library Division.

[20] Matthew Henry's conclusion confirmed Miller's sense of purpose. "The remembrance of having done our duty will be pleasing afterwards; so will not the remembrance of having got worldly wealth, when it is all lost and gone... May we learn the difference between justifying ourselves and being thus justified by God himself. [N]otice that others have passed this dreadful gulf; and though they found it hard to believe that God would hear or deliver them, yet he rebuked the storm, and brought them to the desired haven."

household surrounded by loving parents, several siblings, and a doting grandmother. He attended a Presbyterian school where Reverend Willard Richardson contributed to his ethical moorings.

In Chapter Two: "A Vastly Different Life Opens: 1880–1889," the shy and awkward young adult is no longer tugging at his grandmother or mother's apron. His proficiency in math won the admiration of other students, and sensed his ability had a divine purpose and responsibility. Known for his lightning-fast mathematical prowess, he applied his remarkable talents to a range of scientific disciplines, including astronomy and physics. As the chapter ends, Miller boards a train for Howard University in Washington, D.C., the city that would be his home for the remainder of his life.

Chapter Three, "Introduced to a New World: 1890–1918," witnesses Miller's progression from a student to a Howard University mathematics professor, from a bachelor to a Miller morphed from a mathematician to a sociologist, author, journalist, and social critic, and became an apostle of classical, industrial education. His Howard experience infused Miller with a greater desire to promote racial uplift and provided the platform for influencing generations of black youth. He came to love the university and believed its campus and classrooms were places of transformation. During this period of growth, he confirmed his roles as a leader and daysman for the race. Undeterred by negative comments from some of the race leaders, he remained committed to the ideological middle ground as the means of racial uplift.

Chapter Four: "The Negro is Scarcely Ever Considered: 1919–1926," presents Miller as an established African American intellectual voice. While education was working and black people were being transformed, the dismal failure of post-World War I era race relations led Miller to consider another method for engaging the issue, and his relationship with the black press afforded him the opportunity to expand his audience.

While the black leaders were divided over methods, Miller believed that they sought the same goal—full citizenship and equality and conceived of his Negro Sanhedrin, a confederation of organizations based on the Hebraic model. Unfortunately, the organization that was intended to resolve methodological schisms, did not survive beyond its first meeting. Miller traveled nationally to stump for Howard, and was actively involved in the Howard Alumni Association. His outspoken nature earned the disfavor of Howard President J. Stanley Durkee, resulting in his demotion from dean to department chair. The chapter closes with an aging Miller who is demoralized yet refuses to surrender to defeat.

Chapter Five, "A Yardstick of Progress: 1926–1939," examines the effect of his failed Sanhedrin Council and his media war with President Durkee. When Baptist preacher Mordecai W. Johnson replaced Durkee, Miller disagreed with him on a variety of issues, and the disputes, health issues, and changing projections of younger men resulted in Miller's retirement. Chapter five closes with Miller's death in 1939.

Conclusion

Employing the model of a daysman, Miller's contribution to African American educational and intellectual history presents us with an alternative model of engagement that sought to harmonize ideas and ideologies. He believed his generation would lay the intellectual, organizational, and moral groundwork for the reconstitution and direction African Americans needed through self-improvement and education, for he insisted that, the salvation of any overshadowed race will depend upon what they are rather than what they do, upon character more than enterprise, upon endurance rather than endeavor. For the Negro race I regard the development of the moral nature as fundamental and supreme.[21]

In 1935, Miller looked for an endowment to support the production of his biography. He obtained $1,200.00 from the Rosenwald Fund and was instructed by its president, Edward Embree, to inquire with other agencies. In his follow-up letter, Miller succinctly explained the daysman ideology that had characterized his life:

> My thought is to use my own life as a yardstick in terms of which to measure the progress of the Negro race from emancipation to the present time. I was born in July 1863, six months after the Emancipation Proclamation. My life, therefore, has touched, directly or remotely, the intervening events which have shared the progress of the Negro race. My idea, as developed up to the present time, is to lay the chief stress of emphasis upon the events weaving in my own life incidents as they have been influenced by, or have influenced them; in other words, to portray the history of the Negro race as a human document with my personality in the background. I am convinced that such a treatise, properly documented, and set

---

[21] Kelly Miller "Word to the 20th Century Negro," *Voice of the Negro*, 1905, 678.

forth in becoming literary style, would constitute a valuable contribution to Race literature.[22]

---

[22] KMP Box 71-2 folder 38, 1.

One
Entry to a Land Made Sick by Strife: 1863–1879

Man is a creature so formed and fashioned that besides his grasp upon the present, he has a power of historic life, which sends forward his influence far beyond his own times and makes him an agent of might and even of responsibility in other generations."
Africa and America: Addresses and Discourses.
Alexander Crummell

The early 1860s was a pivotal period in American history. In 1861, the election and inauguration of President Abraham Lincoln fanned the glowing embers of Southern contention toward this northerner. Southern politicians viewed his opposition to slavery as a threat to their lifestyle, and their fears were realized when the first shots of the Civil War were fired on Fort Sumter, South Carolina, on April 12, 1861. Lincoln's effort to replace the South's aging agrarian system with the rising industrial scheme was not intended to ameliorate the vile, inhumane practice of chattel enslavement. It was simply an option for embracing the new form of economic organization, beginning with the removal of African people from America.[1]

---

[1] Lerone Bennett, Jr. *Forced in Glory: Abraham Lincoln's White Dream* examines the intentions behind Lincoln's Emancipation Proclamation as an attempt to outmaneuver "the real emancipators" to contain the emancipation tide, which reached a dangerous intensity, threatening his ability to govern.

When Lincoln issued the Emancipation Proclamation on January 1, 1863, Reverend Jonathan C. Gibbs, pastor of the First African Presbyterian Church of Philadelphia, reported:

> Today, standing on the broad platform of the common brotherhood of men, we solemnly appeal to the God of justice, our common Father, to aid us to meet manfully the new duties, the new obligations that this memorable day will surely impose. The Proclamation has gone forth, and God is saying to this nation by its legitimate constitute head, Man must be free.[2]

As fighting intensified, so did the death toll. On July 18, 1863, General Quincy Gilmore led an assault against Fort Wagner on Morris Island, South Carolina, to capture it and the remaining territory known as "Coffin Island," an antebellum leper colony. A small Confederate garrison held the fort, which was protected by a narrow approach up the beach that limited surprise attacks from Union forces.

On that day, these forces repeatedly bombarded the fort, raining down upon its troops every 30 seconds for hours. The 54th Massachusetts, a regiment of free African American men under the direction of Colonel Robert Gould Shaw, charged the fort with fixed bayonets. The fierce artillery fighting and hand-to-hand combat left heavy casualties over the next 58 days. On that same day, in the state's northeastern corner, Kelly Miller drew his first breath. As he would later describe that event:

---

[2] Jonathan C. Gibbs, "Freedom's Joyful Day" *A.M.E. Christian Recorder*, January 17, 1863.

I, the sixth child, escaped the stigma of a slave birth only by the beneficence of the Emancipation Proclamation. On January 1 of 1863 President Abraham Lincoln had signed the Emancipation Proclamation... my eyes opened amidst these tragic scenes. The circumstances surrounding my birth and the promise and prospect which lay before me in that slave mother's cribs were as gloomy and foreboding as ever befell the lot of any member of the human race. At that time the Emancipation Proclamation, according to Lincoln's own estimate, had no more influence upon the existing status of things than the Pope's bull against the comet. The fact that my father was a free man in no wise altered the status of the offspring which followed that of the mother. In light of retrospect, I can fully appreciate the pronouncement of Frederick Douglass - "You must not judge the progress of my race by the height which it has attained, but by the depth from which it sprung.[3]

Miller's birth on the day on which the 54th Massachusetts demonstrated such courage and valor, indelibly marked him with a numinous sense of balance and talents that he would employ in advocating for the fair treatment of black people. The circumstances surrounding his birth order and place contributed to his life philosophy. Born between slavery and freedom and between enslaved and free-born siblings, he seemed planted in the middle. Recalling the context related to his birthday infused Miller with an urgent and unique sense

---

[3] This quote is a combination of both copies of the autobiography. The first sentence is from chapter 1 "My Entry into a Land Made Sick with Strife and KMP Box 71-2 folder 39, 1.

of purpose. These circumstances, augmented by his family's contributions, gave him a sense of self and the realization of a calling to restore African Americans to the family of humanity.

His story inspired reminiscence about the biblical battlefield of Ebenezer, which the Israelites memorialized as "the place where God met us." His biblically inspired location between Mizpah—a watchtower of the future and Shen—a sharp rock of change during the period of enslavement made him a daysman—an arbitrator or mediator—for his race. His experience of learning and ignorance, victory, and defeat, made him aware that two extremes were linked by time and circumstances.

His early experiences and education provided the standard to which he cleaved for the remainder of his life. Reconstruction-era schools operated by the Presbyterian Church offered him much greater opportunity than had been available to his parents.

As a boy, Kelly rarely encountered white people. Still, in seventeen years in Winnsboro, he did not experience the cruelty or injustice he had read about. And in his few encounters with white people, he saw only friendship and kindness. Moreover, he recollected that relationships between Confederate veterans, former slaves, free-born African Americans, and Scotch-Irish immigrants in northeastern South Carolina were amicable. He pitied racist white people, loved black people, and tempered his opinion with Calvinist Christian ideals. His pity stemmed from their irrational hatred of people they did not know, for he could not understand how, in a supposedly Christian country, ostensibly based on the brotherhood of man, the fatherhood of God, and biblical ideals, people could love an unseen God while hating certain people.

Information about the Miller family begins with his paternal grandparents, Isaac, born in 1780, and Milly, born in 1784. Their union produced six free-born children: Rebecca, Elizabeth, Thomas, Kelly, Mary, and Isaac. Miller's uncle Isaac served as a South Carolina State Senator during the Reconstruction era, from 1872 to 1874, and became an ordained African Methodist Episcopal minister in 1880.[4]

The 1860 census lists Miller's father, Big Kelly, as a mechanic, and later census records list him as a farmer and laborer. His inclusion in the South Carolina census informs us that the Millers were free persons for at least two generations. His parents married in the late 1850s, but her slave status precluded the marriage from being recognized by the local government. Yet marriages such as this were not uncommon in the antebellum South. In describing the union, Miller wrote, I never learned… the circumstances involved in [my father's] marriage to my mother, a slave woman." [5]

In *Long Memory: The Black Experience in America*, Mary Frances Berry, and John W. Blassingame assert that,

> [the black family grew out of a complex combination of African traditions, Christian beliefs, and adjustments made to slavery."[6] For them, "[t]he enslavement of the Africans led to new familial practices. Men were forced to share authority with women and parents no longer completely shaped the destiny of their children; however, monogamy

---

[4] Linda Malone of the Fairfield Archives and History Project
[5] KMP, Box 71-2 folder 39, 4.
[6] Mary Frances Berry and John W. Blassingame, *Long Memory: The Black Experience in America*. This book examines Black relationships during enslavement. In particular, kinship ties and strong communal institutions, such as family, were impacted by enslavement, and the West African culture afforded some adaptable skills.

remained a norm although the law did not recognize slave unions.⁷

Regardless, Kelly's childhood home provided a stable environment, for his parents, paternal grandmother, aunts, uncles, and siblings were a close network of support and intimacy. His relatives extended into notable South Carolina families, including the Martins and the Byrds, many of whom had achieved top positions in the state legislature. Miller believed that the family's success contributed to a happy childhood and added a permanent sense of confidence and independence, for he later claimed:

> Although I never learned anything about my paternal grandfather, I have every reason to believe that all six of my grandmother's children were of the same paternity. Nor did I ever learn where my father derived his Christian name - Kelly. There may possibly have been some Irish invasion somewhere down the line, as Fairfield County was settled by the Scotch-Irish from Pennsylvania.⁸

Home Life in Miller's South Carolina

European influences permeated South Carolina as Welsh, Scotch-Irish, and German settlers populated the state from the 1750s. During this period, Low Country European farmers primarily planted and harvested indigo and rice, though there was a rise in cotton production by the 1790s. To counteract their economic boon, the federal government

---

[7] John Blassingame, *The Slave Community: Plantation Life in the Antebellum South*. 72.

[8] KMP, Box 71-2 folder 39, 4.

encouraged migration from neighboring states such as Pennsylvania, Virginia, and North Carolina, and a few Welsh and Scotch-Irish Americans opted to settle in Fairfield County. With rolling acres of arable land, this area's topography provided sufficient agricultural revenue from cotton, tobacco, corn, and other crop production to sustain local and statewide markets.

Miller's aunts and uncles ranked high in their free black community, where his grandmother was a ruling spirit. However, as Miller recounted, his maternal lineage was difficult to reconstruct since he never met his maternal grandfather, Joe Roberts, for he would go on to say,

> They tell me that my grandfather was trusted and favored beyond other slaves by virtue of his industry and dependability. He was not only permitted the use of a plot of ground but was allotted a worn-out horse with which to cultivate it. I well remember my mother's relating how he used to plow his home plot at night by means of lightwood knots, placed at the end of the furrow. Endowed with natural intelligence, she was every inch a queen among women; tall and slim... graceful, whether at work in the cotton field or toiling with pick and shovel while she helped prepare a roadbed for a railroad project to be run through the Western part of Fairfield County, South Carolina, from Spartanburg to Columbia. For years it was a humiliating reflection that my mother worked on a railroad, but when I remember that this was due to the depletion of labor on account of the War, my humiliation of feeling became somewhat mollified. During the labor dearth of the World War, I saw with my own eyes, free white women working

with barrow, pick and shovel in Pennsylvania Railroad, just outside of Pittsburgh.⁹

In autumn 1863, two months after Kelly's birth, General Braxton Bragg defeated General William Rosecrans at Chickamauga. By year's end, the battles of Lookout Mountain and Missionary Ridge proved to be the proverbial writing on the wall that the war was ending. In the waning months, southerners did not embrace the ideas of their northern captors. Losing the war and their cultural identity disturbed their sense of community. Moreover, while attempting to stomp out Confederate ideals, northern troops did not elevate the condition of black people and held paternalistic, derogatory ideas about women, as Miller wrote:

> I was sixteen months old when Sherman captured Atlanta and entered upon his famous march to the sea, devastating the country on a sixty-mile front. Troops on his left flank passed through the Laban Chapelle plantation in the Western part of Fairfield County, where I was born, causing grave consternation among white[s] and blacks alike. My mother often recited to me how the Yankees fondled me on their knees and asked her to let them take me North where they would make me stand on my head.¹⁰

Kelly was born on the Laban Chappell plantation in Winnsboro near Shelton, South Carolina. According to him, Chappell was an enslaver of moderate means and circumstances who only owned a few slaves, including

---

⁹ KMP, Box 71-2 folder, 39, 2-3.
¹⁰ KMP, Box 71-2 folder, 39, 1.

Miller's mother. He did not affect the aristocratic pretensions usually ascribed to the more wealthy and powerful slaveholders, and neither Elizabeth nor her older siblings recounted any brutal treatment. His two youngest sons were killed in the war, while the oldest was not drafted and served as his father's overseer. Miller wrote about the family:

> All that I know about my mother's master, his family, and their circumstances I learned from my mother. I never saw any member of this family except Mr. Chapelle, and then it was only a momentary glimpse. Among my earliest recollections, at the age of three was the sight of my oldest sister, seated on a white horse behind her former master, who had ridden over to the free colored settlement, where we had moved immediately after Emancipation, to negotiate for the employment of this ex-slave girl of 12, to assist his wife in her household duties. But her return was as a free agent, to work in the home of her former master and be paid a weekly wage. Such an occurrence caused much comment among members of our race. It was an object lesson, demonstrating that the old order of things had passed forever. Now the Negro was not subject to the beck and call of the white man, but like the whites, he could demand and receive pay for services rendered.[11]

Numerous plantations gave witness to Fairfield County as home to an agricultural tradition. The roots of Winnsboro's inhabitants, mores, and neighborhoods could be traced to the Revolutionary War era when, in 1785, Richard Winn of

---

[11] KMP, Box 71-2 folder 39, 5.

Virginia moved to the area and petitioned that the land he occupied be laid out, chartered, and declared his property. John Winn, John Vanderhorst, and John Richard assisted Winn. Though by 1870, four years after the close of the war, Winnsboro was a prosperous agricultural community, its African American residents experienced significant disruption and displacement, as Miller described:

> It must have been soon after the surrender of General Lee, and when the Confederate troops were disbanding, that my father rejoined my mother and we moved from the plantation to the free settlement upon the farm owned by his brother-in-law, John Byrd, with whom my grandmother lived. I was soon to learn that we were on land which belonged to members of my father's family. At the top of the hill, in the "big house," lived John Byrd with his wife, Aunt Harriet, and their six children, with whom my grandmother made her home.[12]

Though, like Winnsboro's other African Americans, enslavement and war fractured the Miller household, they faced the 1870s with hope. For, amid swirling change, their nuclear and extended families remained a close unit. Within it, his grandmother and mother exemplified the importance of racial pride and integrity and their influence contributed to his sense of identity and purpose. These women engaged in physical labor and their productivity was crucial to the family's well-being and economic survival.

Except for Kelly's father, Milly's six children were literate. She provided a high moral standard for them and her

---

[12] Ibid.

grandchildren by rewarding good comportment, punishing poor behavior, and building their self-esteem with kind words. At the same time, Elizabeth delivered moral lessons through practical examples. And because of them, Miller admired the tenacious spirit of African American women and encouraged and celebrated his wife, Annie, and their daughters, May and Irene.

Scholars assert that women are the main transmitters of culture within black society and provide living bridges to African folkways such as food, clothing, song, medicine, and history. In the Reconstruction era, African American families and women provided examples of endurance, strength, grace, and fortitude. These customs were learned from their mothers and older women and passed to their children through informal education while cooking, grooming, or playing.

At the age of five, his father moved the family from the Byrd plantation to an African American settlement owned by Mr. Beard, a sharecropper and Confederate veteran with whom Big Kelly had served, and with whom there existed that kind of relation that such common experiences evoke. Beard later relocated because he did not care to live under "carpetbag and Negro rule." His disdain for black people did not impact Kelly's recollection of kind relationships with Fairfield County's white people.

While racism and hatred remained present, African Americans in the South continued to build viable communities. When running short on manpower, the Confederacy conscripted enslaved and free black men into service. Big Kelly was free, not enslaved, but strategically moved to ensure that his family would not suffer from being misinterpreted as Northern sympathizers or overly ambitious black people. He served in Company F, 12th Regiment of the South Carolina Infantry under Captain John Bell. Company F,

12th Regiment of the South Carolina Infantry formed in Lightwood Knot Springs in July 1861. They provided costal defense on Edisto Island in October 1861. Over the course of two days in August 1862, they engaged in the Second Battle of Manassas (Bull Run) and lost 146 of their 270 men. In July 1863, for three days under the command of Captain John L. Miller they participated in the Battle of Gettysburg. Over 100 men were wounded, 26 died and four were missing from their regiment of 366 men. By April 9, 1865, there were ten officers and 149 enlisted men of Company F, 12th remaining.

His First Suit of Clothes

Industrious living required black people to provide basic food, clothing, and shelter for themselves. So Kelly assisted in making his first suit. This project further contributed to his daysman understanding of the connection between practical elements of industrial education and theoretical aspects of classical education. In his eyes, both contributed to the whole person through service, humility, and thriftiness.

The making of a suit was a twofold process. First, during the day, the siblings picked cotton—the raw material for the fabric. This required filling a basket with the "fluffy white substance" they carried home. Then, at night, they separated the cotton lint from the seeds. As Miller explained:

> When you consider the production of three pounds of lint a day was considered a grown person's task, you will begin to get some understanding as to how slow and painful the finger ginning process was.[13]

---

[13] KMP, Box 71-2 folder 40, 6.

Miller circa 1880

After picking and separating the shreds of cotton, the raw materials were given to their mother, who carded the lint into rolls which she drew into threads, wound into a broach on the spinning wheel. Then she sized the threads must be with a glutinous substance made from corn or wheat flour to give it luster, dyed it with walnut stain or some other dye stuff to prevent the fabric from displaying a drab uniformity. Manufacturing three yards of cloth was considered a good day's work.[14]

The final cloth was woven, cut, fitted, and made into dresses for Elizabeth and the girls and coats and pants for Big Kelly and the boys. Elizabeth mastered the dying process to produce striped and checkered patterns, and though Kelly was proud of his mother's craftsmanship, his clothes did not compare with the "fashion-plate outfits" of his classmates, and he felt out of place at school.

Miller noted that the homespun age continued longer for rural people whose livelihoods did not enable them to purchase fancy fabric, but that materialism contributed to the downfall of craftsmanship within the southern African American family, asserting that,

> I have since owned several swallow tail suits, such as the president wears at his levees. It is a far cry between the backwoods schoolboy bedecked in his mother-made homespun and the college Dean arrayed in the latest evening style at a gala reception; but when I reflect that my race has made no progress in the textile industry since my mother fitted me out for that log schoolhouse in the backwoods of Fairfield County, I find little room for boasting or elation. Black hands performed the complete manufacturing process, from producing the raw material to manufacturing it into fabric, then fashioning it into finished garments; but the only part which Negro workmanship contributed to my evening dress was

---

[14] KMP, Box 71-2 folder 40, 6-7.

the production of a few threads of raw cotton which were necessary to hold the woolen fabric together.[15]

Miller's reflection on rural clothing manufacturing contributed to his ideas on industrial education. In his view, the independent, homespun industry had a dual effect on morality and economy, for according to him:

> After the Negro finger plucks the fleece from the bowl, the race has no further part or parcel in the textile industry. Reflecting upon the part which my mother played in the production of my first suit of clothes, and the present status of the race in the textile industry, I am able to understand the meaning of Mahatma Gandhi when he advises his Hindu fellow countrymen to eschew the whole process of British manufacture and to revert to the more primitive stage of the spinning wheel and the hand loom. Great havoc [occurred] in the shifting of the manufacturing process from the family to the factory and played with the industrial opportunities, possibilities and outlook of backward races and groups.[16]

His First Days at School

In his early days, Miller, his brother Isaac, and their cousin's children attended school in one room of a house built and occupied by his uncle, Joseph Thompson, a free black master carpenter. At the start, four months out of the year, Thompson and one of his daughters alternated as teachers. As the number of pupils increased, Miss Letitia Jackson, a

---

[15] KMP, Box 71-2 folder 40, 7.
[16] KMP, Box 71-2 folder 40, 7.

graduate of Hampton College, became the lead instructor. As Kelly remembered:

> Upon entering this school, I was made acquainted with the second textbook of the hundreds, yes thousands which I have perused during my life of almost continuous study and research. Not only did this little book influence my life, but it may be said to have influenced the lives of all young Americans, because it taught parental and filial affection, frugality, integrity, religious fervor, and patriotism; and between the years 1836 and 1920 it was studied in its various editions. McGuffey's New First Eclectic Reader is the book to which I owe a great deal of my educational training.[17]

Eventually, Kelly's education moved from his Uncle Joe's house to Reverend L. M. McCurdy's one-room schoolhouse, where his thirst for learning increased. As he reminisced, those were seemingly magical days, for,

> [w]hen we left our cabin to enter school, I was proud of my two-piece suit, also proud of a pair of new shoes. Every child in the family was allowed one pair of shoes a year. That may seem to have been a hardship, but it was not, because we could go barefoot at least six months in the twelve, which meant a great saving in soles and uppers... The schoolhouse was one large room equipped with benches. Moreover, the physical building was an abandoned Negro cabin built of pine logs with mud

---

[17] KMP, chapter 6 "My Second School," 51-53.

dobbing between them to keep out the wind, a mud chimney at one end and a window at the other. There were no desks and each pupil had to safeguard their own spelling book, slate, and pencil. The principal instructor was Reverend L. M. McCurdy, a colored man from Biddle University in Charlotte, North Carolina, and a Presbyterian minister."[18]

Eventually, a white woman, a one-armed former Confederate veteran, and more instructors from Biddle University came to the school. The University was started in 1867 in North Carolina by two ministers—Samuel C. Alexander and Willis L. Miller—who sought to inspire the best and brightest African American minds to higher attainment. Over time, they changed the classical curriculum into a theological program and encouraged students to become teachers and preachers to elevate other African Americans.

In 1891, Daniel Jackson Sanders, founder of the *African American Presbyterian*, became Biddle's first African American president, incorporating his printing business with that of the school to increase the university's outreach. He left a legacy of a steady stream of African American leadership well into the twentieth century. The second president, Dr. Henry Lawrence McCrorey, dubbed an ambassador of Christian education, served for 40 years. During his tenure, enrollment and finances increased, and, in 1927, Biddle changed its name to Johnson C. Smith University.

Miller had never experienced any animosity from white instructors. He recalled that though violence and distrust marred Reconstruction in South Carolina, Biddle's white

---

[18] KMP, Box 71-2 folder 41, 3.

instructors were as "kindly, patient and sympathetic" as their African American colleagues, and treated students fairly.

There were 50 girls and boys aged 6 to 16 from all parts of Fairfield County. Regardless of age, however, all students in McCurdy's school began with the rudimentary, including learning the alphabet. Miller recalled the classroom format.

> Our teacher stepped upon a platform and held up a small book so that all might see. It was a book, he said, which Abraham Lincoln had studied, and if we would faithfully study what that book contained our lives would be made much easier and there was no telling what we might accomplish. The book was The Elementary Spelling-Book…by Noah Webster…The day I learned how to spell 'boy' was one when I took great pride in myself because I realized that I was an entity which met with recognition in that wonderful book; and of a certainty I felt more affection for the furry animal cuddled by my side at night when I learned that c-a-t spelled cat. It was slow progress at the beginning; however, due mainly to the fact that school was in session only four months in the year. Children could not be spared from farm work when there was work to be done. Even I, at the age of 6, had chores to perform and my nimble fingers made me useful when cotton was ready for picking. July and August were slack months for farmers; therefore, school was in session eight weeks during the mid-summer. As the cotton had been [picked by the end of November, the mid-winter term embraced December and January] Reverend McCurdy shared a special relationship with me, because he seemed to take special pains with my education. He whipped

me only once and then so lightly that I barely felt the blow.[19]

Although Kelly was empowered by and hungry for learning, he sometimes succumbed to peer pressure like any young boy, and . once, he and some classmates opted to skip school. To contemporary eyes, his infraction was simply youthful playfulness, but Kelly viewed his disobedience as a seedbed for possibly greater waywardness.

On a sweltering day in August the big boys decided to build a dam across a creek which flowed near the schoolhouse, and thus create a pond where we could go swimming. The little boys were told to join them and that afternoon we all played hooky. Not a prudent idea. Those were days when lessons were taught to the tune of the hickory stick, only in our school birch switches took the place of hickory. Next morning the teacher was ready with his switch and blows fell heavily on the shoulders and legs. Finally, it came my turn, and the lightest blows were issued. Reverend McCurdy knew that there was good fishing and swimming was a pastime all boys enjoyed…Each season offered a pleasantry, in the fall we enjoyed a hooked watermelon, spied growing between the rows of corn. To open this treat, the watermelon dashed against a fence post, and we all ate it with juice dripping everywhere. We also helped ourselves to apples growing on the farmers' trees and were ready at any moment to "cut and run" should the owner appear on the scene. My mother must have

---

[19] KMP chapter 3 "My First Day of School," 22, 27-28.

known about these boyhood antics, but never punished me.[20]

Though white fears of a literate enslaved population led to the creation of local and state laws against teaching black people to read, sympathetic enslavers taught some the skill, while some others devised learning strategies for themselves without letting enslavers know. So, for example, while Phyllis Wheatley was formally trained by her enslavers, Frederick Douglass parsed the meaning of the words of the white children with whom he played.

Knowing that enslavement had rendered his maternal ancestors illiterate, Miller saw his life and accomplishments as a yardstick for measuring the progress of the race. He was the first of his generation to learn the use of letters without penalty of the law. So his entrance into school "marked not only the beginning of an individual's education but of a race," and he regarded himself as the first fruit of America's reparation to formerly enslaved persons.

> There is a race thirst, just as there is an individual thirst for knowledge. Comprehensively speaking, the education of the Negro race inaugurated the morning I entered that little log schoolhouse in the backwoods of Fairfield County. Up to that time a handful of Negroes in the North, and in a few favored cities in the South, had scanty educational opportunities, but only a few favored individuals had been permitted to partake of the tree of knowledge… [This tree] was zealously guarded by the flaming sword of wrath lest the servile population should partake thereof and

---

[20] KMP chapter 3 "My First Day of School," 28

should thereby learn of good, evil, and become "as one of us." But these efforts to keep the race from literacy were in vain. Here and there a favored slave was taught to read and write by a kindly master or mistress, who ignored the law...It is like entering into a new world where none had gone before to prepare the way.[21]

Mutual Endearments - Grandmother and Mother

Kelly's relationships with his grandmother and mother strengthened his resolve to be a productive part of society. Both required the young child to do moderate farm labor and help produce the necessary elements for making clothing. Millie Miller provided a refuge for her grandchildren, and Miller wrote fondly of her:

> "I... fell under the charm of my grandmother and became her favorite pet. I experienced all the mutual endearments which existed between grandmother and grandchild."[22]

On the occasions when minor accidents caused him to need her help, her marvelous salve cured all. When, for example, he was afflicted with what he called "grits" in the eye, she would insert a grain of flaxseed or placate Kelly with her gingerbread and comfort. And he remembered an occasion,

> ...when I became too familiar with a hen and her brood that the enraged mother flew in my face and

---

[21] KMP, Box 71-2 folder 41, 2-3.
[22] KMP, Box 71-2 folder 39, 6

knocked me flat on my back. I ran screaming to my grandmother who soothed me in her arms; put me to sleep, whence I awake oblivious to my recent predicament…As has happened to many a child, the influence which she impressed on me in those days, remains more vivid than that impressed by my mother.[23]

Like other African American children of his time, Kelly wore a loose-fitting Mother Hubbard gown during his early childhood. But when he was about four years old, Grandma Millie heard him humming a popular tune. Pleased with his talent, she promised him a pair of pants if he sang the whole song for her. In anticipation of this "bifurcated garment" to replace his one-piece torn shirt, he practiced fitting words and tunes together for several days in the hope of winning the prize. His first attempt contained trembles and a boyish bashfulness, but Kelly recalled that the song emerged:

Come along, my brother, come along,
the time is drawing near;
the angels say there is nothing to do
But ring dem chiming bells.

Chorus:
We are almost home, almost home,
We are almost home, to ring dem chiming bells.[24]

After finishing triumphantly, he received the mark of true boyhood—his first pair of pants. His last recollection of his grandmother was several years after they had moved from

---

[23] Ibid.
[24] KMP, Box 71-2 folder 39, 6.

the Byrd farm to a larger plantation, and she presented him his own calf, representing "the highest expression of interest, affection, and goodwill."[25] In discussing what went into making the pants he obtained from his grandmother, Miller relayed:

> To clearly understand the situation when the announcement was made, that I must have suitable clothes for attending school, one must bear in mind that during the War, and for some time thereafter, no manufactured goods were shipped from the North [to] south of the Mason-Dixon line. There was plenty of cotton in the South, but all the machinery for its manufacturing was in the Northern states. Clothing could be had at prices prohibitive to all save the well-to-do; and the backwoods folks, poor whites as well as Negroes, do their own spinning and weaving, their cutting and fitting or go naked.[26]

Miller saw his mother as endowed with fine qualities of mind and soul and his esteem for her ingenuity and creativity was evident in his writing:

> Mother could cut, sew, clean, patch worn garments, can and preserve fruits and vegetables for winter use; dry apples, peaches, and blackberries; make soap from bones and resin; manufacture starch out of green corn; convert hickory ashes into soda and parched corn into coffee. She was the best gardener in the neighborhood; she kept a cow, pigs, and a flock of chickens...At times food was very scarce and on

---

[25] KMP, Box 71-2 folder 39, 7.
[26] KMP, chapter 2 "My First Suit of Clothes," 5.

many a day my mother caused a rabbit or a squirrel to so flavor a dish heaped with dumplings that it served as a meal for all the family. She was the family doctor and was skilled in brewing teas from plant leaves and concocting pain killers and poultices from roots and herbs with which she treated the ills and complaints of the family. When the children went to her complaining of pain or suffering we felt satisfied when she rubbed the afflicted part with her soothing hand, treated the bruise or cut with homemade salve, prescribed a drink of sage, sassafras or pennyroyal tea for fever and ague, and applied poultices to relieve pain... Whatever qualities of mind and heart which my mother may have possessed were not derived from contact with the white man's culture.[27]

He likened her to Frederick Douglass' mother, as representing the field hand rather than the household servant. He attributed his mother's fine qualities to her indigenous African alertness of mind and soul. For Kelly, her innate human goodness was not simply a human desire to "live a good life" but a divinely placed moral compass. Miller insisted that the love for gardening she implanted in him influenced him to lead a pious life. In sum, he saw his mother's influence as shaping the moral direction of his life, for in his words:

My mother never had any intellectual or religious tutoring after the white man's model. I do not believe that she ever attended church, for there was available no church for her to attend. She experienced no

---

[27] KMP, Box 71-2 folder 39, 6-7.

evangelical fervor and had no conception of the theological mysteries. She implicitly believed in heaven as the home of the good and hell as the place of the wicked. I suspect that these conceptions of ultimate human destiny were derived from African lore or conveyed through plantation melodies which were then in vogue as they are today... I have heard my mother croon practically the whole repertoire of these spirituals which made such deep impression upon my memory that I can now cite and sing them from beginning to end. One wonders after all if music is not the best medium through which to impart moral and spiritual values... My mother took it for granted that all her children should and would be moral and upright... The climax of moral maxims was expressed in a single formula – 'God does not love ugly.'[28]

Each season, the community knew that Elizabeth grew a variety of vegetables. Her garden on a quarter-acre plot, a space one-fourth the size of a football field, contributed to the family's well-being. More importantly, her love of the venture contributed to Miller's enjoyment of Washington. As early as 1894, he established a household garden modeled after his mother's. He believed he was the only or largest garden cultivated by a black person in the community during the mid-1920s. This love of gardening provided catharsis throughout his life when he was not reading or writing. Moreover, it reawakened, deep inside the man, the country boy who picked the cotton that his mother wove into his first suit.

---

[28] KMP, Box 71-2 folder 44, 2-3.

Miller highly regarded his beloved mother's moral sensibility, intuition, and influence. Though by the time he penned his autobiography at 72, he had heard notable preachers and theologians, he concluded her simple candor and guidance imparted through her moral precepts and direction was what compelled him.

His Father's Industrious Example

Although unschooled, his father firmly believed in education. So Kelly, Jr. attended one of the first public schools under the South Carolina Reconstruction government. While some black parents would not send their children to school because they saw education as useless for farming and industrial production, Big Kelly sought schools for his children to attend.

When leaving the Byrd plantation, he took the family and their belongings in a two-horse wagon across five miles of forest to his new home. Since the Beard shack was more dilapidated than their previous cabin, his first task was building a new house. Because the children were too young to help, the craftsman hewed trees, cut logs into suitable sizes, crafted shingles, raised the rafters, and built the chimney. Further, he made most of the household furniture, farm tools, baskets, bread trays, and the framework for their beds.

> Big Kelly was especially adept with the fro, the maul, chisel and drawing knife. The fro was a blade made of steel, sharpened on the lower edge, to which a handle was fastened at a right angle at one end. The maul was a mallet, the head piece being oak, hickory,

or some other hard wood. After a tree had been felled, father would saw it into blocks of varying sizes.[29]

Big Kelly had always lived on a farm where he paid rent, and his thrift was responsible for the family's charmed life. The cruelties and hardships of Southern tenant farming were foreign to him. However, his craftsmanship made him highly esteemed by neighbors, and he had many friends among the white men who had served with him in the Confederate army.[30]

Sunfish, Sojourn and Sorrow

Miller credited his independent spirit to growing up in a stable farming community where hunting, fishing, and scouring the countryside for plums, wild grapes, and walnuts was a major pastime. In the summer, the plantation was lush with watermelons, peaches, collard greens, black-eyed peas, corn, and cowpeas. Livestock contributed an abundance of buttermilk, and the slightly sour and tangy clabbered milk that was preferred when refrigeration was not an option. He recalled drinking an entire bottle and placing the empty jar

---

[29] KMP, Box 71-2 folder 40, 2.

[30] KMP, Box 71-2 folder 40, 3. When Miller was called back to South Carolina after his father died at the age of 97, it fell on him to arrange for the funeral. On his return, a Confederate veteran who lived on the adjacent property asked permission to ride Miller to the funeral stating that he regarded Big Kelly as a comrade, the same as the other soldiers and the two of them had been the only survivors of their old regiment. He asked if there would have any objection to his placing a Confederate flag on the coffin and Miller consented to man's request but not without some misgivings. When the neighbor procession passed by his house to find the Confederate flag, he a Union flag instead, stating that this was perhaps better since the stars and stripes wave over all. Miller responded only with a silent nod, though with a loud inward, Amen. So when father's coffin was taken from the hearse it was covered with the stars and stripes, placed there by this Confederate veteran.

near the cats, telling his mother they drank it! While this incident did not incur a thrashing by his parents, it evoked some residual guilt.

Recollections of childhood foodstuffs brought fond memories of an easier life. Breakfast consisted of cornbread, molasses, bacon, buttermilk, or dried corn coffee. Once store-bought coffee was an option, the family purchased it, but preferred the parched corn coffee. Dinner was primarily vegetables, cornbread, and bacon. Supper—or lunch—was frequently porridge, cornbread, and bacon.

> Parched corn caused many a boy to go astray in a small way. Whenever possible, during fall and winter months, groups of children could be seen hurrying into the woods where a quick fire soon was blazing. Then from under tow shirts and coats would be taken ears of corn which had been filched from our fathers' cribs, and a roasting bee would follow. Parched corn and sweet potatoes, such was the menu, and the memory of those feasts still lingers with me... My mother smoked a pipe, even as did my father. Cigars and cigarettes were unheard of. At times they used home grown tobacco leaves, ground fine, but after a measure of prosperity came to the Millers, they used tobacco bought at stores. On one of those days when I was struggling with the intricacies of the blue-backed speller I filled a pipe with tobacco, struck a light and smoked away as I had seen my elders do - smoked until the entire contents of the cob pipe had been consumed. Five minutes later the world commenced to turn over and over, faster, and faster, then I became unconscious for several hours. This was my one and only smoke during 70 years. I have

no use for another, because I can always taste tobacco when I think of that day. We stored up hickory nuts and walnuts like the squirrel, for use during the chilly weather months.³¹

The family of twelve lived in a three-room cabin: Father and mother, sisters Liza and Mathilda, occupied the rooms. The seven boys slept in the narrow wooden structure where corn was kept. They used Corn husks, silks, cobs, and kernels for various purposes. Leaves were chopped into fodder for the cattle. Used shucks were made into chair cushions, padding for the horses' collars, or stuffing for mattresses. Kelly never recalled sleeping on a softer bed than one newly filled with these shucks. He recalled the corn husk mattress as "delightfully cool during the summer; and warmer than if tucked between feather beds." in winter.

Though the bittersweet country life produced what they carried to market, Miller remembered his childhood as a cup of joyful delight. And this sense of satisfaction is seen throughout its text, as when he writes,

> I can hardly appreciate the attitude of pity for the hardness of the lot of a country boy. As I look back over my life, when I was playing with my brothers, about the farm, fishing in the streams, hunting in the woods, roaming over the hillsides, it is hard for me to conceive of a boy whose life was happier than mine. It is true that my surroundings and circumstances were of the poorest and crudest type; clothes were scanty. One pair of shoes had to last the whole year. There were little or no social contacts of an elevating

---

³¹ KMP, chapter 4 "My Home Life," 36-37.

character, and yet, this narrow range of life sufficed for one submerged in it and knew no other. There were no degrading and humiliating contrasts. Where all are poor, the sting of poverty is not keenly felt.[32]

The cornfield was a precarious place for children, and Kelly bore many cuts on his hands from stripping its stalks. Occasionally, bugs would sting him, or the keen edge of a leaf would cut his palm, inflicting knife-like wounds. But Elizabeth's magical salve seemed to cure every affliction.

It was a mile and a half to the mill, which was on a bank of Mill Creek, and one had but to walk three or four miles upstream to learn why it had been given that name. There were four mills within a stretch of four miles. Above each mill was a dam which caused the water to form an artificial pond, and a current diverted from the pond and running through a sluice would give motion to the overshot wheel, which consisted of a series of buckets fastened to a circumferential frame... The miller kept a percentage of the meal, called toll, as his bill for grinding, and the remainder was placed in the bags for me to take back home. Later I learned that the pond held other attractions, it being fairly well stocked with small size fish. At first, I used to a bent pin at the end of a piece of string, with an angleworm for bait, and was quite jubilant when, after an hour's persistence, I drew out a minnow. Then came a day when I possessed a genuine fishhook, which I had bought in Winnsboro for the expenditure of half a dime received for a

---

[32] KMP, Box 71-2 folder 42, 4.

gallon of blackberries. In honor of the fishhook, I cut a pole in the woods and obtained from my mother a longer and stronger piece of string. A cork made from bamboo root, served as a bob, which would indicate when fish were biting, and thus equipped, I assured the miller that he could be as long as he liked grinding our corn, as I was in no hurry.[33]

The water yielded a bounty of pleasure and food: sunfish, minnows, and perch. Lightwood, small roots, and branches provided revenue at times. When the pin knots bound together, heavily saturated with resin, and lit, they provided poorer people light sources as a fair-sized knot would burn for half an hour and give a steady flame.

His rural boyhood years were a mixture of work, play, and sport, but the country boy was attracted to city curiosities. The five-mile Saturday trips to Winnsboro were a great time to visit town. Though he worked on the farm or was in school through the week, he always attempted to double up on his tasks on Friday to be available for these outings. But there were other also sobering memories from this time:

> [It is believed] that the ages from 5 to 12 constitute the happy period of life. This is the time of detached enjoyment... Ideally there should be no vexatious problems in youth. Nevertheless, the poet Horace, tells us that death with equal hand, knocks at the palace of the rich and the hovel of the poor... No human being, young or old, has experienced the essential realities of life unless death has invaded his

---

[33] KMP, chapter 5 "Happy Days of Childhood," 64-66.

early or late experience...Twice death invaded our family circle. First, he took away two of my younger brothers, who died at an early age, when I was only seven years old. They died within two weeks of each other, the victims of diphtheria. I cannot say that their passing made any profound lasting impression upon me beyond the pangs of the occasion, which I may have forgotten in a few months' time. Their sudden death illustrates the danger to which every country family in straightened circumstances is subjected. There was no physician within a radius of five miles. The family never learned the nature of the disease until sometime afterward... But I had an elder brother, five years older than myself. His name was Adam. Among all the members of the family, I was his favorite, and he was mine. I thought the sun rose and set in him...At his death, in March 1877, when I was 13 years old, the light went out of the world for me. I begged to be buried in his grave... It wore upon me and marked the turning point in my life.[34]

This was a "great grief" for Miller, and although he needed help on the farm, his father let him continue in school, where he encountered Reverend Willard Richardson, who opened a new prospect of life for him. Richardson's guidance and compassion challenged Kelly to not view Northern white people as solely the speculators he expected in the years after the War.

Although born into a family with ten children, the quiet and introverted child did not mix with others. Outside of school, he was shy and timid and lacked the social qualities

---

[34] KMP, Box 71-2 folder 42, 4-5.

necessary for leadership. He admired his older brothers, Isaac and Adam. Isaac, two years his senior, was debonair, full of personality, and mixed well with other children. He was a dancer and skilled in talking to girls. He defended Kelly when other children teased him. Conversely, Adam, who was one year older, was his number one fan, and he was Adam's. Their closeness in age and intimate relationship deeply influenced Kelly, and Adam's untimely death ended his childhood innocence and taught him that life was fragile while propelling him to value the opportunity school afforded him and excel even more. The pain of loss made him realize that learning was transcendent, for as he recounted:

> ... because I persisted in the study of Webster's Blue Backed Speller and supplemented this with continuous study of other books, I can look back upon a life in which, rung by rung, I mounted the ladder of power student, alumnus, instructor, professor, vice dean, then dean of one of the great universities in the land. I live in comfort with members of my family in a home which I own, and we shall never know want because of the retirement pay which comes to me for the reason that I qualified myself with an education.[35]

His concept of the interaction between industrial and classical education was birthed when he wore homespun clothing made from cotton he picked and thread and fabric his mother made. He considered the education received while working on the farm before and after school during the four-month session and industrious activity during the eight-

---

[35] KMP, chapter 5 "Knowledge is Power," 48-49.

month "vacation" as the foundational fusion of intellectual stimulation and manual labor that produced a person fit for servant leadership. He saw his birth at the close of the Civil War, between enslaved and free-born siblings, his affinity for finding the medium between opposing views, his innate curiosity, and mathematical skill as the seedbed of his daysman ideology, balance-mindedness, and dedication to finding resolutions to situations many considered unsolvable.

A Christian Journey

As a child, Kelly never read the Bible because no such book was on the family table. He received his first religious instruction from a divinity student from Biddle University's seminary. And his first great moral and spiritual lessons came through reading songs. He recounted sweet memories in singing such soul-melting lyrics as "Oh, you must be a lover of the Lord if you want to get to heaven when you die;' "Around the throne of God in heaven ten thousand children stand;" "I want to be an angel with the angels stand, a crown upon my forehead and a harp within my hand;" and "Jesus loves me this I know, for the Bible tells me so."[36]

Throughout childhood, Kelly had an ardent desire to know God, experience divine visitation, and ensure his soul's salvation. But though he never joined a church, he affiliated with the Presbyterians, for they held a special place in Miller's heart since their schools provided an opportunity to move beyond the confines of Winnsboro. His Uncle Joe served as a church school superintendent and builder whose efforts resulted in the formation of the Shiloh First United Presbyterian Church in 1880.

---

[36] KMP, Box 71-2 folder 44, 2.

Later, he realized his instruction in morality was Bible-based as he had learned from community elders that "the Bible was a holy book, written by holy men inspired by the Holy Ghost."[37] Miller credited his reverence for Scripture for providing his faith in the milk of human kindness and employed biblical stories throughout his writings.

> The Bible became a sacred book, and thus it has ever remained in my mind and imagination. The sacred and secular education took place in the same schoolhouse building. I regularly attended Sunday School and once a month attended church, as often as the minister filled this station on his circuit. My Sunday School teachers were recruited from the two or three colored men who had learned to read and write under the slave regime. The scripture lessons and song service made a deep and abiding impression upon me. I became a regular attendant of the little Sunday School which, at first, was held in Joe Thompson's house, and afterwards, transferred to the school building. Often, I was the only pupil in the Sunday School. I well recall the prayer which Joe Thompson was accustomed to utter on such occasions. "O Lord, we are too many to be lost, and not enough to be saved.[38]

Kelly learned several scriptural passages and gospel hymns in Sunday School. Ministers would line out the hymns, verse by verse, for those who could not read or didn't have a hymnal. By simply repeating what was heard, he acquired a body of scriptural and lyrical literature, but he was convinced

---
[37] Ibid, 3.
[38] KMP, Box 71-2 folder 44, 3-4.

of a need for centered spiritual values and a relationship with Christ at an early age. When, on one occasion, he was brought to tears and asked why he was crying, he stated that he feared his soul might be lost. Of his early spiritual experience, Miller would later write that:

> Conversion by experience was universally required of those who wished to join the church. Candidates were expected to see sights and hear sounds. Revivals and experience meetings were held at several churches. I tried all I knew how to "get religion" according to the prevailing mode, without any positive success. On one occasion I walked home by myself through the woods, to and from [a variety of] revival meetings, with the express purpose of receiving a visitation on that lonesome trip, but the coveted light was not vouchsafed to me. I used to wonder at the suddenness with which the same individual could get religion during the revival season in the wintertime and backslide to join the dancing brigade and the baseball players as regularly as the summer season arrived.[39]

In his longing for holiness, the young Christian experienced a divine visitation that drew him closer to the sacred world. This desire for a close relationship with Christ gave him a sense of truth, service, mission, and purpose that would be fulfilled by a life dedicated to education and reconciliation. This sense of purpose characterized who he would become as a daysman who harmonized divergent viewpoints.

---

[39] KMP, Box 71-2 folder 44, 5.

Part of his spiritual heritage came from witnessing camp meetings where people came by mule, horseback, or country wagon. In these settings,

> [a]ll of the preachers within reach would gather and display their sermonic powers at this religious feast. But the camp meeting was as much a secular consort as a religious meeting place. All the young men would be there to show off their fine clothes and to escort their lady-love. The religious excesses and grotesque performances of these camp meetings were disgusting to me, as a boy." They very aptly fulfilled Robert Byrnes description of "The Holy Fair" where "some were filled with the grace of God, and some were filled with brandy.[40]

He remembered the country church he attended from age nine to fourteen as a fusion of community and culture. Rural black Christians were unconcerned with what they considered superficialities such as a minister's educational background or the congregation's size. Instead, they focused on their eternal souls. They were led by country preachers who felt called to preach by the Lord or popularity. Though many were illiterate, Miller never doubted their genuineness and sincerity, for he said,

> A youth of ten or twelve years, caught up in such environment, was almost certain to be swept beyond his conscious moorings. Such happenings constituted my religious experience and observations while I was submerged in the country until my fourteenth year.

---

[40] KMP, Box 71-2 folder 44, 5-6.

> But, fortified as I was in firm moral convictions derived from my mother, I was held to decent behavior without evangelical influence... I had received a touch of the Presbyterian influence which looked with disdain upon the noise, confusion and grotesque carryings-on of the more ignorant Methodists and Baptists.[41]

He believed this moral and spiritual atmosphere shaped his character and life projection.

> I am not vain enough to suppose that my personal experience would be of any importance or significance to any considerable number of readers, but just as I have taken my life as a yardstick to measure the advancement of the Negro race. So, I regard my experience as typical of those passed through by thousands of Negro youth just after Emancipation who were subject to the same sort of environmental conditions as myself.[42]

During Reconstruction, most of the African Americans held a strong rural Christian worldview. Protestant and denominations sought to educate newly freed black people. For they believed that though Christianity had been hijacked by enslavement, it could raise the moral level that would make them fit citizens. This first legally educated generation was linked to enslavement through parental history or personal experience, but saw that the God of Exodus, who provided the end of enslavement, would provide greater

---

[41] Ibid., 6.
[42] Ibid. 44, 6.

future opportunity. As James Weldon Johnson's *Negro National Anthem* articulated:

> Lest our feet stray from the places, our God, where we met Thee. Lest our hearts, drunk with the wine of the world, we forget Thee. Shadowed beneath Thy hand, may we forever stand, True to our God, true to our native land.[43]

This hope infused Miller with a sense of responsibility to live his life shadowed beneath the hand of God. For he saw himself as the living embodiment of the hope of the entire race of formerly enslaved people and the bridge to a better tomorrow.

Just as the race started at school on the same day that I did, in a comparable manner, this experience gained its moral and spiritual awakening. The whole race was coming into a new moral life and a new sense of religious value. Indeed, I saw and experienced the race in the making, of which I formed a part.[44]

---

[43] "Lift Every Voice and Sing" Words by James Weldon Johnson and music by John Rosamond Johnson, 1900.

[44] KMP, Box 71-2 folder 44, 6.

Two
A Vastly Different Life Opens: 1880-1889

Let not conscience make you linger - Nor of fitness fondly dream —All the fitness He requires is to feel your need of Him.

Come ye Sinners Poor and Needy
Kelly Miller[45]

The 1880s were pivotal for Miller. Within six years of arriving at Howard, he received a degree and went on to become the first African American student admitted to Johns Hopkins University.

Reverend Richardson encouraged Kelly to pursue higher education and a career in Christian ministry where he could extract the talents of other African Americans. The young man embraced his commission without a heady sense of pride, but as a humble servant. Like his enslaved ancestors and the survivors such as his mother, he felt constrained to contribute to future generations. For him, education was the key to unlocking this future and equalizing the playing field. As he said,

> Picture me, nearing 14, when the great change came into my life. I never had seen a newspaper, or a magazine, never heard a lecture, never had received what today is meant by "instruction" from a teacher. All those who had taught during the eight years in

---

[45] "Come ye Sinners Poor and Needy" in B W Stone and T Adams, compilers, *The Christian Hymn-Book*. Lexington KY: N L Finnell, 1829, 3. Transcribed in KMP, Box 71-2 folder 46, 5.

the first and second schools, had been almost ignorant as their pupils, and they repeated, parrot like, the words and sentences found in textbooks.[46]

Fairfield Institute and Reverend Richardson

Miller saw the benevolence of white Christians in his interracial community as atonement for the injustice experienced by African Americans. To him, Richardson was one such person who was motivated to establish Fairfield Institute to elevate students' moral and religious development. After the Civil War, mainline denominations flooded southern states to open schools and assisted in reconstructing a semblance of normalcy, including the education of all youth. In Winnsboro, the Presbyterian church was represented by both black and white missionaries in pulpits, classrooms, and community. These men and women enlightened the population of Winnsboro by their presence and connections beyond South Carolina.

Richardson observed Kelly's math skills and selected the talented young man for special attention, for he had not met anyone in Fairfield County with such mathematical ability, and he was connected to his destiny.

> It happened one day that a stranger visited our school. He was a white man, advanced in years, a kind, courteous gentleman. I was told he was missionary from the northern states. This meant little or nothing, except that it coupled his calling with that of a man named Francis who several years before had conducted revival meetings while standing beneath a

---

[46] KMP, Kelly Miller "I Am Introduced to a New World," *Autobiography*, 71.

brush arbor which had been hastily constructed in the woods. I never had attended the services conducted by the evangelist; but from a distance had heard him shouting exhortations and lending his powerful voice during the singing of gospel hymns; and the announcement that the school visitor was a missionary caused me at first to liken him to the man with the voice that cried in the woods.[47]

The elderly, northern missionary had been born in Pennsylvania in 1815. His father was an ordained Presbyterian minister and founder of the University of Harford. By the close of the 1840s, the younger Richardson had attended the Franklin Academy, Hamilton College, and after becoming principal at the Academy at Franklin, Pennsylvania, Auburn Theological Seminary.

After completing Seminary, he continued his relationship with the Academy and returned there in 1848 as a mathematics and natural sciences professor. He influenced his pupils so much that many were prominent in national affairs.[48]

On Sundays, he preached throughout the Catawba Synod, into which all the Presbyterian missions to Africans had been organized. The abolitionist prophesied more than once during the 1840s, '… the day is not far distant when the government will extend equal rights to all men."[49] In 1852, he stopped teaching to assume the pulpit at Conklin Church in New York. During the Civil War, he served as a chaplain for the 86th New York Infantry Regiment, then returned to a

---

[47] Ibid., 72.
[48] *The History of the Conklin Presbyterian Church*, 56. Vertical file on Reverend Willard Richardson. Fairfield County Library, Winnsboro, South Carolina.
[49] Ibid., 58.

subdued life of home, family, and church in Delaware for a while.

When the Presbyterian Home Missionary Society began organizing schools throughout the South in 1866, they asked Richardson to help educate Winnsboro's newly freed African Americans. He accepted the role of lead instructor at the Fairfield Academy and established a grade school system that became a model for other southern towns. Thirteen years later, an article in the *Fairfield News and Herald* noted his work:

> Improvement in the country schools is very marked. The credit is chiefly due to Mr. Richardson. He came here eight years ago as a missionary and teacher for colored people. Quietly pursued his duty, never prostituting his profession by making it a steppingstone to political preferment... He brought order out chaos. Advanced money from his pocket, his worth is appreciated.[50]

When he died from pneumonia at age 82, his daughter Clara Richardson Pierce wrote to the *Fairfield News and Herald*:

> ... Father loved Winnsboro very, very much, and the last thing mother read to him was the news in the *Winnsboro News and Herald* the day before he died. Mr. Richardson came to this place as a missionary and teacher to the colored people at a time when there was much bitterness between the sections of the Union. Many who had come on similar missions exerted an evil, rather than a good influence. But through his earnest and sincere attention to his duties

---

[50] Ibid., 60.

his unobtrusive, upright life, his broad-mindedness and his sincere interest in the welfare of the whole community, he first disarmed enmity and then inspired respect and regard. His work in elevating the character of his pupils is seen to-day.[51]

Though able to receive instruction and glean from Richardson's spiritual leadership, the duplicity of some northern missionaries contributed to Kelly's disdain for "organized" religion.

> Indeed, these two cultural forces have served to keep the Negro race divided from the days of emancipation to now, when all the missionaries coming from contact with high modes of life often sought to belittle or eliminate the natural and normal culture which the race derives from its inheritance and environment. The missionaries looked upon the Negro in the same way that they look upon the heathen in Africa, and in other parts of the world [and that is]. Their indigenous culture must be uprooted to make place for the high culture brought from contact with European civilization. They would substitute for what they regarded as ignorance and superstition a more excellent way. They made no allowance for the peculiar religious genius of the Negro which exists in revelry and explosion.[52]

---

[51] *Fairfield News and Herald* March 31, 1897. Vertical file on Reverend Willard Richardson. Fairfield County Library, Winnsboro, South Carolina.
[52] KMP, Box 71-2 folder 45, 4-5.

The missionaries he encountered carried the Bible in one hand and a textbook in the other and could easily shift emphasis from the church to the school. For he noted that,

> [a]fter a generation of trial and failure they practically gave up the attempt to gather Negroes into religious denominations after their own pattern and confined their efforts chiefly to educational development. The great institutions which survive as monuments to this early missionary endeavor are of an educational character. Although they planted church and school together, the school has increased, and the church decreased.[53]

While he was encouraged by his Uncle Joe and Biddle student, Lethia Jackson, Richardson was the first formally educated white man to show interest in his educational pursuits. He suggested that Kelly's parents allow him to pursue his education unfettered by farm chores. So, in the fall of 1876, Kelly enrolled in the Freedmen's Institute, where sessions were held for nine months in the year instead of four. Miller remained at the school for three years, the first two as a commuter traveling 10 miles roundtrip. The trek often left him feeling tired. Yet, his desire to learn compelled him to attend as many sessions as possible after completing long days of farm chores. And as he points out, he was rewarded for his effort.

> I well remember the morning when I started far too early for my first day's attendance at this new school. I sensed that I was adventuring upon a new life,

---

[53] KMP, Box 71-2 folder 45, 7.

although I could not have expressed my meaning in language. But it was not the school as a school which attracted me, but the personality of the man who was its head. I can see him now as he welcomed me with a kindly clasp of the hand. And then I learned that I was not to be seated in the lower room but would join the more advanced pupils under Dr. Richardson's personal guidance.[54]

His last year was as a boarding student, an opportunity that prepared him for dormitory life at Howard University. As he described his change in circumstance:

On quitting the farm for a boarding school, one always feels a sudden transformation in his life as if shifting from one plane to another. There always exists a certain semblance of a nobleman to those who have once attended a boarding school. This becomes a badge of distinction upon which they look with endearment and fond recollections through the rest of their lives.[55]

Kelly deeply enjoyed the favor and special math instruction he received from the principal of Freedmen's Institute. Richardson's bible-based lessons enhanced Kelly's mother's influence and grounded him in the Christian faith. He also became acquainted with the history of people whose lives predated his and the world of thought about the millions who were contemporary. He wrote:

---

[54] KMP, "I Am Introduced to a New World," 75.
[55] KMP, Box 71-2 folder 46, 5.

To understand what this wealth of information meant to me it must be recalled and that heretofore a small section of Fairfield County had been my entire world, and I had no concept that anything lay beyond. This complete metamorphosis of my intellectual faculties no doubt will with difficulty be understood by the youth of today, who through the media of the cinema, the radio, newspapers, and magazines, is introduced not only to the world but to the universe by the time he reaches the age when I was taught that a cat is spelled c-a-t-.[56]

At first, Kelly considered a profession in the ministry or mathematics and commented that:

A teacher-ship was the highest position to which the ambitious young people of the county might aspire. A few of the older men who claimed to have heard a voice in the sky occupied pulpits in the Baptist and Methodist denominations. Their educational advancement consisted of the ability to read the scriptures and line the hymns. These were too vain and conceited to attend a secular school to learn how to preach the gospel. The students at Fairfield Institute constituted the intellectual elite of the County. Under the building hand of the Fairfield Institute, the Presbyterian ministers were supposed to pass through the regular course of training before entering upon ordination.[57]

---

[56] There are two citations 54 and 55 both are from his public biography. Some chapters are titles others are not. Seemingly, this is from the chapter, "I am Introduced to a New World."

[57] KMP, Box 71-2 folder 46, 2-2a.

His mathematical gift made him the teacher's favorite. Though this attention allowed him to experience "a newness of life," other students were initially ridiculed by his homespun clothes. When, finally, he overcame the ridicule and made a favorable impression on fellow students, he wrote:

> The scornful laughter which greeted me on my first appearance, on account of my peculiar [clothing], was changed into admiration when the pupils sought my assistance to help them with their knotty problems in arithmetic.[58]

Miller's learning led him to reflect deeper: Why had he been gifted in math? Why had his brother Adam died? Why had his parents allowed him to attend school and encourage his innate ability? Many other questions perplexed him, and Richardson tried to explain the meaning and purpose of religion.

The family held no formal religious beliefs, so he was left to select the path that suited him. Though he never formally joined a church or affiliated with a denomination, the Presbyterian Church markedly influenced him. At age 15, he listened to Richardson's biblical explanation about the purpose of life. He understood that acceptance of the principles of the Christian life was all that Jesus required, for Richardson held that one's need for God would be met when one reached out to God and was fond of saying.

> "Let not conscience make you linger – Nor of fitness fondly dream – All the fitness He requires is to feel your need of Him."

---

[58] Ibid., 3.

Kelly could not embrace the emotional abandonment of many holiness groups nor the rote Episcopal or Catholic liturgy. And his "spiritual awakening" did not conform to any denominational structure. Instead, he sought conversion through "angelic visitation," "opening skies," and other signs or voices from on high. Though none of these happened, his writings and observations are infused with Christian imagery and allegory, and his non-conformist ethical code embodied an African American spirituality that blended bible-based morality with a desire to live a life of service to God and humanity. Miller believed that while many black people embraced the Methodist and Baptist churches and, as time progressed, also joined the Presbyterians, Congregationalists, and Episcopalians, they had harmonized African, European, and indigenous religions to form their own with Christian cosmology.

The fusion of his mother's wisdom, his father's industrial fortitude, and Richardson's moral temperance nurtured him into a principled, diligent, and compassionate man. These elements, coupled with education, provide the sense of purpose he incorporated into his teaching style. Within "moral pedagogy." That extended beyond the classroom into practical living. Education was more than simply learning letters and dates. It was a holistic commitment to elicit the best from the teacher and student.

From Fairfield Institute to Howard University

Richardson believed the brightest African American intellectuals belonged in the pulpit, where they could infuse others with a sense of moral duty, Christian temperance, and solid values. For him, these were the building blocks for productive citizenship. Thus, those fortunate enough to obtain an education were ambassadors of and to the race.[59] His support landed Kelly a scholarship from the Presbyterian Board of Missions for Freedmen to attend Howard University. So, at age 17, he left Winnsboro for "something" more educational:

> Imagine a rustic lad from the backwoods of an upland county in South Carolina suddenly transplanted to the City of Washington in the year of 1880. My experience was nothing less amazing than those according to Alice in Wonderland. I received my larger education from the city of Washington and its cultural opportunities while pursuing my intimate tuition at Howard University.[60]

Big Kelly and Elizabeth were delighted when he received the scholarship. It provided a reason to purchase a new suit, other clothing, a small trunk, and a tin bucket full of food and gave him about $10 in his pocket. The 392-mile journey to Howard marked a physical and emotional separation from all that was familiar to him. This was the first time he had ridden a train or traveled outside South Carolina, for his world had been circumscribed within a five-mile radius in any direction from his father's farm. Washington began a new, adventurous life with high hopes in his heart.

---

[59] Ultimately Miller decided against a career in ministry in 1914 he penned an article encouraging the talented tenth to pursue the ministry as a career option instead of government or politics. "The negro preacher has a larger influence and function than his white confrere... Almost every feature of leadership and authority comes within his prerogative." Talented Tenth in Ministry in Kelly Miller's *Out of the House of Bondage*, 1914, 203-204.

[60] KMP, Box 71-2 folder 49, 1.

On to Washington

His travel companion, Clarence Dillard, a former student at Fairfield Institute, was returning to the city after attending a relative's funeral. The two left Winnsboro at 4:00 p.m., October 31, and arrived at the Pennsylvania Railroad depot at 6th and B streets in Northeast Washington at noon on November 1, 1880. Of his arrival, he would write:

> Then, as now, the Pennsylvania Railroad furnished the only gateway between the north and south. The Pennsylvania depot was standing on B Street near the edge of Pennsylvania Avenue in full gaze of the Capitol. The old station is noted as the place where President Garfield was assassinated just seven months after my arrival in the Capitol. The contrast between Washington and Winnsboro of that day was scarcely more striking in many particulars than that between the capital city during the last half century is a fair gauge of the advancement of the nation along the line of municipal improvement.[61]

The two hired a horse-drawn carriage to travel the 2.1 miles to the campus. Miller would have walked the distance had he known his destination and not had luggage. At that time, this was the only means of transportation within the city, and these fancy carriages dotted the Washington landscape of a place whose sights and sounds were very different than in Winnsboro.

However, the campus was a half mile from the city's boundary, and since neither had money to hire a horse and

---

[61] Ibid.

buggy beyond that point, they had to walk the remaining distance with their luggage.

The cosmopolitan atmosphere of Kelly's new home filled him with awe and excitement. Its spaces were occupied by nationally and internationally known people, including educated African Americans who had elevated themselves and their race. But the intra-racial strife that he witnessed between the city's newly freed and pre-Civil War free persons and between light and dark-complexioned black people fascinated and disturbed him, and he sought to understand them and see them destroyed.

Beginning College Life: Becoming a Howard Man

Kelly was assigned a room on the fourth floor in Clark Hall with two other students, one of whom had also been a student of Richardson.[62] Adjusting to this space that would be his home for six years was easy because of his boarding experience at Fairfield Institute. Adjusting to the schedule of the college pace, however, proved more difficult. The day began with the six a.m. morning bell, followed by breakfast at seven. Then, students had an hour and a half to tidy their rooms and prepare for the day. Courses, held from nine a.m. until three p.m., involved alternating study with recitations of lines of poetry, history, and mathematical formulas. Dinner was served at 4 p.m. From five until seven p.m., students were free to entertain themselves. At seven p.m., the bell summoned them to the study hours until ten p.m.

---

[62] Howard's campus in 1880 was located outside of the official federal city more than ¼ mile from the city boundary line at present day Florida Avenue. The campus was an agrarian space sitting atop a hill on a knoll overlooking Washington and the entire city could be viewed from the spire atop Clark Hall. This captivating view of the city and surroundings from the dome surpassed those from any other point in or about the city.

Remaining an aloof introvert, Kelly enjoyed exploring the campus environment and visiting downtown Washington alone. He was not the typical college man who played sports or engaged women. He never learned to dance and was shy with women. Thus, he lived in self-imposed seclusion in his room during the unscheduled time. Once, he jotted poetic lines in a trigonometry book:

> What though I can in number rant - Derive a cosine from a secant. Construct a logarithmic table - Translate both Greek and Latin fable. Since all of these are nothing able - To comfort me without my Mable.[63]

Temporarily forgetting his note, he lent his book to a classmate who exposed his secret and subjected him to his classmates' teasing and laughter. This incident pushed him deeper inward and fostered more of his preferred solo outings. Other times, his sole companions were English literature, poetry, and mathematics books.

Though his siblings could write, he received few letters from home, except an occasional message from Isaac, who served as the family correspondent. There was no financial support because there was no money to spare.

Howard's tuition fluctuated according to government appropriations. During any year, fees cover charges for dormitory\care, laundry service, meals, and a small amount for toiletries, a total outlay of approximately more than $150.00.[64] His scholarship from the Presbyterian Church paid his tuition. Still, the expense of clothing, food, books, school supplies, and occasional treats, such as his favorite

---

[63] KMP, Box 71-2 folder 51, 3.
[64] Or Approximately $5,000 in today's market.

gingerbread, depended on his efforts. Since most historically black colleges employed students as janitors, cooks, tutors, and in other perfunctory roles to subsidize their education, Miller cut grass, worked in the University garden, and did odd campus jobs, including scrubbing floors and washing windows. This work allowed him to dress as well as the average student since the competitive style and reputation of Howard students required Miller to "fit in." It also afforded him the luxury of an overcoat when the weather warranted more than a sweater. And though financial issues did not detract from his enjoyment of the intellectual rigor of college life, he spent many holidays on campus since he could not afford to travel home.

Students were forbidden from smoking or drinking alcohol in the study hall or dormitories from dancing, playing cards, or attending theaters. But these regulations were often broken, and his classmates lodged many youthful antics to get around the strict rules. In one instance, Kelly imbibed his first and possibly last social drink when some students brewed eggnog on Christmas Eve in their room. The episode resulted in a riotous event, and the next day, there was an investigation. When questioned, he admitted to participating in the incident. The punishment was a mild reprimand.

After a series of reprimands, however, he resolved that following the rules was easier than facing disgrace or expulsion. As he recalled:

> [It was] difficult for an uncontaminated country lad to preserve his delicacy of conscience when thrown in promiscuous contact with a student body, the majority of whom not like minded as himself. Unless he is a good mixer and joins in the sports and frivolities and mischief of the crowd, he incurs the

jibes and ridicule of his associates. Fortunately, among my classmates was a boy of my own age, William R. A. Palmer, of Charleston South Carolina, who at that tender age, had consecrated himself to the Christian ministry of the Methodist Episcopal Church. He was more rigid in his conduct and observances of the moral and ethical code than myself and set a hard pace for me to follow. As a rule, we were separated from more frivolous and sporty boys by a self-distance of our own imposing. Palmer always kept Good Friday religiously as a day of fasting. We were both fond of "Washington pie" [cake layers filled with jelly or jam] On a certain Good Friday I bought a luscious slice of Washington pie and placed it on the table to test how serious his profession was. The next day he gave me an upbraiding which my shabby conduct deserved.[65]

Howard's preparatory department was a pre-collegiate program to equip students for college-level work. It exposed students to languages, math, and literature they might not have had in their earlier education because, generally, instruction in most local African American schools only included late elementary school-level instruction.

Work at the Pension Office

After completing the preparatory curriculum in 1883, Kelly became a full-fledged freshman. In January of that year, Congress adopted the civil servant examinations for hiring government employees throughout the country. In the autumn of that year, 14,000 people took these tests, hoping to

---

[65] KMP, Box 71-2 folder 50, 3-4.

obtain federal employment. The following spring, Kelly completed the second round of examination takers, but several months passed before he was informed about the results.

In the summer of 1884, he worked as a waiter at Camp Bello, a Canadian resort near Eastport, Maine. His obvious displeasure with this work led to several reprimands and multiple disciplinary actions before a telegram informed him that he had passed the examination and obtained a position as a clerk in the Pension Office. The salary of $900.00 was a year, and he was ecstatic for, in his words,

> No person inheriting a fortune could feel more elation than did I upon receipt of that telegram which assured me a government position and salary of $900.00 a year. To me who had walked five miles to sell a bushel of blackberries or a pack of lightwood for a dime and had passed many an afternoon mowing a lawn for a quarter, it was a princely sum. Indeed, it was a goodly wage, for at that time a dollar would go further than two dollars at the present writing… "I rejoiced fully as much because of my delivery from the servitude of waiting upon guests at tables. The repugnance I felt toward this task was no doubt due to the fact that we had led an independent life back home. Only once had a member of the family acted as a servant… when Liza for a short time returned to the old plantation as a domestic. I detested waiting on tables. Once I was a bellhop for a spell in a hotel at Wesley, Massachusetts and that I enjoyed. It was sport rather than work. But the toting of food from the kitchen and the removal of soiled dishes was a job I disliked more than anything I ever had undertaken.

My pay was $25 a month which was supposed to be increased by the receipt of tips from the guests. But my many mistakes cut me off from this source of revenue, indeed in all fairness; I should have paid those upon whom I awkwardly waited for the annoyance I caused them. When I received the cable about the civil service job [I left immediately].[66]

Kelly had previously met Professor James Gregory, an Oberlin College graduate who tutored in mathematics in that department. Gregory considered him "a member of his family" and entrusted Kelly to house-sit during his travels away from campus. This closeness led to Miller standing as godfather to his daughter and tutoring his two sons, one of whom graduated from Harvard, the other from Yale.

James M. Gregory

---

[66] KMP, chapter 18 "Both a Clerk and Student," 135-136.

While Miller received congratulations from the Howard community on landing the position, Gregory assured him that his study and recitation hours could be rearranged so as not to interfere with his work duties. So, he entered another phase of life, thankful for the opportunity to improve himself.

His first position was as a copyist, but he was quickly promoted to a clerkship. For the next two years, he balanced full-time work with full-time study. He worked from nine am to four pm for four years. His double role was tedious but a relief for his financial woes. Howard University embraced its working students' schedule by adding night courses. Further, his professors gave him instruction outside of scheduled hours so he did not have to use sick days or vacation leave to finish schoolwork.

The election of 1884 promised to provoke celebration for Howard students. When they asked President William Weston Patton[67] if they could host a bonfire, he persuaded them to hold off until after the election. But election results doused plans for a bonfire, silenced speeches, led Miller to delete a poem he had written for the occasion, and began to open the political eyes of black people. Their leaders protested President Grover Cleveland's policies that promoted bigoted responses to issues of racial equality and an open-door policy to ex-Confederate veterans.

Moreover, Cleveland's opposition to integrating New York public schools emboldened racial conservatives and signaled his abandonment of liberal ideals. His administration divided the political allegiance of the black community so that one faction sought to sway federal government leaders to enforce the 14th Amendment, which was being nullified by extralegal measures. The others sought

---

[67] The ardent abolitionist and scholar served as the fifth president of Howard University. His tenure ran from 1877 to 1889

political solutions that opposed governmental policies. The 1880s were fraught with other challenges to post-Civil War legislation that abolished slavery, proved equal protection under the law, and enfranchised black men. In 1883, the United States Supreme Court consolidated 5 cases because of their similarities. The court declared the Civil Rights Act of 1875 unconstitutional, which empowered Jim Crow laws. So, the nineteenth century closed with *Plessy v. Ferguson,* instituting a separate and unequal America.

Kelly's response to the election was to move from the Republican party to Cleveland's Democratic party and eventually to non-participatory independence. He saw politics as an ugly business and reasoned that he could not become a partisan party member since both groups could be swayed with the strongest wind to gain political office and held representation of the people as secondary. This stance reflected his daysman ideology, for he saw the purpose of leadership as charting a course for others. For him, Americans —especially African Americans—needed to build character without vacillating political ties. As he put it,

> [m]y sympathies veered from the Republican to the Democratic Party, under the liberal leadership of Grover Cleveland. My position in the Pension Office enabled me to observe and understand the policy of President Cleveland and felt convinced that, as far as, the Negro was concerned, there was no great difference between the two parties, that, although the race had been given its freedom and rights under the Republican administration, still they would not be jeopardized by the triumph of the Democratic party in national politics. Grover Cleveland emancipated the minds of the Negro and marked a turning point

in the political outlook of the race. From that time until now I have steadily striven to convince my race, as well as, my white fellow citizens, that the advancement and permanent place of the Negro in American life [was] not dependent upon any political party, but the goodwill and cooperation of all right-minded American citizens, regardless of party label.[68]

Graduation, Home Visit, and New Career

In 1886, the only three graduates were William R.A. Palmer, Josephine J. Turpin, and Miller who missed being valedictorian when the faculty abolished this honor for the first time. He believed that the non-resident character of his last half of courses contributed to their decision, but that he understood the import of his accomplishment, for he said,

> every Negro college student, in my day, looked upon himself as a marked man and was so regarded by the faculty... students in other departments, and... the outside world. There were not a hundred Negro college graduates in the whole country at that time. The Negro collegian was led to suppose that liberal culture would confer upon him a charmed life and talismanic power.[69]

During the nineteenth century, higher education had been unavailable to most black families. Farming required manual labor that called for all available hands to work to maintain livable conditions. So, for every African American child of enslaved parents, born into, or on the cusp of, emancipation, college graduation was a recurring

---

[68] KMP, Box 71-2 folder 54, 5-6.
[69] KMP, Box 71-2 folder 53, 3.

emancipation. These children of enslaved parents, born into, or on the cusp of, emancipation reach that propelled them to hitherto unfathomable heights. They were bridges between the chasm of the dark past of legalized illiteracy and a future of bright possibilities. Miller understood this empowering moment as divinely fitting him to serve his family, the race, and the nation. Nevertheless, he described his sense of disillusionment when, after the long-awaited graduation day arrived, life seemed no different:

> I left the dormitory that eventful morning after graduation. I heard birds singing, but their [song] was not more musical than it had been on the day previous, I saw flowers in bloom, but their colors were not more gorgeous, the green of trees was the same, no additional sheen was on the leaves. I said goodbye to my classmates who were seeking a place in the arena of the world's work, if haply, they might find it. I shook hands with other students, also professors, and their demeanor was as it had been. The driver did not salute me; neither did the policeman at the corner. I observed the buildings, they had not altered. Flags were out, here and there, but so they had been on other days. Yet, I Kelly Miller, had been graduated from college![70]

Miller questioned where he would go from there and what he would do with what he had learned. In the interim, he turned down an offer of a math professorship at the University of Louisville and returned to the Pension Office. Though he still wrestled with financial issues, he reasoned

---

[70] Ibid., 4.

that a calling should not be gauged by the profit one could make. Yet, since he enjoyed his work there, he could have stayed with the goal of contending to render public service. But Kelly believed that these were times when "fields [were] white unto harvest" for those willing to work toward a brighter future for the race. Further, he felt he should not bury his education and talent in a government position when they might give light to the world and wrote:

> The greater the need for service the readier should be the response, without regard to material reward. I have striven to carry forward and persist in the ideal derived from my early tradition and missionary environment, despite the allurement and temptations of the fleshy minded day and generation. As a toiler in the vineyard of service I have been more anxious about the worthiness of the laborer than the attractiveness of the hire.[71]

Before plotting his future, Kelly revisited Winnsboro, where he had not been in six years. The separation from family heightened his humility, and once there, he used most of his savings to purchase the 100-acre farm known as Kelly Miller Place that his family had cultivated as a graduation gift to his parents. The 800-dollar purchased allowed his father to work the land on his own terms rather than as shares for as long as his parents lived, and he recalled:

> It was good to be with the old folks again, and with my [siblings]. It was good to walk over the farm and recall memories of childhood, and to meet the few

---

[71] Ibid., 5.

neighbors whom I had known as a boy. I remained for two weeks in South Carolina visiting old scenes and renewing my boyhood acquaintances among both races. Six years' time had worked a wonderful change in my earlier environment, and in my own point of view.[72]

When Kelly returned to Washington, he sought advice from noted astronomer and mathematician Simon Newcomb concerning his educational and career direction. [73]He recommended Miller to British mathematician, Edgar Frisby, under whom Miller was privately tutored in analytical geometry and differential and integral calculus for a year as a non-traditional student. Kelly also sought instruction in French and German in preparation for postgraduate studies and, after a year, asked Newcomb if Hopkins was a good place to further his studies.

At the urging of the two mentors, Miller began communicating with Hopkins as early as 1885, informing school personnel of his soon-to-be-completed degree from

---

[72] Ibid., 6.

[73] Newcomb had risen from rural Nova Scotia to international prominence as an astronomer with the United States Navy and a professor at Johns Hopkins University. He retired as a Rear Admiral but was a "paper and pencil" officer at the Nautical Almanac Office at the Naval Observatory. In his memoir, *Reminiscences of an Astronomer*, he recounts that his father, who was his first instructor, was a country schoolteacher" in Nova Scotia and Prince Edward Island, two agrarian communities that valued farming, raising cattle and production of industrial materials above book knowledge. At 16, he was apprenticed to "Doctor" Foshay of Salisbury, New Brunswick, a quack herbalist. Two years later, Newcomb ran away to join his father in the United States. He found teaching jobs in Maryland, that gave him allowed to the Smithsonian Institution, and eventually became a founding member, and the first president, of the American Astronomical Society. He also served as president of the American Association for the Advancement of Science from 1876 to 1878, president of the American Mathematical Society from 1897 to 1898, and vice president of the National Academy of Sciences in 1883.

Howard and expressing interest in obtaining a doctorate in mathematics. Miller indicated that he wanted to study as many courses as possible in several fields as a candidate for a Doctor of Philosophy in mathematics, physics, and astronomy.[74] He also informed them of his special circumstances, including needing funding and off-site housing since he lived in Washington. When he did not receive an answer, he sent another letter which read:

> I have received your circular and register but do not find therein the direct information… Please have the kindness to answer the following questions: 1. If one wishes to become a candidate for the degree of Doctor of Philosophy and chooses some official branch- mathematics for example - how many other branches will he be compelled to pursue, and how far? 2. Upon what conditions can one become a candidate for this degree Ph.D. not residing at the Univ.? 3 In what branches must one pass the competitive examinations to procure a scholarship or a fellowship? 4. Has the Univ. By answering the above questions, you will greatly oblige one who desires to become a student at Johns Hopkins University - at an early date. Respectfully yours, KM July 1885.[75]

Hopkins' Quaker roots were attractive to Miller because, like the Presbyterians, the Quaker's abolitionism resonated with him. For them, race was not a barrier. Thus, Miller was accepted and enrolled in the two-year postgraduate program

---

[74] Ferdinand Hamburger Archives of The Johns Hopkins University, Record Group 13.010, Office of the Registrar, subgroup 1, series 2.

[75] Ferdinand Hamburger Archives of The Johns Hopkins University, Record Group 13.010, Office of the Registrar, subgroup 1, series 2.

in math, physics, and astronomy. He was admitted after Frisby approached President Daniel Gilman to present Miller's application to the Board of Trustees, and as Hopkins first black student, all the opportunities and facilities of the University were open to him. Kelly's first courses were in spherical and practical astronomy, mathematics, theory and functions, differential equations, and physics. The following year, he took astronomy, quaternions, analytical geometry, physics, celestial mechanics, introductory mathematics, the theory of numbers, and the theory of substitutions.

Hopkins to High School to Howard

During those two years, Miller pursued his interests without conflicts with instructors or students. For, of his Hopkins experience, he recalled,

> ... I was treated with cool, calculated civility. The fact that Professor Newcomb was personally interested in me became known throughout the institution and undoubtedly, inured to my advantage.[76]

At first, Kelly was able to meet his expenses out of the savings from his Pension Office job, supplemented by Commissioner Black, who allowed him to work during vacation months. However, since he was also sending money to his family, after two years, tuition became prohibitive. So, he didn't complete his graduate study. At this seemingly unfortunate moment, however, Francis Cardoza, principal of

---

[76] KMP Box 71-2 folder 53, 8. Miller's October 3, 1887, application to Hopkins states his reason for pursuing the degree. "I wish to enter as a candidate for Doctor of Philosophy in mathematics (leading subject) physics and astronomy." Ferdinand Hamburger Archives of The Johns Hopkins University, Record Group 13.010, Office of the Registrar, subgroup 1, series 2.

Washington's notable M Street High School, offered him a teaching position in math.

Francis Lewis Cardoza

Miller had known Cardoza from Howard. Moreover, their association and fondness for each other's high intellectual attainments and moral qualities knitted them together. He accepted and enthusiastically entered his career teaching geometry and algebra at a salary of $1000.00 a year in September 1889.

The M Street High School brought Miller into contact with Washington's African American elite and pretentious society.[77]

> Washington's colored folk possessed unusual opportunity to differentiate themselves into upper and lower classes. All class distinction in the world will sooner or later be based upon occupation and income. The thousand or so Negro clerks, schoolteachers, doctors, and lawyers drew a sharp line of demarcation between themselves and the bulk of their fellow race men who were confined to manual service.[78]

The prominent, influential school provided leaders for most of Washington's black community, and many of his students later became principals and head teachers in the city's public schools and colleges. Still, Kelly felt that his talent for math and broader interests were blunted when confined to high school-level topics, and. needing a challenge, he began to look elsewhere to teach.

---

[77] The school began in the basement of the Fifteenth Street Presbyterian Church in 1870. The Church, located several blocks from the White House, was founded by Reverend John F. Cook a private school teacher. First named the Preparatory High School, became M Street School in 1891, and Paul Laurence Dunbar High School in1916. From 1872-1916 the school moved to several locations throughout the city By the close of the nineteenth century, the school had risen to prominence as a notable collegiate high school. Its proximity to Howard University contributed to cross-fertilization of faculty and students. Many Howard faculty members taught, attended, or sent their children there. Miller taught mathematics and Carter G. Woodson taught Spanish and history.

[78] KMP Box 71-2 folder 56, 4. Miller believed the "Negro Aristocracy" looked with condescension and disdain on the less fortunate members of their community. In *Aristocrats of Color: The Black Elite, 1880–1920*, Willard B. Gatewood notes that most major cities with African American populations experienced similar cliques.

On a streetcar ride a year later, he noticed a dignified, courtly clergyman who graciously volunteered to speak to him. Kelly knew of him via his eloquent sermons on national issues and the rights of African Americans. Because of his patriotism and eloquence, many presidents, cabinet officers, judges, and senators frequented his church and listened to his sermons. This seemingly chance conversation resulted in Kelly being invited to Howard University. Friendly fellow Dr. Jeremiah Rankin, the principal preacher at the First Congregational Church of Washington, was elected President of Howard University in September 1890.[79]

Kelly was selected to occupy an endowed professorship in math, which the Howard University Alumni Association had recently created, and, on Rankin's recommendation, was made a professor of mathematics. The position began a 40-year relationship with his alma mater in teaching, administration, and publicizing.[80]

Miller's interests soon expanded beyond the classroom, and issues of broader education, employment, and civil rights began to consume as much of his time, energy, and enthusiasm as his teaching duties. He plunged into activities related to the overall betterment of black people and he began authoring articles and speaking on topics that expressed his deep concern about issues such as the abrogation of African American constitutional rights.

---

[79] Abolitionist, hymnist, and minister Jeremiah Eames Rankin, served as the sixth President of Howard from 1890 to 1903. During his tenure, he oversaw the construction of the Andrew Rankin Memorial Chapel, named after his brother.

[80] Miller continued for the rest of the year on the Howard University Alumni Association, but the organization's enthusiasm to raise funding required the University to absorb the cost of the position. An alumni professorship was proposed in 1890, and Miller was elected to the chair. Shortly afterwards, the University assumed responsibility of this chair.

My first important public address was delivered before the Association of Educators of Colored Youth, held in Atlanta University in February 1890, on "The Higher Education of the Negro." At that time the Negro college was on the defensive. The advocates of higher education had to prove that the Negro possessed the capacity to take in the higher forms of European culture. Much of the educational discussion of that day was devoted to proving this proposition, that the Negro possessed sufficient intellectual capacity to master and assimilate the most exact and abstruse phases of higher education, as set forth in the curriculum established for the most choice, white collegians. During the succeeding decades, while this issue was under discussion, I defended the negative, through voice and pen. [Meaning that Black people did not have to prove themselves proficiency they simply needed an unobstructed opportunity to exercise their mental facility] The Association for the Education of Colored Youth was a prototype of all educational organizations among Negro educators.[81]

Since Miller's educational interest had been inspired by missionaries in the Reconstruction South, he felt he owed much to rising generations of African Americans and saw his service at Howard as repaying the debt for the opportunities he had been provided, replenishing the resources those opportunities had cost, and influencing others to reach higher goals. He saw himself as an "epistle read of men" and a living

---

[81] KMP Box 71-2 folder 56, 7.

testimony of the benefits of higher education and dedicated himself to the uplift of African Americans. He wrote:

> I had imbibed a full measure, a double portion of the missionary spirit, from the day I entered Howard University [as a student and eventually as a faculty member]. Nevertheless, I had deliberately eschewed the ministry as my chosen field; medicine and law made no appeal to me, but during my whole college course I looked forward to teaching as a life career, believing that therein I would find a larger field of service, fitted to what I deemed to be peculiar gifts and faculties than might be found in any other pursuit or calling. My fondness for mathematical studies seemed to indicate the field to which I was called.[82]

As the twentieth century dawned, he added interest in the new field of sociology to his love of math. This provided a unique perspective on his effort to elevate the race. Using rational and logical principles from math and religious ethics, he gave students tools to deconstruct faulty notions of black inferiority and develop self-confidence and racial pride.

His work afforded him a canvas to recreate an image of African Americans infused with a zealous desire to embody the words of the biblical prophet Habakkuk, "Write the vision, and make it plain upon tables, that he may run that readeth it."[83] He also drew on the history of African people, the sense of purpose of his generation, and a hope for an unborn future. As Miller expressed it,

---

[82] KMP Box 71-2 folder 53, 3.
[83] Habakkuk 2: 2

I found myself plunged into the general activities for the social betterment of the people and began to write articles and make speeches on broad educational and social topics.[84]

Howard University became Miller's living laboratory where he could meld hand and head with a heart of succeeding generations of African Americans to produce grounded, servant leaders. Kelly wrote

[l]et us distinguish between the moral and spiritual nature of man and regard those faculties as moral which express themselves in terms of obligation and duty, and those as spiritual which manifest themselves in worship, reverence, adoration, and devotion, and which crave the higher satisfaction by longing after God.[85]

At the same time, he grew into a daysman who learned to live a life of mediation and harmony with poor and rich, educated and illiterate, northern and southern, white and black. This middle-ground position provided room to locate the similarities, differences, and universal threads of human life.

---

[84] Ida E. Jones, *The Heart of the Race Problem*, 57
[85] KMP, Box 71-6 folder 147, Moral Pedagogy, 3.

Three
Introduced to a New World: 1890-1916

> I see him who was once deemed sickened, smitten of God, and afflicted, now entering with universal welcome into the patrimony of mankind, and I look calmly upon the centuries of blood and tears and travail of soul and am satisfied.
>
> *Out of the House of Bondage.*
> Kelly Miller

After arriving in Washington, Miller's horizon expanded beyond that of one who occupied the social shadows to that of a budding intellectual as the city and Howard University provided him an opportunity to meet black leaders about whom he had heard and read. He engaged some of the brightest African American visitors to the Howard campus. Over the following decades, he encountered leading race men such as Booker T. Washington, W. E. B. DuBois, John Mercer Langston, Carter G. Woodson, Paul Lawrence Dunbar, Alexander Crummell, and women such as Mary Church Terrell, Mary McLeod Bethune, Nannie Helen Burroughs

A Professor of Mathematics cum Sociologist

Miller's primary method of instruction was classical lectures. This differed from the more common method of student recitation that other universities were using during this time. Each student took turns demonstrating theorems in arithmetic, algebra, or geometry on a large blackboard.

What memories are conjured by those blackboards, by the crayons of chalk and the felt covered erasers, with which, first as pupil, then as instructor, many years of my early life were passed. Hundreds, yes thousands of faces pass in retrospect as I visualize those who came under my tutelage, most of them eager for knowledge and a few who were laggards. Many of those whom I taught hold positions of trust and responsibility in Washington and elsewhere. I wonder how the others fare.[1]

A Harmonizer Discord: Washington & DuBois

In Miller's estimation, black educators had to be bilingual multitaskers and articulate in their subjects. Further, he felt they should factor in the burden of historic injustices such as poverty and lack of access to resources that impacted their stunted students' intellectual growth.

Two men he highly respected—Booker T. Washington and William Edward Burghardt (W. E. B.) DuBois—advocated distinctly different ideologies regarding African Americans' education. Washington, a graduate of Hampton Institute, advocated industrial training. Conversely, DuBois, a graduate of Fisk University, promoted classical training, believing it would provide leaders who would advance the cause of their unenlightened brethren. But Miller saw the benefits of both schemes and proposed a synthesis:

> Unless such higher education [is] taught, the Negro could not enlighten the ignorant, restrain the vicious, care for the sick and afflicted, administer solace to

---

[1] KMP, chapter 28"As A Professor of Math," *Autobiography*, 197.

weary souls, or plead in litigation that cause of those who had been wronged. In some sections even fierce resentment flared. Had not these men and women of darker skin been machines, incompetent to do anything unless under a master's direction? Of what use could they make of an education? Knowledge would make them upstarts and rebellious. I heard much of this when advocating my principles and became the shaft for much ridicule. Strange to say, even members of my own race decried my efforts and maintained that the only education necessary for a Negro was the one which would make him more dexterous with the use of his hands.[2]

When Miller proposed a modified version of the two ideologies, leaders from both camps dismissed such moderation with vitriol and stinging accusations. They questioned his intellect and loyalty and denounced him as a "trimmer" who lacked the courage to take sides, and that label followed him for many years. Though it would have been far easier to align himself with either side since neither option completely satisfied him, Miller held to his conviction, reasoning that,

> [a]s one looks back upon the history of those days... it clearly can be seen that a damaging mistake was made by both apostles of ultra-education and those who favored industrial training by each assuming that their doctrine and theirs only would solve the race problem. Both were wrong, as events have shown... I sensed that they were wrong and gave

---

[2] KMP, "Higher Education," *Autobiography*, 204-205.

voice to my views at a time when such sentiments caused one to become anathema, but now I must be pardoned if I make use of the trite expression "I told you so." Each doctrine had its merits, but as a cure-all neither was sufficient... Tersely expressed, my views were these, higher education was necessary for those Negroes who would administer to others of their race as clergymen, editors, teachers, lawyers, doctors, dentists. And industrial training was necessary for those who planned certain work with their hands within the limited sphere allotted them. But even as the boundary of endeavor for the Negro of higher education would be the color line, so the Negro expert craftsman could not expect to co-mingle with the whites who even in that day were forming trade unions in effort to limit the supply of skilled labor. Early proponents of higher education believed that knowledge as gained by extensive schooling would prove the open sesame into all walks of life, and proponents of industrial training thought that skilled labor could enter fields of labor which would be taboo to the less favored."[3]

The two remained connected throughout their professional lives, and Miller corresponded with him until his death. Irrespective of personal politics, they shared a similar background, having been born in the South and becoming self-made with missionary assistance, as Miller shared:

Much of the difference between us was due to the influences in our early lives. I entered the realm of

---

[3] KMP, "Raging Contest Over Higher and Industrial Education," *Autobiography*, 208-209.

books in the years when the missionary spirit was at its height, when these good people from the North treated the Negro as the equal of the white man and insisted that he be given every educational advantage. This enthusiasm was fading during the early life of Booker Washington and the wedge of segregation was being driven. He had not been inspired with the almost fierce desire for knowledge which had come to me and to others during those days immediately following the Civil War, a desire which was a flame fanned by the zealots from the North.[4]

From the perspective of a daysman, Miller did not discount Washington's view, for he appreciated his rational mind and providential favor and acknowledged that,

The desire for knowledge became in my mind a necessity when the gradual social separation of the races emphasized for me the imperativeness that the professional classes among the Negroes should be recruited from their own ranks. In America, when the religious fervor which included equality commenced to wane then the necessity for promoting professional men and women of our race became apparent and this became the burden of my lectures and my writings upon the subjects of higher education for the Negro.[5]

Though he admired Washington's tenacity, he saw him as unable to expand his access to other African American

---

[4] KMP, "Higher Education," *Autobiography*, 203.
[5] KMP, Box 71-2 folder 56, 7.

leaders or whites or to create a dialogue about long-term measures for ameliorating the results of enslavement and conditions of Jim Crowism. His displeasure with Washington's tactics is further evident in the following:

> You have the attention of the white world. You hold the passkey to the heart of the great white race. Your commanding position, your personal prestige, and the magic influence of your illustrious name entail upon you the responsibility to become the leader of the people, to stand as daysman between us and the great white God, and lay a propitiating hand upon both of us... A noble soul is big enough to invite candid criticism and eschew sycophantic adulation.[6]

Miller felt that discussions about black higher education often devolved into a debate about the value of industrial training. Since he saw both forms of training as symbiotic and beneficial for the black community, he felt they should be considered "on the basis of relative, not rival claims."

Washington, the Wizard of Tuskegee, held a Svengali hold on black newspapers, organizations, philanthropists, and popular opinion. Yet, his popularity with whites caused some black people to bristle. Though Miller respected the commanding authority his larger-than-life reputation held in both circles, he was frank about his seeming indifference to racist affronts from presidential administrations as well as his placation of white philanthropists.

Yet, the debates raged on until Washington's sudden death in 1915 left a void in the crusade for industrial

---

[6] KMP, "What I have Done to Abate Race Prejudice," *Autobiography*, 194.

education. Though several acolytes continued to spread his philosophy, no one rose to the same level of prominence.

A Peculiar Relationship

Washington first mentioned Miller in a letter to Howard University affiliate John Mercer Langston on January 14, 1886.[7] Then Cromwell mentioned Miller to Washington in his January 19, 1896 letter informing him of the formation of the American Negro Academy.

Miller saw his mathematical training as suiting him to craft the direction of African American higher education and believed that the Christian-inspired philosophy of heart, head, and hand was the best solution to problems experienced by the "backward race." who had been kept ignorance[8] For him, these three components were foundational, so while industrial education humbled a student's haughtiness while wrestling with Greek, and math stimulated the mind. But his outspoken nature created

---

[7] John Mercer Langston, the son of a Virginia planter and slave mother became dean of the law school and vice-president of Howard University. In 1888, he was elected to the U.S. House of Representatives in a close race in by appealing to black Virginians to elect him because of his race. A decade later he was optimistic about black-white relations in the South and concluded that blacks would solve the "Negro problem" though intelligence and acquisition of wealth. His biography, *From Virginia Plantation to Nation's Capital,* was published in 1894.

[8] Miller referred to African Americans as a backward race because of the enfeebling and intellectual theft that resulted because of enslavement. His 1899 speech at Hampton University entitled "The Primary Needs of the Negro Race," explained that "[t]he progress of the race must be provokingly slow as compared with that of the individual. Education prepares for a [static] rather than a dynamic condition of society. And yet... every educated Negro *must* be a reformer, a positive, progressive influence in uplifting the masses... although he belongs to a backward breed that has never taken the initiative in the progressive movements of the world. He must, therefore, be aroused to a consciousness of personal power, the energy of the will, the individual initiative, that subtle, indefinable quality which has always exerted a controlling influence upon human affairs, despite the theories of doctrinaires and the formulas of philosophy."

tensions between the two. Not one to be contradicted, Washington responded to Miller with a defense of industrial education. On March 2, 1899, T. Thomas Fortune wrote Washington that,

> Dr. Frissell will injure Hampton and the industrial education interests if he does not muzzle Kelly Miller and Hugh Browne on the political phase of the situation, and unless they are muzzled, I am going to open up on them in the *Age* and *Independent* [two black newspapers]. It is not necessary to give [a]way the *whole* political case to propagate the industrial idea.[9]

Miller's January 27, 1901 letter to Washington about a recent work of William Hannibal Thomas[10] concluded that leading race men needed to devise effective counter strategies to mute opportunistic voices. Thomas' work so troubled Miller that he toyed with the idea of protesting against McMillan Press for publishing it.

As Washington and DuBois each hoped to win the minds of black America, Miller became a focal point of their debate. His position at Howard made his endorsement ideological gold because it implied the tacit approval of the rising institution. In August 1903, Washington's colleague, Emmett J. Scott, wrote him about Miller.

---

[9] Booker T. Washington Papers, T. Thomas Fortune, March 1899. Throughout the remaining document the Booker T. Washington Papers will be referred to as the BTWP.

[10] William Hannibal Thomas. *The American Negro: What He Was, What He Is, and What He May Become: A Critical and Practical Discussion*. McMillan Press, 1901, 74.

Dear Mr. Washington:

No doubt you have noticed that four of my editorials appeared in the Colored American last week. I was especially desirous of placing Kelly Miller in direct opposition to DuBois, which I succeeded in doing. A report from [the Herald and Transcript] will weigh I think with the Negro press, and they should have firsthand information upon which to base any comments they may make.[11]

In September 1903, Miller corresponded with Scott about his admiration for Washington's efforts on behalf of the race:

You have seen the article in the *Boston Transcript* of Sept. 18 & 19, headed "Washington's Policy" and signed "Fair Play." I authored these articles. It was my aim to be fair and impartial to all sides of the controversy and to suggest the absolute necessity for some common ground. I trust that the plain speaking which I deemed necessary to full and frank discussion of the points in issue will be accepted in the spirit of kindly candor, in which it was employed...Trusting that the great and good work of Tuskegee will go forward with increasing influence and effectiveness and wishing you the fullest possible personal success.[12]

---

[11] BTWP, Letter to Emmett Scott, August 3, 1903.

[12] BTWP, to Kelly Miller September 24, 1903. These articles written by Miller took a middle position between Booker T. Washington and his critics. Miller observed that Washington was "not a leader of the people's own choosing" and that "few thoughtful colored men espouse what passes as Mr. Washington's policy, without apology or reserve." He concluded: "The Negro's lot would be sad indeed if, under allurement of material advantage and temporary easement...

Scott relayed Miller's sentiments to Washington, who, in response, wrote in August 1905:

> I am quite sure it will interest you to know that Kelly Miller and Grimke have broken off completely from DuBois and his crowd. DuBois has insulted both. Grimke had a long talk with me and went over many of the details covering the devilment of the whole gang. He seems more than anxious now to line up with us. Kelly Miller feels the insult very keenly and resents it in extraordinarily strong language, but he is mushy and cannot be depended upon for a straight-out fight.[13]

Scott remained loyal to Washington and kept surveillance of the anti-Bookerites. In a February 1905 letter to Charles William Anderson, he spoke openly about the rising skepticism among younger men.

> You were sent a wire today advising you to be in Washington during the inauguration to keep your eyes on the enemy. The particular point is that DuBois, Kelly Miller, Trotter, Grimke, and some of that crowd are to have special meetings during the inauguration and are planning, among other things, to call upon the President... The Wizard [Washington] believes that it would be well for you to be on hand and if possible as you easily can, secure an invitation

---

but it would be sadder still if intemperate insistence should engender ill will and strife, when the race is not yet ready. See Hugh Hawkins, "Booker T. Washington, and His Critics: Black Leadership in Crisis. Boston: D C Heath & Co, 1962.

[13] BTWP, Letter to Emmett Scott, August 7, 1905.

to the Pen and Pencil Club banquet so as to meet the enemy on any ground that may be offered.[14]

Francis J. Grimke

Miller's friend, Francis Grimke wrote to Washington in January 1906 regarding the Committee of Twelve. The Committee of Twelve & [DuBois] relations to it. I have seen

---

[14] BTWP, Letter to Charles William Anderson, February 20, 1905.

Kelly Miller & asked him to reply to it in *The Voice*. He had not at the time seen the article, & so could not say that he would comply with my request. It seems to me that Kelly is the best member of the Committee to make the answer, which it appears to me the time has come to make once for all. Will you not write Kelly & second my request? That is of course if you think reply is called for on the part of our Committee. DuBois & The Guardian people would like to involve us in a controversy, at least they would like nothing better than to involve you & me, for against us they are especially bitter.[15]

That year, Miller and Washington expanded their correspondences to address overall racial injustice beyond education. That November, Miller wrote to Washington about his impending meeting with President Roosevelt. Miller thought that Washington should present the conditions of African Americans without apology to refute stereotypical assumptions, but Washington remained indifferent to that idea. Miller wrote:

> I have been thinking deeply over the situation which seems to me is about to be seriously complicated by the proposed treatment of the Negro as a criminal race in the President's forthcoming message. The more I think of it the more I am convinced of the lasting hurt that this utterance will do the race. The Negro is held up as a race of criminals and rapists, banded together to uphold one another in crime, with only occasional individual exceptions. This utterance from the White House will do more to damn the Negro to everlasting infamy than all [other] the

---

[15] BTWP, Letter to Francis Grimke, January 6, 1906.

maledictions... His message becomes a part of the documentary history of the nation. The Negro will thus be branded as a lecherous race, with the authority of the President of the United States. This will be the most serious official blow that the race has ever received. As the acknowledged spokesman for the race, you will be held responsible for the President's utterances in these matters. When Mr. Roosevelt requested you to act as his adviser and when you accepted that delicate responsibility, the world may be expected to believe that he is guided by the advice of his own seeking... In the minds of many you are held responsible for the dismissal of the colored soldiers, [regarding the Brownsville affair] although few fair-minded men could believe that you counseled it... Pardon me for writing so freely. I deeply appreciate the gravity of the situation.[16]

Washington reminded Miller that he was an educator, not a presidential advisor:

Of course, all of us could have discussed the President's Message in a little different light if we had any idea of his intended action regarding the Negro

---

[16] BTWP from Miller November 7, 1906. Kelly was referring to the Brownsville Affair, a skirmish involving returning Buffalo soldiers of the 25th infantry regiment who faced open racial hostilities. They were not allowed to leave the military base or mingle with local people. In August 1906, shots were heard near Fort Brown and a white bartender was found dead. Towns people rioted and rogue military personnel raided the town. After an investigation, President Roosevelt dishonorably discharged the entire 200-man regiment, most of whom were decorated veterans. With the discharge, they lost their retirements and other military benefits. Washington, who was appointed as part of a commission to review the initial findings, supported the dishonorable discharge, stoking disappointment within the black community. Nearly 70 years would pass before the US government rescinded the dishonorable discharge.

troops. He did not mention the matter to me until I saw him that evening, and then told me that the matter had been decided. I tried to persuade him to take a different course but without success... I have never seen a time when the whole race has been so stirred and hurt on a subject as it seems to be on this one. As for anybody holding me responsible for any such action. I would state that in this case and in others, I simply fall back on the old doctrine, obsolete but nevertheless potent, that truth in the last analysis always asserts itself, and I confess that more I am finding myself having implicit faith in that doctrine. The President or no one else has ever asked me to be his official adviser regarding race matters...I have felt in the past and feel now that no Negro should refuse to give whatever advice or information the President of the United States might seek of him. To fail to do so would be acting cowardly... [My] experience in life so far has taught me that if one is right and square, everything usually comes out all right.[17]

In December 1909, Miller again wrote Washington, now a member of Howard's Board of Trustees, regarding President Thirkeld's desire for students to perform plantation songs during an anniversary of the Emancipation:

President Thirkeld in several eloquent appeals urged the singing of plantation melodies as an important part of the University's musical repertoire. A considerable number of our students do not feel that it is becoming to this Institution devoted to the higher

---

[17] BTWP, Letter to Kelly Miller, November 19, 1906.

aims and ideals of the race to emphasize these melodies as a part of the mission of Howard University. It has become in mind that unlike Fisk University, [in Tennessee] Hampton [in Virginia]... Howard has no sentimental tradition based upon the plantation melodies. We have never made a feature of singing them. Our student body comes largely from the North and West where these melodies are not appreciated because, their spirit and meaning is not fully understood. My personal attitude toward these melodies is set forth in *Race Adjustment* in the chapter entitled "Artistic Gifts of the Race."... To urge the singing of these melodies at this time would unnecessarily divide our student body [,] Faculty, Alumni and Trustee Board. There are numerous and strong opponents in all these bodies. I have urged President Thirkeld in the interest of internal harmony and good will to drop the proposition entirely for the present at least. I fail to see the wisdom of arousing a bitter a[nd] long drawn-out controversy when no corresponding good is to be accomplished whichever set may triumph. I have ventured to present this matter to you knowing that as a Trustee of the University, you are interested in all our activities.[18]

In May 1912, the last letter between the two men, marked personal and confidential, concerned the possibility of an African American being appointed to Howard's presidency. Though Miller's popularity, love for his alma mater, and influence with students and alumni positioned him as a viable

---

[18] BTWP, Letter from Kelly Miller, December 1909.

candidate, Washington questioned the university's "readiness" to select a black president, but offered his opinion on who the candidate might be.

> Of course, this is highly confidential and is not to pass from your hands. There are two questions to be decided: First: has the time come when a colored man should be at the head of Howard University? Without committing myself to this point, I would say it has, still I confess I am open to argument. Second, if a colored man is to be put in charge, I have thoroughly made up my mind that you are the person. *You are the logical man* [author's emphasis] and I find the country unanimous on this point. If the main question as to the advisability of putting in a colored man is decided in the affirmative, I do not believe there would be any opposition to amount to anything to your being appointed and I would do whatever I could to further that end. If a white man is to be chosen, I am very anxious to have a conference with you before I enter any meeting looking toward the choosing of a white man.[19]

On June 28, 1912, another white man, Stephan M. Newman, was elected president, and the Trustee Board voted to give six candidates "honorable mentions." Three of those were African American men—Howard University deans George W. Cook, Lewis B. Moore, and Miller.

In this work, Miller portrayed Washington as one who began his career with a narrow educational bias toward

---

[19] BTWP, Letter to Kelly Miller, May 1912.

industrial training but who grew to accept various modes of education. At one point, Miller characterized his colleague as:

> One who has come up from slavery [and] the coal caverns of West Virginia, struggling up against narrow theories, lack of early education and bias of environment, tactfully expanding the prudential restraints of a delicate and critical situation, rising upon successive steppingstones of past achievements and past mistakes, but ever planting his feet upon higher and higher ground... [His] noble soul is big enough to invite candid criticism.[20]

The American Negro Academy

In March 1896, the pan-Africanist religionist, Alexander Crummell[21] invited Miller, John Wesley Cromwell, Paul Lawrence Dunbar, and Walter B. Hayson to join him in forming the American Negro Academy as an organization of intellectuals who would host conferences, present and publish papers, and invite the black community to engage in ideas, plan strategies to combat white supremacy.

---

[20] Kelly Miller, *Radicals and Conservatives and Other Essays on the Negro in America*, 18.

[21] Crummell was born to an enslaved father and a freeborn mother in New York in 1819. Throughout his life, he witnessed the injustice and degradation of enslavement. As a young man, he studied for the Episcopal priesthood and sought ordination in the Diocese of Massachusetts, but was rebuffed by the church because he was black. In 1844, after the 25-year-old was excluded from a meeting of priests of the diocese, he went England, 56then traveled to Liberia, where he hoped to establish a black Christian community. His work there met with opposition and indifference, so he returned to the United States to find and strengthen urban black congregations.

Alexander Crummell, John Wesley Cromwell
Paul Lawrence Dunbar

As its historian, Alfred Morris detailed:

> The failure of the Afro-American League, a national coalition of black organizations committed to racial defense, the hand-to-mouth existence of black publications of the day, and the rapid demise of the black literary society he had helped found in 1877... these and other negative examples may have influenced his thinking[22]

---

[22] Alfred A. Moss, Jr., *The American Negro Academy*, Baton Rouge, LA: Louisiana State University Press, 1981, 21.

However, Crummell's doubts disappeared, and he felt that the society was a "possibility and... imperative necessity" whose spiritual center would result in greater moral grounding and social services for the black community. As a consummate race man, Crummell strove to inform, unify, and direct African Americans into a fruitful and fulfilling endeavor and conceived the idea of the American Negro Academy to empower black people through models of success.

Crummell was disgusted with "black opportunists who [would] jump at anything a white man says if it [would] give [them] notoriety and help jingle a few nickels in their pockets."[23] On December 18, 1896, Crummell met with Walter B. Hayson, Cromwell, Dunbar, and Miller to join him in "establishing a learned society" of Colored authors, scholars, and artists." His goal was to promote literature, produce publications, and collect archival materials that refuted negative stereotypes of black people, and addressed aspects of the "race problem."

The proposed society would be limited to 40 members of academic, literary, or distinguished professional groups. In a series of resolutions, the five men endorsed Crummell's proposal and adopted the constitution presented to them as the initial members. Crummell selected men of varying ages to ensure the furtherance of the society. "In [his] mind, Miller and other stable, honest, hard-working black young men of genius were the people on whom the burden of leading and representing the race fell and the future of their people depended."[24] Cromwell died two years later. The American Negro Academy served as a bellwether on issues of racial

---

[23] Ibid., 22
[24] Ibid., 34

matters for 31 years until it ceased operation in 1927. Miller remained an active member, carrying out administrative duties, serving as an officer, researching topics, and occasionally writing papers. He also embraced Crummell's vision of researching, gathering, and preserving historical documents and approached Howard University to consider collecting materials from prominent faculty members.

Early in 1890, he attracted the attention of Francis Cardoza, principal of Washington's renowned M Street High School, where Carter G. Woodson and Mary Church Terrell had taught. But Miller was soon called from the high school classroom to Howard.

> My selection for this position had been made by the alumni and for a brief time I was under the direction of this graduate body. Their financial plan failed and within a year, 1890 I became a regular employee by the Board of Trustees at the annual salary of $1,200 plus housing. Being a bachelor, I recalled free quarters in Clarke Hall in lieu of a house. The actual salary was $1500. This appointment as professor of mathematics was a departure from the custom that had prevailed and which had thrust double and occasionally triple duty upon my predecessor, who frequently had taught physics together with mathematics and occasionally chemistry in addition to the two other studies. My duties, however, were not confined to the college proper, for I also taught mathematics in the Preparatory School, and this double duty necessitated my presiding over an average of six classes daily.[25]

---

[25] KMP, Box 71-2 folder 58, 7-8.

Former Miller student George M. Lightfoot described Miller's mathematical ability, stating,

> the field of pure and applied mathematics fascinated him, while the power of his inspiration and personality made him a veritable idol of his students. His fame soon extended far beyond the campus of this University. Early in his career as a mathematician, it was soon apparent to him and to his discriminating friends that the problems and processes of mathematics with their exact limitations and absolute definiteness of result did not offer sufficient scope for the satisfaction of his type and temper of his mind.[26]

Lightfoot also noted that in his math courses, Miller "became deeply and sympathetically interested in various problems affecting the Negro race." The quantitative nature of math and the qualitative elements of life stirred his desire to blend both concepts to explore and expound on the condition of black people. The advent of sociology provided him with the language to articulate his beliefs about race. Thus, he left the Department of Mathematics to create the Department of Sociology, where he established formative courses in this field at Howard University.

In 1901, Miller sought funding from Howard's trustees and others for a series of studies the ANA wished to conduct and publish in its proposed journal.[27] Though the board approved the measure, the ANA ultimately failed due to a lack of broad-based support. Despite being supported by an

---

[26] KMP, Box 71-1 folder 10 "Biographical Sketch..." George Lightfoot.
[27] Ibid. 200.

academic institution, it was perceived as an elite men's scholarly club that excluded women and produced no ideas or any concrete action that effected the welfare of the masses.

Involvement in the organization helped Miller to see race issues from a multi-faceted perspective, contributed to his moderate stance, and made hm aware of the dearth of literature available to teach on the subject. His desire for a progressive, empowered black community limited his partnerships with others who confronted race issues. Instead, as a daysman he sought to mediate the different opinions among black leaders while contributing to the growing corpus of race literature and maintaining a presence at Howard University.

Miller circa. 1900

Author, Pamphleteer, and Polemic

Being a faculty member with a steady paycheck afforded Miller some latitude, but he still had to be frugal. In a lapsed moment, he cosigned a $600 loan for a friend who defaulted, leaving Miller with the entire responsibility so that.

... with my curtailed salary of $1,200 a year I was compelled not only to pay this debt but maintain myself in keeping with the position which I held. Fortunately, I had acquired no extravagant habits and frugality had become a second nature during my student days. It was less difficult than it might have been for me to redeem the paper to which my name had been signed. However, it was several years before the final payment was made. The drag on my financial resources affected me in more ways than one.[28]

By 1900, Miller began writing-for-hire and authored book reviews, newspaper columns, articles, books, and pamphlets exploring a variety of topics such as race, gender, education, and current events. Though he began this endeavor to supplement his income, the opportunity placed his thoughts before other race men, but also engaged lay people in intellectual and academic discourse regarding the race.

Miller's writing and publishing increased his income and garnered him a national audience, granting respite from campus politics and a refuge from ideological partisanship. Moreover, he was able to capitalize on them through lecture tours. He loved speaking to rural people and inspiring elderly people, families, and youth through the life he lived, wrote, and spoke about.

Miller's Calvinist daysman ideology of head, hand, and heart as divinely proscribed by God infused his writing, and his earliest published work was an essay in *From Servitude to Service* that examined the impact of leading black colleges and universities such as Fisk, Howard, and Hampton.

---

[28] KMP, chapter 28 "As a Professor of Math", p198

When the smoke of war had blown away, when the cessation of strife proclaimed the end of the great American conflict, when the "war drum throbbed no longer, and the battle flags were furled," there emerged from the wreck and ruin of war four million of human chattels, who were transformed, as if by magic, in a moment, in the twinkling of an eye, from slavery to freedom... These people were absolutely ignorant and destitute. They had not tasted of the tree of knowledge which is the tree of good and evil. This tree was guarded by the flaming swords of wrath, kept keen and bright by the avarice and cupidity of the master class.[29]

Discouraged by numerous rejections and in need of money, Miller attempted to publish an article entitled "Political Plight of the Negro" in *Outlook* magazine. That article was initially returned with a note from the editor that it was too analytical for its purpose, referring him instead to an English magazine, the *Nineteenth Century and After*. Miller followed the recommendation, and it was subsequently published.[30]

His most notable poem, "I See and Am Satisfied," which appeared in the *New York Independent*[31] and was reprinted in the *London Contemporary Review*, depicts the history of African American people with biblical overtones. In it, the daysman

---

[29] Kelly Miller, et al "Howard University," in *From Servitude to Service: Being the Old South Lectures on the History and Work of Southern Institutions for the Education of the Negro*. Boston: American Unitarian Association, 1905, 3-4.

[30] Kelly Miller, "Political Plight of the Negro" *Nineteenth Century and After*, 1910.

[31] Kelly Miller, "I See and Am Satisfied," *The* [New York] *Independent*, August 7, 1913

illustrated the history of African Americans, seeking to harmonize the pre-enslavement past with then-contemporary life. The poem paints images of enslavement, the defilement of black women, the Civil War, lynching, and racial betterment, yet acknowledges liberal whites who contributed to the struggle for African-American equality.

> I see the man-catcher, impelled by thirst of gold, as he entraps his simple-souled victim in the snares of bondage and death, by use of force or guile.
>
> I see the ocean basin whitened with his bones, and the ocean current running red with his blood, amidst the hellish horrors of the middle passage...
>
> I see the swarthy matron lavishing her soul in altruistic devotion upon the offspring of her alabaster mistress.
>
> I see the haughty sons of a haughty race pouring out their lustful passion upon black womanhood, filling our land with a bronzed and tawny brood...
>
> I see the great Proclamation delivered in the year of my birth of which I became the first fruit and beneficiary.
>
> I see the assassin striking down the great Emancipator; and the house of mirth is transformed into the Golgotha of the nation...
>
> I see his body writhing in the agony of death as his groans issue from the crackling flames, while the

funeral pyre lights the midnight sky with its dismal glare. My heart sinks with heaviness within me.

I see that the path of progress has never taken a straight line but has always been a zigzag course amid the conflicting forces of right and wrong, truth and error, justice, and injustice, cruelty, and mercy.

I see that the great generous American Heart, despite the temporary flutter, will finally beat true to the higher human impulse, and my soul abounds with reassurance and hope…

I see him who was once deemed sicken, smitten of God, and afflicted, now entering with universal welcome into the patrimony of mankind, and I look calmly upon the centuries of blood and tears and travail of soul, and am satisfied.[32]

Another poem, "The Afro-American Plea,"[33] later renamed "Plea of the Oppressed" and scored to music by J.T. Layton, also documented the black condition:

O Thou who heard the wailful plea.
Of our forebears on bended knee,
And broke their bonds and set them free.
To thee we pray, to thee we pray.

In broken word and wailing tone,
In deep, unutterable groan,
They made their tribulations known,

---

[32] Kelly Miller, "I See and Am Satisfied," *Out of the House of Bondage.* 240-242.

[33] Kelly Miller Plea of the Oppressed in Race Adjustment, p154-155

Hear us we pray; hear us we pray.

In this dark day of sore distress,
In deepest gloom of wilderness.
When threat'ning ills so hardly press.
Help us this day, help us this day.

If scorn and race disdain would seek,
Its vial of wrath to venge and wreak.
Upon this lowly folk and meek,
Spare us we pray; spare us we pray.

No people yet have fallen prey,
Who love Thy Law, walk in the way,
When all the world could look and say,
Behold they pray, behold they pray.

But when we stray from Thy command
And feel Thy sore afflicting hand,
We humbly bow; we understand,
We must obey, we must obey.

Plea of the Oppressed
"Lord, Teach us How to Pray"

Words by KELLY MILLER
Music by J.T. LAYTON

O Thou who heard the plaint-ful plea Of our for-bears on bend-ed knee, And broke their bonds and set them free, To Thee we pray, To Thee we pray.

In brok-en word and wail-ing tone, In deep, un-ut-ter-a-ble groan, They made their trib-u-la-tions known; Hear us, we pray, Hear us, we pray.

3
In this dark day of sore distress,
In deepest gloom of wilderness,
When threatening ills so hardly press;
   Help us this day,
   Help us this day.

4
If slighting scorn of race would seek
Its vial of wrath to venge and wreak
Upon this lowly folk and meek,
   Spare us, we pray,
   Spare us, we pray.

5
They need not fear, our Strength and Stay,
Who keep thy Law, walk in the way,
When all the world might look and say:
   "Behold, they pray"
   "Behold, they pray!"

6
But when we stray from Thy command,
And feel Thy sore afflicting hand,
We humbly bow; we understand:
   May we obey,
   May we obey.

7
If some Thy saving help deny,
With wild, inane, distracted cry,
Like Job's wild wife, would curse and die,
   Forgive, we pray,
   Forgive, we pray.

8
Thy righteous Law is all our trust,
Who builds on else but builds on dust;
The Mighty should, the Lowly must
   Rely alway,
   Rely alway.

Copyright 1906 by J.T. Layton.

If some Thy saving help deny,
With wild, inane, distracted cry,
Like Job's wild wife, would curse and die,
Forgive, we pray, Forgive, we pray.

If time-taught wisdom nostrums find,
In cunning hand or knowing mind,
Show the blind leaders of the blind,
Tis vanity, Tis vanity.

Thy righteous Law is all our trust,
Who builds on else but builds on dust.
The Mighty should, the Lowly must,
Rely always, rely always.

And since of stones Thou raiseth seed
As choice as any boasted breed,
Vouchsafe to us the larger mead,
We humbly pray, we humbly pray, Amen.[34]

Miller's work, such as "Oath of Afro-American Youth," also encouraged children to appreciate their opportunities. This piece was crafted in 1914 and recited in all fourth-grade classrooms in Washington.[35]

---

[34] Kelly Miller, "Plea of the Oppressed," *Race Adjustment*. 154-155.
[35] Board of Education District of Columbia , Annual Report of the Board to the Commission, 1917. During the school years copies of the "Oath" by Professor Kelly Miller, of Howard University... The Oath was committed to memory by all pupils above the fourth grade... That these sentiments may be wrought into the minds and hearts and conduct of the children and youth of the colored public schools of the Capital of the Nation is my earnest prayer. Roscoe C. Bruce, Assistant Superintendent of Schools. Charles Sumner School Archives.

I will never bring disgrace upon my race by any unworthy deed or dishonorable act; I will live a clean, decent, manly life, and will ever respect and defend the virtue and honor of womanhood. I will uphold and obey the just laws of my country and not allow prejudice, injustice, insult, or outrage to cower my spirit or sour my soul but will ever preserve the inner freedom of heart and conscience. I will not allow myself to be overcome with evil but will strive to overcome evil with good. I will endeavor to develop and exert the best powers within me for my own personal improvement and will strive unceasingly to quicken the sense of racial duty and responsibility. I will in all these ways aim to uplift my race, so that to everyone bound to it by ties of blood it, shall become a bond of ennoblement and not a byword of reproach.[36]

The Oath was also applauded in Baltimore, where Mason Hawkins, the Principal of the city's Colored High School, wrote:

Dear Professor Miller

I took the matter of the introduction of your OATH in the schools in Baltimore up with the Superintendent some time ago. He informed me that he had the question under advisement. I might say that he expressed some doubt as to the likelihood of obtaining the Board's sanction of its introduction. The

---

[36] Kelly Miller, "The Oath of Afro-American Youth," *Out of the House of Bondage*. It also appeared in the "What to Read" column. *Crisis* June 1913, 92.

Oath was committed to memory by all pupil's 4th grade and above.[37]

Miller's titles include:

1. *Race Adjustment; Essays on the Negro in America.*[38]
2. *Out of the House of Bondage,* [39]
3. *Progress and Achievements of the Colored People: Containing the Story of the Wonderful Advancement of the Colored Americans: A Handbook for Self-improvement Which Leads to Greater Success.*[40]
4. *An Appeal to Conscience; America's Code of Caste: A Disgrace to Democracy.* [41]
5. *Kelly Miller's History of the World War for Human Rights; Being an Intensely Human and Brilliant Account of the World War, and Why and for What Purpose America and the Allies Are Fighting, and the Important Part Taken by the Negro, Including the Horrors and Wonders of Modern Warfare, the New and Strange Devices, Etc.*[42]

---

[37] Letter from Mason Hawkins to Kelly Miller, On January 8, 1915, Kelly Miller papers, Box 1 folder 19, Manuscript, Archives, Rare Books Library (MARBL), Emory University.

[38] Kelly Miller *Race Adjustment; Essays on the Negro in America.* New York, Neil Publishing Company, 1908.

[39] Kelly Miller, *Out of the House of Bondage.* New York: McMillan Press, 1914.

[40] Kelly Miller and Joseph R. Gay, *Progress and Achievements of the Colored People: Containing the Story of the Wonderful Advancement of the Colored Americans: A Handbook for Self-improvement Which Leads to Greater Success.* Washington, D. C: Austin Jenkins, 1917.

[41] Miller , *An Appeal to Conscience.*

[42] Kelly Miller, *Kelly Miller's History of the World War for Human Rights; Being an Intensely Human and Brilliant Account of the World War, and Why and for What Purpose America and the Allies Are Fighting, and the Important*

6. The Everlasting Stain[43]

Several of these books were compilations of earlier essays, and they garnered the attention of numerous news outlets, including The *Overland Monthly,* which said of *Race Adjustment,*

> Mr. Miller brings to his subject a much deeper study and greater wisdom in education than has ever before been dedicated to a work of this kind by any member of his race. It is a volume that will become increasingly valuable as years advance.[44]

Miller's writing encouraged his readers to consider the origins of racial injustice and social inequity. The *Boston Transcript* said *Out of the House of Bondage* was "clear and decisive, with a comprehensive and convincing command of the subject." It noted that he did not denounce nor condemn anyone but offered analyses and possibilities for the betterment of mankind. For, it said,

> [n]o man of his race has so sure a power of pruning the fallacies with passionless intellectual severity from the pernicious arguments of the prejudiced demagogues.[45]

A review of the work in *The Portland Telegram* remarked that,

---

Part Taken by the Negro, Including the Horrors and Wonders of Modern Warfare, the New and Strange Devices, Etc. Washington, DC: Austin Jenkins Co., *1919.*

[43] Kelly Miller, *The Everlasting Stain.* Washington, DC: The Associated Publishers, 1924.

[44] Kelly Miller, *Race Adjustment, Essays On The Negro In America.* New York: Neale Publishing Company 1908, dust jacket.

[45] Dust jacket comments copy from *Race Adjustment.* From the 1908 edition.

To those not versed in the Negro question, this book would surely appeal strongly. The subject is treated from the standpoint of one who knows what he is writing about." Yet another review of *Out of the House of Bondage in* the *New Orleans Times-Picayune* commented "Those who are interested in the study of the Negro cannot ignore this volume.[46]

A review of *The Everlasting Stain* in the *Journal of Negro History* portrayed the struggle common men faced when seeking to better their position in education, employment, and society. It commented that Miller addressed the common man and offered practical and inspirational essays, and lauded him because he was,

> primarily concerned with combating the ideas of men who, in compromising with the forces arrayed against the man far down, make it almost impossible for the race to present its case to the world. In this chosen field of controversy, Kelly Miller is most successful.[47]

Miller published four volumes of a journal entitled *Kelly Miller's Monographic Magazine,* which marketed a copy for ten cents and solicited agents to sell the product. Agents were wanted throughout America. The first volume, released in April 1913 and entitled "Education for Manhood," focused on the importance of wholesome education.

The highest concern was to develop man as a rational being - a creature capable of thinking, hoping, loving, believing, craving, striving for higher things... The old

---

[46] Dust jacket comments from *Out of the House of Bondage.* From the 1914 edition.

[47] Book Reviews *Journal of Negro History,* 9:4, October 1924, 573.

definition of education, namely. The process of unfolding the seed of immortality which God has implanted in men," was perfectly consistent with this idea.[48]

In Miller's mind, education both developed personal human qualities and encouraged service to humankind. Thus, for him, true education developed a person who delighted in inspiring others. He believed the failure to grasp its dual aim led to confusion and delusion, for, in Miller's mind, a principled life with divine inspiration and focus provided the character of the Black college student.

> The educated Negro must express his manhood in terms of courage, in the active as well as the passive voice: courage to do, as well as, to endure; courage to contend for the right while suffering the wrong; the courage of self-belief that is always commensurate with the composed task. The world believes in a race that believes in itself; but justly despises the self-bemeaned.[49]

The May 1913 issue was entitled "The Political Plight of the Negro." The third issue, "Social and Industrial Capacities of Negroes," Part I, by Thomas Babington Macaulay, was released that June. The final issue, "Social and Industrial Capacities of Negroes," Part II, by Macaulay, appeared that July.

Though his consuming passion was the status and progress of the race and the quality of black people's lives to earn income for his growing family, Miller also published numerous newspaper articles, pamphlets, and open letters. He sold the pamphlets for between ten and twenty-five cents

---

[48] KMP, Box 71-6 folder 127, 5.raternity
[49] Ibid., 17.

and promoted them through subscription services and independent dealers.

In a 1914 article titled "The Ultimate Race Problem," Miller compared the outcome of racial mixing to de facto segregation.

> After the red and brown races shall have perished from the face of the earth, after the fragmentary people have been exterminated, expelled, or absorbed, after the diffusion of knowledge has established a world equilibrium, there will be left the white, the yellow, and the black as residuary races each practically distinguished in its ethnic identity, and occupying its own habitat. We can only prophesy amity, peace and good will among these types who will more fully appreciate than we do now, that God has made of one blood all nations to dwell upon the face of the earth, within assignable bounds of habitation. Whether this will be but a stage in the ultimate blending of all races in a common world type transcends all our present calculable data and must be left to the play of imagination.[50]

Miller's independent, activist, and non-partisan thought in several areas of scholarship appeared in some form in over a million copies of his publications, and an excerpt from the *Journal of Negro History* extols.

> He has perfected the epistolary style of the polemic, beyond most writers of this age. His open letters to Thomas Dixon, to President Roosevelt, and to President Harding will take rank with the best

---

[50] Kelly Miller, *Out of the House of Bondage* "Ultimate Race Problem," 231-239.

literature of this sort of all times... His transient style, logical treatment, and comprehensiveness of presentation give his work a distinct place in the discussion of the race problem.[51]

Miller's writings drew accolades from across the nation, such as one Bethune penned to him in October 1917:

I read with a great deal of interest and appreciation your letter to Pres. [Woodrow] Wilson. In the "Disgrace of Democracy." We are very happy to know that the race has a man like you to so ably champion its cause. I shall do all in my power to distribute the letter and have as many of them read as possible. I shall place one in the hands of my club women of the state. I am sending you my check for $1.00 for which please send me twenty copies. I shall be glad to get them as soon as possible. I shall be glad to have you visit our work in Daytona sometime and see what we are doing on this end.[52]

After his death, Carter Woodson characterized Miller's writing as obituary prophetic, claiming that:

Like most educated Negroes of his day, he was drawn from his chosen field to battle for the rights of his race during the years of reaction when it seemed that all that the race had won immediately after emancipation would be swept away. Miller's analytical mind, then, centered on the race problem. He ceased to teach mathematics and took up sociology. On

---

[51] Book Review *The Everlasting Stain*, *Journal of Negro History*, 9:4 (October 1924). 573.

[52] Letter from Mary McLeod Bethune to KM, October 6, 1917, Kelly Miller papers, Box 2 folder 6, MARBL, Emory University.

every important public question concerning the Negro he delivered a lecture or wrote a pamphlet. His style was highly literary. Because of his commanding position at Howard, what he produced was widely read. He lectured more extensively probably than any Negro who has ever lived, and he thus demonstrated the capacity of the Negro to profit by higher education at the time when others sought to restrict the race to the study of fundamentals and practical pursuits.[53]

Miller with Epsilon Boule Sigma Pi Phi Fraternity

Some white people, including Mary O. White, sister to former Howard University president Jeremiah Rankin, supported Miller's writings, and he welcomed her warm words about his position on women:

> I notice you have acknowledged in the course of your letter that "men are not considered good enough to govern women." Let me congratulate you on the fact that you have reached this wise conclusion. It is true that no man, white, black, brown, or yellow are good enough to govern women. I have profound respect

---

[53] Carter G. Woodson *Journal of Negro History* 25:1, January 1940. 137.

for the things that women of your race are doing to help other women. I trust that woman suffrage will come to us all soon, and that it will give women of the colored race, who have even more to contend with than the women of the white race, the opportunity they so much need. Hoping you will fight with us and for us to bring this quickly.[54]

Wrestling with Colorism

Another issue that disturbed Miller, a dark-skinned person who prided himself in being of African stock, was intra-racial colorism. He claimed that his African heritage was more pronounced than his European one since his maternal grandfather was a continent-born enslaved African. Since many blacks also equated dark with ignorance, backwardness, poverty, crime, and inappropriate behavior, they sought to separate themselves from dark-complexioned people.

In an essay entitled "Is the American Negro to Remain Black or Become Bleached?" Miller explored the problem of colorism and questioned whether black people would not retain as dark skin as the inhabitants of Africa. To him, the pathological obsession with complexion was tied to a degree of privilege lighter-skinned blacks enjoyed during enslavement that entitled them to lighter workloads and assignments closer to their master's enslaver's house.

After emancipation, the desire for fairer complexions seemingly dominated black communities in cities such as Philadelphia, Boston, Baltimore, and Washington, where colorism was attached to social advancement. In select circles

---

[54] Letter from Mary O. White to KM, Kelly Miller papers, Box 2 folder 2, MARBL, Emory University.

within these places, the acceptable black person had a complexion comparable to a brown paper bag.

Though Miller's membership in the Sigma Pi Phi and Alpha Phi Alpha fraternities provided him some entre, colorism remained an obstacle to full acceptance in Washington's society. Yet, he appreciated his ebony color and embraced his maternal grandfather's link to an African past. His love for the race and his dark-complexioned led him to query the whole issue that dark-skinned linked black Americans to Africa.

Miller was not the only one who recognized this trend. In writing about Washington. DC, Langston Hughes recalled hearing about pink teas—social gatherings for fair-complexioned women. He felt that many deemed complexion, as well as class and lineage as important for success, and he lamented about the unspoken color line to darker-complexioned friends. The grandnephew of John Mercer Langton, Hughes dashing looks afforded him entrée into circles that most people of Miller's complexion struggled to enter,[55] but he questioned the practice of some people marrying to lighten the complexion of their children, writing:

> Is the Negro race to preserve its physical identity or to be bleached white within any calculable time. The white man made it possible that such a question could be asked. In America, for nearly three centuries, he preached by day against miscegenation and practiced it at night. Therefore, his blood permeates the black race to a greater or lesser degree and will continue doing so for all time to come. But the laws enacted against this intermingling of races and the

---

[55] Audrey Kerr, *The Paper Bag Principle*, 52.

fiat of social custom have practically put an end to the evil which was glossed over when the overlord of a plantation assumed command of the bodies of his female slaves, many of whom alas, yielded.[56]

The vaudeville minstrel performances of white and black actors with skin darkened with burned cork to act out misinformed parodies of black plantation and Reconstruction life perpetuated demeaning caricatures of black people and warped opinions of northern whites and immigrant communities. To him, viewers saw these depictions as true interpretations of black culture.

A Nod to Black Women

Miller indicted miscegenation and white men's sexual exploitation of black women while exonerating those whose enslaved status left them open to such assault. He loved black women and appreciated their struggle for recognition and respectability. Yet, some scholars characterize Miller as misogynistic because of his article entitled "Negro Surplus Women" in response to an article by Charlotte Gilman entitled "The Duty of Surplus Women."[57] Though Gilman's article spoke only to white women, Miller's concern was that some black women might believe themselves able to experience the freedom she illustrated. He feared that when Southern black women migrated to the North and found it

---

[56] "Is the American Negro to Remain Black or Become Bleached?" *South Atlantic Quarterly*, 1926 25(3): 240-252, 5.
[57] Charlotte Perkins Gilman, "The Duty of Surplus Women" *Woman's Journal*, May 12, 1900.

hard to earn a living, they might be forced into prostitution, for he said, [58]

> [w]hat of the lot of those surplus women who are not white, and not so very free? Is the ennobling sisterhood of woman to be limited to the color line? The struggle of colored woman towards purity and refinement involves as deep and as dark a tragedy as any that marks the history of human strivings... These left-over, or to-be-left-over, Negro women, falling as they do in large part in the lower stratum of society, miss the inhibitive restraint of culture and social pride, and especially, if they be comely of appearance, become the easy prey of the evil designs of both races... The great bulk of colored women in our cities, [are] being shut out from higher avenues of work, must seek employment in domestic service... The Negro woman is handicapped by such an unfavorable environment that it seems almost inhuman to make her the butt of witticism and ridicule as is sometimes done, because from the depth of her lowliness she dares aspire to the highest and best things in life.[59]

---

[58] Cheryl D. Hicks author of *Talk with You Like a Woman: African American Women, Justice and Reform in New York 1890-1935* explores the social landscape that black women faced in New York during the Progressive Era. Young women who worked menial jobs and socialized in ways Hicks calls "harmful intimacy" resulted in black women being arrested on suspicion of prostitution. The stigma attached to most working-class women rendered them more susceptible to public scrutiny. During World War I, these women were of particular concern to the federal government because they feared the spread of venereal disease. Nevertheless, Hicks asserts that these women continued to live their lives with degrees of wisdom to avoid being arrested or placated as prostitutes.

[59] Kelly Miller, "Negro Surplus Women," *Race Adjustment*. 168-167

His article entitled "The Emergence of Negro Women," celebrated the leadership of Mary Church Terrell[60] whose sense of racial pride and unity came from racist affronts she endured in the South. In 1896, she and other women crafted the National Association of Colored Women's Clubs (NACWC), a social justice organization, that created day nurseries, kindergartens, and mother's clubs to ameliorate the harsh conditions and provide opportunities for young black working-class women. In her over 90 years, the fair-complected, educated Terrell did not concede to color privilege but empathized with darker and economically challenged members of the African American community, and her awareness of discrimination led her to speak, write, and protest on their behalf. Miller recounted about her speech at the International Women's Congress.

---

[60] Terrell was born on September 23, 1863, in Memphis, Tennessee into a family of privilege. Her father's investment in real estate made him a millionaire. Terrell was born on September 23, 1863, in Memphis, Tennessee. Her father's investments in real estate made him a millionaire. She obtained a degree from Oberlin University in Ohio in 1884. She moved to Washington, D.C. and taught at the M Street School. She was the first president of the National Association of Colored Women's Clubs (NACWC) in 1896. Her advocacy advanced the race and sought better opportunities for working women and rising generations of young black women. Fair complexioned, educated and privileged she did not concede to color caste within the black community as a place of refuge from empathizing with the economically or aesthetically marginal groups in the African American community. She was a suffragist and participated in the 1913 Suffrage March with a delegation of Howard University women. Miller was the Dean and approved the students attending the march with a chaperone professor Thomas Montgomery Gregory The mutual affection and respect she had for Miller negates mischaracterization as an ardent anti-suffragist. Miller held an antiquated perspective however he acknowledged the maturity of women a benefit over men. Furthermore, in true polemic style his essay "The Risk of Women's Suffrage" has been narrowly read placing him in a chauvinistic light.

Mary Church Terrell

The article read I part:

> In the culture of carriage, dignity of manner and brilliance of utterance, Mrs. Mary Church Terrell, of Washington, D.C. who came from the slave environment some 50 years ago, enjoyed this distinction. This brilliant daughter of a despised race, stood in her place amid this celebrated assembly and pled the cause of her sable sisters in English, French and German, with such ease and eloquence that each delegate from those nations could hear and understand the sad story in her own tongue. The effect of one who herself had come up from lowly conditions which she so eloquently portrayed voicing the miseries and wrongs, as well as, the struggles and triumphs, of black womanhood filled every heart with pity and melted every eye with tears... The case of colored man is often yoked with that of white woman by reason of the common denial of rights and withholding of opportunities on account of race, on the one hand and sex on the other.
>
> But the case of the colored woman stands alone in its pitiable helplessness. She is the most unfortunate of all the despised elements of our complex society. The sins and inequities of the male portion of both races are visited upon her. She bears the burden of their transgressions. If the situation and circumstances of the colored man awaken such anxious solicitude, and call so loudly for remedial endeavor, what should be said for the Negro woman who staggers beneath the weight of a much severer load? The mere

contemplation of her condition fills the soul with infinite pity.

Under the slave regime her native delicacy of sex was ruthlessly outraged. She was forced into the closest intimacy of contact with the coarsest and most imbruted men of both races. As one of the most thoughtful of her own race has said: But from the day their fetters were broken and their mind released from the darkness of ignorance to which for more than two hundred years they had been doomed, from the day they could stand erect in the dignity of womanhood, no longer bond, but free, till now, colored women have forged steadily ahead in the acquisition of knowledge, the cultivation of those arts that make for good... These are but samples of the higher aspirations of black, brown, and bleached womanhood. Are not such shining emergencies from so dark and forbidden a background, striking and encouraging indications of a higher and better life to which this race is aspiring.[61]

In the same article, he celebrated Nannie Helen Burroughs,[62] who, in 1909, founded the National Training School for Women and Girls in Washington.

---

[61] Article "The Emergence of Negro Women," Kelly Miller papers, Box 19 folder 3 MARBL, Emory University.

[62] Burroughs was born on May 2, 1879, in Orange, Virginia. When her father died unexpectedly, her mother's Jennie Poindexter Burroughs, moved the family to Washington to seek employment and education for her young daughter. She attended the M Street School where she identified with teachers such as Terrell. Burroughs was disappointed when one of her instructors failed to apprentice her and left her scrambling for employment.

While attending school, she was committed to the Baptist tradition, and as a member of the prominent Nineteenth Street Baptist Church, she worked as a

Nannie Helen Burroughs

The school, whose motto was "work, support thyself, to thine own powers appeal," offered domestic science and missionary training. Burroughs was dedicated to racial uplift and the empowerment of women. As the two became close friends, she dubbed him the "Sage of the Potomac" because of his prolific and insightful writing. In return, Miller wrote of her:

Baptist missionary while seeking an apprenticeship in domestic science. When that did not materialize, she poured her energy into church work and advancing the position of women, publishing articles, lecturing, and advocating for biblically mandated social justice.

As an orator Miss Burroughs is simply irresistible and sweeps all before her with the impetuosity of cyclonic power. Her effectiveness does not end in mere oratory. She is tireless practical worker. By indefatigable energy, she has established in the city of Washington a school for training of Negro girls in household duties and domestic service. When we consider that domestic service is practically the only avenue open to colored girls on an unlimited scale, it will be readily agreed that there is no school in all the scope of Negro philanthropy that is more worthy of aid and encouragement than this.[63]

Miller's positive perspective on women stemmed from his love and respect for his mother and grandmother. He willingly highlighted women's contributions and gave them equal coverage as larger topics such as race, politics, and cultural criticism.

Along with cordial relationships with Terrell and Burroughs, he interacted with fellow educators, Mary McLeod Bethune and Charlotte Hawkins Brown.

---

[63] Article "The Emergence of Negro Women," Kelly Miller papers, Box 19 folder 3, MARBL, Emory University.

Charlotte Hawkins Brown.

He also thought highly of Sadie Daniels, whose book, *Women Builder*, one of the first titles written by a black woman, presented a roll call of worthy women.[64] Miller wrote of her work:

---

[64] Bethune was founder of Daytona Educational and Industrial Training School for Negro Girls in Tallahassee, Florida. Brown founded the Alice Freeman

Miss Daniels justifies this limited list by a word of caution: "Of thousands we cannot write the full story. We shall note here only a few towering personages. This volume will restrict itself to Negro women who are pioneers–hose who are builders of educational, financial, and social institutions... I do not think that even the women themselves will find occasion to quarrel with the author by reason of the limited list, which, with two unaccountable exceptions, is complete within its category. We are thankful to Miss Daniels for giving us this plain, simple, readable volume and for justly extolling these seven race builders whose work attests their worth. But we cannot confine our thought to the excellent portrayals presented. We lay down the volume more deeply impressed by what we read between the lines.[65]

A Husband and Father

Shy, uncoordinated, and simply dressed, Miller desired to have a wife and family. In 1894, he met the girl he desired to marry. To him, it was a case of "love at first sight," but he lacked the courage to ask her out even after she had initially shown interest in him. Annie May Butler, who was five years his junior, taught at the Normal School in Baltimore. Miller knew that a wife and children required financial resources and a means to secure an income.

Palmer Memorial Institute in Sedalia, North Carolina; and Slowe served as Howard's first dean of women.

[65] Kelly Miller "Sadie Daniels Extols Seven Women Builders," New York *Amsterdam News*. March 30, 1932.

Engagement Photo

During the days and nights while I was equipping myself for my chosen profession I often looked forward to the time when I should become a member of a university faculty as a period when I could cease worrying about money matters, be able to save something against a rainy day and perhaps make some small investments which would prove an addition to my income.[66]

Miller's debt and lack of financial resources caused the wedding plan for 1891 to be delayed for three years. Reverend Francis Grimke officiated the wedding.

Continuing financial restraints did not allow the couple to purchase a house, so they lived in his Clarke Dormitory quarters for the first three years of their marriage. The tight dormitory space was comfortable enough until within the first year of marriage, the couple became parents, and it became cramped. So, they took advantage of the University's offer to move into a residence at 430 College Street in 1896.

> From a second story window in this house I would often look down upon the premises adjacent, one of the largest and best-appointed frame houses at that date in Washington. A house surrounded by a spacious garden in the rear, a barn and stable from where handsome horses were led to be harnessed to the equipages [necessary equipment] in use before the automobile destroyed the picturesque street panorama, in evidence during my early days in the Nation's capital. I was not covetous, nor envious, but as I gazed at this property, I wished that someday it might become mine. The wishing had something to do with what happened, but I am forging ahead of the sequence of events.[67]

---

[66] KMP Box 71-2 folder, 8.
[67] KMP, chapter 41 "My Home Life," 1. John Mercer Langston built the house.

When finances improved, the Miller's moved to 2225 Fourth Street, a "fine house" with gables and a sizable garden. A sycamore tree given to John Mercer by Charles Sumner and believed to have been planted by Frederick Douglass remained in the front yard until 1934. Its connection to great men and early Howard history infused Miller with a sense of continuity and pride. Miller usually spent eight months each year engaged in gardening. Each spring, he grew enough vegetables to supply the table throughout the rest of the year. The remainder of the yard was covered with grass and flowers.

> My wishes came true. I acquired the property in 1915, by purchase from the heirs of Dr. Langston, who died in 1908. The house had thirteen rooms, but as the basement is practically divided into two sections it might well be said that it is a house of 15 rooms. One of the basement rooms, and by far the largest is my sanctum, where I may browse among my books, undisturbed, or peck with two fingers at the keys of my typewriter. At other times I have the service of a most able clerk, who takes well from dictation, and between us we turn out daily a goodly amount of copy for newspapers and magazines. On the shelves of my library are more than 1500 books and a thousand brochures, covering every subject under sun. On the hottest day in summer this retreat of mine is cool and on the cool and on the coldest in winter it is well warmed by heat from a Latrobe.[68]

---

[68] KMP, chapter 41 "My Home Life," 2-3.

When Kelly Miller, Jr. was born, the child was affectionately called "Scrump" by his father, who directed him to "consecrate him to God." This sentiment was Kelly's desire for all his children, who he believed should serve humanity as educators or ministers. He graduated from Howard University and completed a Master of Arts degree at Clark University in Massachusetts. Though he intended to teach, he became interested in medicine. When World War I came, he enlisted and served until honorably discharged. Following this, he taught for two years in Lynchburg, Virginia, before becoming a dentistry. For many years, he was the editor of *Howard Medical News*.

Miller's second child, Isaac Newton Miller, affectionately called "Pike," was born in 1896. He showed interest in physical training and was "a fine specimen of what proper exercise can do for a person." Kelly privately applauded the discipline and success of his son. He took a course in physical training at Harvard,"[69] then taught at West and Armstrong high schools in Washington. According to sister May, he was a talented basketball player. He entered World War I, but the Armistice was signed before his regiment was deployed. His sudden death at 32 years old from complications of appendix surgery devastated Miller, who wrote,

> [o]f all my children he gave the greatest promise, yet he was the only one to be taken from us... My eyes dim with tears as I write these lines. He was my best beloved. In him was the making of a great man, a splendid character. But it was not to be as I had hoped and planned and all that I can say is "God's will be done."[70]

---

[69] KMP, chapter 41 "Home Life," 5.
[70] KMP, chapter 41 "Home Life," 3

The grieving father authored a poem to commemorate Isaac's death:

> In Memoriam, Isaac Newton Miller
> 'Tis Two Years Since
> Time will assuage the deepest grief.
> an age-old maxim of belief
> the ticking clock will weaker grow
> these well-worn saws which are not so
> I placed him there beneath the sod.
> and left him there alone with God.
> when sad October comes again
> It prods my self-renewing pain.
> Were there no power to compensate.
> frail flesh would sink beneath the weight.
> this ever-growing grief of mine
> but waxes with the lapse of time
> the preacher on the mount has said.
> who mourneth shall be comforted.
> the offspring of his loins shall be
> the promised solace unto me.[71]

Miller published an excerpt from Isaac's obituary entitled "Meet My Son" in the *Amsterdam News*. This article exhibited his life and accomplishments, provided Miller with a catharsis, and proclaimed his son worthy of national acclaim for his work with the youth in Washington.

> I make no apologies for presenting these columns an extract from the eulogy of Professor G. David Houston, principal of Armstrong High School of

---

[71] Poem, In Memoriam, Isaac Newton Miller, Kelly Miller papers, Box 28 folder 1, MARBL, Emory University.

Washington, D.C. over the remains of my son Isaac Newton Miller, who died October 3, believing as I do that the simplicity, sincerity, serviceableness, and beauty of his short-circuited life will be a benediction of those who learn of it. In memory of a life that has been short but serviceable in fitting tribute to a character that merits emulation, and for an inspiration to our youth, we gather here today to pay our final respect for Isaac Newton Miller, whom we all knew merely as 'Newt'... That made Newton Miller a most valuable leader of impressionable youth. It was his hearty, jovial, sincere disposition that won his pupils...He developed a rare genius for dealing with adolescent boys and could handle 150 boys as he handled fifty. Though Newton was abruptly removed from us, in the physical sense, in the April of his career, he was, nevertheless, permitted to tarry long enough amongst us to enhance a beautiful philosophy of living, to give both young and old a living picture of domestic felicity, of filial devotion of Christian service...We can neither restore the physical nor destroy the spiritual. We are not going to see Newton daily, but we cannot help from feeling his influence daily. Such an inspiration is immoral.[72]

Isaac's death added three members to Miller's household: his widowed daughter-in-law, Clarissa, and her daughters, Annie and Gloria. Kelly's third child and first daughter, May, nicknamed Tom, was born in 1900. Early in her life, he believed she demonstrated an ability as a writer, having won two prizes from the *Washington Post* for the best grade school composition. Valedictorian of the Howard class of 1922, after a post-graduate course, she taught high school French, Latin,

---

[72] Kelly Miller, "Meet My Son," *Amsterdam News* December 19, 1928.

English, Speech, and Dramatics in Washington and Baltimore into the late 1930s. She was also a successful playwright, and a collection of her works was published in December 1935.

Growing up in Howard University's shadow, her artistry was impacted by her notable classmates. Close friend and fellow writer Zora Neale Hurston applied and attended Howard University at her suggestion. May and her father shared a love of poetry, often engaged in wordplay, and had a remarkably close relationship. She describes it as her heart being especially connected to his. May married and did not have any children. A series of letters between the two from 1906-1922 with observations about cities, race progress, and his travel misfortunes and for home and family concerns are the only extant letters between him and any of his children held outside of the family. In one, he wrote.

May 10, 1906

My Dear Tom

I am now in Dallas, Texas, two thousand miles away…It is not so extremely hot down here. I will be home now within a week…You know, Tom, that you must tell me who has been good. Do you help Mama with her work? Tell the boys that they must be good, or you will tell when he comes. Do you like the cards I have been sending you –
yours true to serve

Goodbye Tom

Papa K[73]

---

[73] Letter from KM to May Miller Sullivan, Kelly Miller papers, Box 1 folder 4, MARBL, Emory University.

Miller with Booker T. Washington and Byrd Prillerman

A month later, Kelly again would write to daughter May, nicknamed Tom, about his travels:

June 10, 1910

Dear Tom

I am now in Houston, Texas, two thousand miles from home. It is extremely hot out here I lectured in Baton Rouge, the capital of Louisiana… I speak here tonight. Then I will work my way slowly up through

Texas and Oklahoma and back home where I expect to arrive July 7th - how is the garden? Are the geraniums blooming - How about the petunias? I will see about your mom when I get back. Be a good girl and write whole lot of pretty stories. Give my love to Mama and everybody else.

Papa K[74]

In July 1913, Kelly visited Byrd Prillerman, founder and president of West Virginia Collegiate Institute. This trip proved difficult when lost luggage, a missed train, and tiredness overwhelmed his senses. [75] Miller informs May about the strenuous journey:

---

[74] Letter from KM to May Miller Sullivan, Kelly Miller papers, Box 1 folder 5, MARBL, Emory University.

[75] Prillerman was born a slave in 1859, in Virginia. He was the youngest of seventeen children and the grandchild of two white men. After the Civil War his family became tenant farmers and at age 12, Prillerman attended school. Eventually he attended Knoxville College in Tennessee earning a B.S., and after graduation, taught school in West Virginia. In 1890, he approached the Governor and superintendent of West Virginia to create the West Virginia Colored Institute which opened its doors in 1892 with Prillerman installed as a professor of English. In 1909 he was elected president and in 1915, its status was elevated from Institute to College and its name change to West Virginia State University.

During his tenure as President, he received honorary degrees including an A.M. degree Westminster College of Pennsylvania and the degree of Doctor of Literature from the Selma University. Prillerman retired from West Virginia Collegiate Institute in 1919 and dedicated the remaining years to Baptist Sunday school work. His mercurial rise from poverty and obscurity to a place of leadership and influence is a similar story to Miller. Moreover, his indelible imprint on the growth of higher education for African Americans in West Virginia brought many race men, including Booker T. Washington, to the campus. In 1912 Dr., visited the Institute. . In part because of Prillerman's dedication to building an institution to produce competent leaders for the race through a curriculum infused with worth, greatness, modesty, and simplicity. West Virginia Collegiate Institute (now West Virginia State University) became the first school for African Americans to receive state accreditation.

My Dear Tom:

Let me tell you of a series of unmerciful disasters which followed fast and followed faster. On leaving Wilberforce [Ohio] I gave the driver my suitcase to put on the top of the bus. He stupidly failed to do so – at the station I have him money and directions for expressing it to me at Cincinnati by next outgoing train - this he also failed to do - I was compelled to buy a change of linen and lecture in dust begrimed clothes – but this was not all. I fell into the hands of some Howard folks in Cincinnati who detained me at a banquet till half past nine.

Luckily no one was injured, but we were delayed two hours.... He landed me at the deport one minute before the train time. I had no time to enquire about baggage or to telegraph people at Institute about my arrival. After boarding the train, I learned that it did not stop at Institute, but went to Charleston eight miles away. I reached Charleston at 4:30 on Tuesday and took an automobile for the depot where the trains for Institute were but found that the last train for the day had just pulled out... The shades of darkness were falling about me.

You may imagine I thought of "Lord Kindly light amid the encircling gloom..." I appreciated this hymn as never before...I brought mathematics to bear on the situation and calculated that I had about 25,000 feet to travel. I calculated that I would have to take 10,000 steps – I knew that every step brought me that much nearer my goal. I arrived finally at President Prillerman's house...The people here marvel at my luck. My dear Tom, do you know the definition of a hero? A hero is a man who can overcome circumstances. Papa[76]

Of a trip to Battle Creek, Michigan, to address a gathering of Howard alums and other black people interested in higher education, he wrote:

Battle Creek, Michigan
July 29-22 My

Dear Tom:

This is... where they make Post Toasties... I am visiting here a while till I reach Flint where I address the Masons on Monday. I am enjoying my vacation. In four weeks, I will be back to Wash. DC which after all is the best of all. I narrowly missed a visit to Idlewilde, the summer paradise of the Afro-American... [are]the grapes and cherries are about ripe and should be preserved. Hear the philosophy of preserving fruit and vegetables? Monk would eat all the sweet and tempting grapes... Where Sill turns them into juice or jelly and relates their use till grapes come again... Show this letter to Sill - she is better in science than she is in philosophy...

With love to all, Papa[77]

Miller's fourth child, Irene, nicknamed Sill, was born in 1902. She graduated from Howard with Bachelor of Arts and Master of Arts degrees and taught math for a year at

---

[76] Letter from KM to May Miller Sullivan, Kelly Miller papers, Box 1 folder 7, MARBL, Emory University.

[77] Letter from KM to May Miller Sullivan, Kelly Miller papers, Box 7 folder 1, MARBL, Emory University.

Petersburg State College, then transferred to Miner Teachers College in Washington as an instructor, where she remained until the late 1930s.

The fifth child, Paul Butler Miller, affectionately called Monk, was born in 1907. At age thirteen, he set up a printing press in the family's basement, demonstrating an aptitude for this craft. In his senior year at Howard, his father opened a morning newspaper to learn that Paul had eloped to Maryland with a classmate. However, Howard students were forbidden to marry during their matriculation, and Paul received no leniency from his father when seeking readmission. In his autobiography, Miller recalled this event:

> They were forgiven and given the parental blessing, but when they begged that I intercede with the faculty to suspend the rule which punished students who married during the University course by a year's suspension I replied "Nay" I made that rule and shall be the last to ask that it be rescinded. When the time expired, they both returned to college and were graduated. Then Paul established himself in a print shop which he now owns and is quite successful. They have two children, a boy known as Kelly Miller III and Suzanne.[78]

According to May, her father was a humorous and affectionate man who was able to stoke his wife's and children's emotional embers with loving words. On Annie's 50th birthday, Miller offered her a brief note of affection.

Dear Mama,

---

[78] KMP, chapter 41 "Home Life," 6.

Things moving well so far. Addressed Chamber of Commerce Spokane yesterday was met there by the Mayor this morning.

Your fiftieth birthday will be pas[sed] before this letter reaches you. I am sending one kiss for each year - kisses. Having given to the world five children who promise decent upright lives, and intelligent, high-minded relationship to the issues of life, you may surely consider your fifty years of existence have been worthwhile. Let us hope that your future years will be relieved of much of the strain and care of former days and that you may enjoy a larger measure of happiness and tranquility.... I must close - with love Papa.[79]

A Living Legacy - The Moorland Foundation

Between 1890 and 1916, Miller's passion for the race led him to collect historical books, manuscripts, photographs, and material culture to preserve scholarship and research and serve as a medium for understanding human strivings and accomplishments. Toward this end, in the 1910s, he birthed the idea of a National Negro Museum and proposed it to the Howard University Board of Trustees by Miller.

The proposal coincided with the establishment of the Moorland Foundation in December 1914. At Kelly's request, the donation of a valuable collection of books, pamphlets, clippings, and other historical items from Howard alumnus and Trustee J.E. Moorland was combined with the material the Library already possessed, including the Tappan and the

---

[79] Letter from KM to Annie Butler Miller, Kelly Miller papers, family correspondence, MARBL, Emory University.

Lavalette Collections.[80] The objectives of the library and museum were as follows:

1. To promote the investigation and study of the life, art, history, and ethnology of the Negro and Negroid peoples.
2. To accumulate, record and preserve all such material by and about the Negro.
3. To disseminate knowledge about the life, art, history, and ethnology of the Negro by publications, lectures, or otherwise and to serve as a Bureau of Information Concerning the Negro.
4. To assist interested students of Negro life and history to pursue the scholarly use of the materials in the collection.
5. To provide a great reference library on every phase of Negro life.
6. To collect and preserve the art, ethnology, and material objects of the past in Negro life and to display those for the enjoyment, aesthetic appreciation and education of students and observers.
7. To assist, guide and encourage the organized research and systematic excavation of areas where archaeological discoveries of the Negro's past are likely to be found.[81]

---

[80] The Tappan Collection included 1,650 items bound in about 300 volumes. Lavalette Collection was about sixty volumes. This collection has grown to more than 10,000 items including books, periodicals, pamphlets, manuscripts, theses, pictures, and curios. Dorothy Porter was placed in charge of the collection in 1933. Through her indefatigable efforts, the original collection was organized and developed into one of the most unique collections concerning black people.

[81] Rayford Logan papers, Box 166-16 folder 16, MSRC. For additional information see Logan's paper "Origins of the Idea," this document giving the history and breath of the National Negro Museum and Library as envisioned by

Miller received support for the effort from Alain Locke, the first African American Rhodes scholar,[82] fellow South Carolinian and Howard educator Benjamin Brawley, other faculty and alumni, as well as the Librarian of Congress.

The interest Miller generated resulted in establishing a committee to investigate the feasibility of creating the institution. Still, the idea languished with the Trustee board for several years as some Trustees did not like the term Negro while others did not care to extend Miller's territory into another location on campus. So, though Miller continued to press the issue of the National Negro Library and Museum, it remained an elusive goal during the early twentieth century.

On January 2, 1915, Howard University issued a press release entitled "Negro Americana Begun at Howard University." It read, in part:

> Howard University has just undertaken to make a collection of books, documents, records, and other available data bearing upon the Negro race on the American Continent. The University already possesses several important individual collections as

---

Kelly Miller and advocated by Howard library, and scholarly colleagues. The Rayford Logan papers will be referred to as RLP in subsequent pages.

[82] Locke's grandfather attended Cambridge University in Great Britain. Locke attended Harvard University and concerned himself with the cultural artifacts and expressions of Africans within African American society. During his global travels he amassed a collection of artifacts that expressed African creativity. Intellectually, Locke's work in philosophy impelled him to construct the framework of the "New Negro movement" which developed into the 1920s Black Renaissance that empowered a generation of writers and thinkers such as Langston Hughes, Zora Neale Hurston, Wallace Thurman, Countee Cullen, and Claude McKay. These young writers and thinkers would move beyond European ideals of poetry and art to create images and stories that were based in the African past and lived black experience during the 1920s. The success of these artists opened the door to self-identity and self-definition stipulating who and what black art was and could become.

a basis of the proposed Negro Americana...The Moorland collection is the largest and most significant contribution to the New undertaking. Dr. [Jesse] Moorland, International Secretary of the Young Men's Christian Association, has been a collector of rare and curious books in this field during the past quarter of a century and has gathered up a collection of several thousand titles. Dr. Moorland has just turned this collection over to Howard University, of which he is an Alumnus and Trustee.[83]

Miller corresponded with prominent alumni and national leaders seeking assistance in influencing the trustee board to fund the project. However, his polemics on issues that exposed university matters muted his effort to bring his dream to fruition. Still, the seeds of the idea percolated until finally, the Founders Library opened in 1939. Still, 75-year-old Miller continued campaigning for his National Negro Library and Museum. Herbert Putman, librarian and the intellectual architect behind the Library of Congress, backed Miller's idea. In a letter to him, Miller wrote:

My proposal for the establishment of a Negro Library and Museum at Howard University, in which you were kind enough to express a generous interest, was unanimously approved by the Board of Trustees at their semi-annual meeting, October 25, 1938, in the following actions.

That the Administration be instructed to proceed with such steps as will bring about the full realization

---

[83] KMP Box 71-2, folder 15 National Negro Museum Press Release, January 2, 1915.

of the National Negro Library and Museum project as rapidly as possible.

I am sure that your interest in this enterprise will be heightened by this authorization, and that all friends of higher education of the Negro race will co-operate with the President and Trustees of Howard University, to bring into full realization this undertaking.[84]

Since he was an instrumental part of the Museum committee, Brawley's untimely death left Miller with more obstacles. However, as interim committee representative, Howard historian Charles H. Wesley continued to promote the project. A May 3, 1939, letter to Guy B. Johnson at the University of North Carolina explains the events that delayed the movement of the Committee on Scholarship and Research.

The sudden death of Professor Brawley, Chairman of the faculty committee of the National Negro Library and Museum, together with the illness of President Johnson have very greatly delayed the progress... Dean Wesley after much research and elaboration completed his assignment and turned it over to the President. I presume that both Professor Wesley's manuscript and my own may have been or will be placed in your hands...To let the iron cool after it has

---

[84] KMP, Box 71-1 folder 31 correspondence "P" A response to Miller's letter was not located, however, the Librarian of Congress did attend the opening of Founders Library and remarked on the high-quality facilities and state of the art to technology the building employed.

been heated to the melting point may jeopardize the success of the entire project.⁸⁵

A month before his death, Miller entrusted documentation about creating the museum to Wesley to preserve as part of its permanent record.⁸⁶ In 1928 librarian Dorothy Porter Wesley was hired to build a world-class repository that chronicled the global African experience. Over her 40+ year career, Dr. Porter Wesley curated the world's most comprehensive collection of primary sources, prints/photographs, artifacts, artwork, and institutional records on the global African community.⁸⁷ The Moorland Spingarn Research Center came into being in 1973.

Like Arturo Schomburg, Miller saw the achievements of black people as crafted by the divine.⁸⁸ Both men desired that

---

⁸⁵ RLP, Box 166-16 folder 16 Correspondence "Miller, Kelly" letter.

⁸⁶ Wesley was a trained historian and multi-talented person. Educated at Harvard University and involved in numerous professional, civic, and African Methodist Episcopal [AME] church organizations, he believed in a fusion of scholarship, faith, and purpose. He served as chairman of the Department of History at Howard from 1921 to 1942. Wesley and Miller both were members of Alpha Phi Alpha and Sigma Pi Phi fraternities.

⁸⁷ Dorothy Porter Wesley was born in 1905 in Warrenton, Virginia. She attended Howard University graduating in 1928. She attended Columbia University where we obtained a Master of Science in Library Science. She was the first African American woman to obtain that degree. President Mordecai Johnson hired her to administer the Library of Negro Life and History donated by Jesse Moorland. Her overwhelming success at Howard resulted in being called to numerous countries in Africa and the Caribbean to establish governmental and national libraires. For additional information see *Dorothy Porter Wesley at Howard University Building a Legacy of Black History*, by Janet Sims-Wood.

⁸⁸ Schomburg was born in Puerto Rico in 1874. His early education began in Puerto Rico. During his formative years one teacher informed him that African people had contributed nothing to humanity except service as enslaved people. This statement left an indelible mark in Schomburg's soul. After his family migrated to New York city In 1891, Schomburg would dedicate his entire life to refuting through documentary evidence the misinformed statement of his elementary school teacher. Miller and Schomburg both pushed for the true telling of black history.

their institutions would leave legacies of racial pride for rising generations. Unfortunately, unlike Schomburg's institution's memorializing his involvement in its creation, the memory of Miller's work in establishing the Moorland Spingarn Center has all but faded from Howard's consciousness.[89]

Historian Rayford Logan described the forty years between 1890 and 1930 as the nadir. This period was characterized by virulent anti-black racism in federal and state legislation as well as de jure encounters. Concurrently, it was also a time of enormous growth for Miller when his name and influence began to stretch across the country. During this period, Miller's daysman commitment to harmonizing disparate views about racial uplift and politics positioned him as a national figure. Major black leaders such as Crummell, Washington, Bethune, Schomburg, and Burroughs invited him to join their organizations and participate in their meetings and often sought his opinion.

---

[89] It is my desire that his ingenious efforts are restored. This would place Miller within the land of giants such as Jesse E. Moorland, Arturo Spingarn, and Dorothy Porter Wesley.

Four
The Negro is Scarcely Considered: 1917-1925

> Life is a continual warfare against internal and external foes which, if unchecked, would speedily lead to death. Man has the same physical necessities... to which he is indissolubly linked, and of which he is a special emergence.
>
> "The Primary Needs of the Negro Race"
> Kelly Miller

A Modern Tantalus 1917-1919

Some scholars assert that the assassination of Archduke Franz Ferdinand, heir presumptive to the throne of Austria-Hungary, was the cause of World War I. Others hold that a shift in the economic and social climate and rising industrialization was its root cause. But regardless of its cause, this was the first man-made catastrophe of the twentieth century. Slated to be short-lived, the failure to implement a strategic battle plan and a deadlock between the American, British, and French forces allied against Germany and the Ottoman Empire led to a protracted conflict and one of the bloodiest, most devastating wars ever seen.

Yet, this war ushered in an era of growth for black men and women who served as supporters, secret agents, and tactical assault forces as they had done in the Revolutionary and Spanish-American Wars. Miller documented their valor and courage In an article entitled "The Negro Place in the New Reconstruction:"

> History abounds in convulsive epochs when the acute evils of society are eradicated. We have but to recall the tremendous outburst of moral energy during the Revolutionary Struggle and the Civil War, to bring to mind the operation of this principle within our own national experience. Each of these great upheavals serves to curb the arrogant assumption of irresponsible power, and to give impulse to the doctrine of the inherent claims of man as man.[197]

He viewed the conflagration as a necessary evil that offered black men an opportunity to assert their patriotism, manhood, and humanity. The shifting political landscape gave rise to new challenges in both domestic and international spheres. It also created fresh economic prospects and a renewed spiritual outlook, which in turn spurred a wave of black migration from the rural South to the urban North. It also allowed black men to become free agents and global citizens, as Miller would explain in *History of the World War for Human* Rights:

> Conditions in Europe intensified when Germany aimed to] throw off the yoke which she claimed England wished to fasten on her

---

[197] Kelly Miller, *The Negro's Place in the New Reconstruction*, 2

world relationships.... Little did Germany dream what moral advantage she gave these overrun lands in the hearts of the millions of Negroes of the world. Germany felt assured that Negroes from all Africa would gloat over the assassination of Belgium...The American Negro, be it said, came to the Belgian relief with money and goods, prayers, and tears.[198]

Miller saw black men's entry into military service as contributing to a conveniently forgotten history and providing an opportunity to elevate themselves.

From such a status of debasement, existing in an intolerable atmosphere of derogation and disrepute, the humble and humiliated American Negro sought the exaltation of international honor. Denied and disavowed at home through vicissitude of international war, he hoped for affirmation of a new world dictum in acknowledgment of his human qualities and worth...He wanted to make good in public. He wanted to demonstrate both efficiency and initiative. He desired that popular belief conceive him as a man, not a monkey. He yearned to reveal his powers in every field of endeavor.... He wished for the world to find in him fitness for survival [and] human relationships... He sought to neutralize

---

[198] Kelly Miller, *Kelly Miller's History of the World War for Human Rights*, 447-448.

the misteachings of Adam Smith, of Darwin and Defoe...These ideas the Negro wished to topple over.[199]

Unfortunately, during this period, Jim Crow ideas and practices still held sway in American society, and the mixture of white supremacy, race hatred and prejudice, injustice, and fear proved to be an intractable, volatile enemy of progress. Yet, black leaders saw involvement in the war as an opportunity for others to view their men more positively and felt that this was worth the risk of human lives.

When Miller and seven other black leaders implored Secretary of War Newton D. Baker to invite three hundred black men to enter any regular training camp, he declined to do so but promised to consider planning a program to train colored officers for their regiments. After the meeting, Joel Spingarn[200] urged white and black men to organize campaigns on black college campuses, with Howard leading the way.

The Military Intelligence Section had targeted Miller as a potentially seditious instigator of black citizens because his writings were thought to undermine patriotic sentiment among them. However,

---

[199] *Kelly Miller's History of the World War for Human Rights*, 435-436.

[200] Spingarn was a professor of comparative literature and civil rights leader. He was active in the military where he became a colonel. His interest in civil rights issues stemmed from his involvement in the National Association for the Advancement of Colored People (NAACP) where he was one of the first white leaders of and Chairman of the Board in 1914. He established the Spingarn Medal still awarded annually by the NAACP for outstanding achievement by an African American.

he was personally interested in the war because his sons, Kelly and Isaac, sought to serve in the military.

Walter Howard Loving[201], the only black agent in the Military Intelligence Section, infiltrated African American communities, reporting racial problems and advising black people of the legal consequences unpatriotic actions might incur. Prior to his employment, the embers of a series of riots had threatened to boil over into full-blown race wars, and federal officials feared that subversive elements of the community might connect to international enemies because of the underlying German-inspired "Negro unrest." Their fears were partially realized in the Bayou City, Texas

---

[201] Loving was born to former slaves in 1872 in Lovingston, Virginia. The family moved to St. Paul, Minnesota before relocating to Washington, DC where he graduated from the M Street High School before returning to St. Paul. In 1893 he enlisted in the Army and throughout his military career, the gifted musician traveled around the world before using his talent to give free vocal lessons and assist in orchestrating the high school minstrels' music program.

As America increased its military readiness during World War I, Loving considered returning to active duty and 1917, again got his chance to serve when he was recruited as a civilian for the Army's Military Intelligence Section that concerned itself with m espionage, counterespionage, domestic surveillance of the nation's racial situation. As its only Black agent, Loving's infiltrated African American communities to determine what racial problems could arise, report them, and persuade African Americans of legal consequences unpatriotic actions could incur. His reports on "Negro activity" resulted in visits by General Winston Churchill to military camps housing black servicemen.

In August 1919, a year after ending his Military Intelligence career, Loving relocated his family to the Philippines where he began directing the Philippine Constabulary Band and approached the War Department about establishing a standing office in Military Intelligence (MI) to survey the African American community. But this idea was ignored, and he dedicated his remaining years to the Constabulary Band. When Japan invaded the Philippines, Loving was taken prisoner and killed, and his body was never recovered.

incident, where black men from the 24th Infantry rampaged the city, killing sixteen private white citizens, four policemen, and four service members. As fear of fighting became a pressing matter and the felt injustice of unprosecuted white supremacy led some black citizens to form militias, the entire battalion was disarmed and transferred from Texas to Ohio.

The 24th Infantry was not the only group to respond to overt racism and governmental indifference with violent outbursts. Many of these encounters resulted in prison sentences, dishonorable discharges, or death for those found guilty, and greatly enflamed the existing discontent of young black men and race leaders with the government.

Loving was seen as a compassionate patriot who understood the racial climate and tenor of his times. In a March 1918 letter to him, Miller explained:

> On yesterday, you were good enough to let me see a paper in which you were directed by the Intelligence Branch of the War Department to investigate me and my activities in connection with my attitude concerning the present war... The extracts contained in the letter which you showed me occurred in my open letter to the President of the US under date August 4, 1917... The extracts quoted by the Intelligence Bureau, are taken from their logical setting, and fail utterly to represent my purpose which was certainly not to "stimulate adverse propaganda," but rather to point out to the President the just grievances of the colored

race and to urge the government to do justice towards this despised people, and thus justify and encourage that loyalty and patriotism which it has never failed to manifest.

As to my general attitude, I can only say that long before this war was dreamed of, I have on numerous occasions and in numerous ways urged the colored people to be loyal and patriotic to the country to which they owe their allegiance, even though for the time being it accords to them only a partial measure of the privilege and prerogative of citizenship. Anyone who will take the pains to search my writings will easily be convinced of this fact. I think it was the second day after America declared war, I wrote the President offering the government such service I might be capable of rendering.

In company with others, I called upon Secretary Baker, and urged the establishment of a training camp for colored officers. I urged the students at Howard University to take advantage of this opportunity to serve their country on an elevated level. I visited the Camp at Des Moines and addressed the twelve hundred cadets urging the utmost loyalty and patriotism.

> During the past six months I have spoken widely throughout the country sounding the keynote of duty to the flag and country.
>
> In view of my utmost endeavor to serve the country at this critical hour, I confess that I am surprised and disappointed on finding myself under surveillance by the Intelligence Department of the Government.[202]

In correspondence to the Intelligence Department, Loving attempted to clarify an inquiry about the influence of Miller's writings on the black community:

> I have been over each paragraph of the pamphlet in question and pointed out to Mr. Miller the phrases which are misleading, especially at this time when the country is at war with a foreign nation. This is the second time that I have had the occasion to approach Mr. Miller on this same subject. I have kept a keen eye on Mr. Miller's writings and speeches since my first interview with him and true to his promise, I have never heard him make a remark in any of his speeches that could have been construed as disloyal or misleading.
>
> The several articles written for the various papers mentioned in his letter, were all

---

[202] Letter from KM to Walter Loving, March 8, 1918. Kelly Miller Papers, Box 4 folder 2, MARBL, Emory University.

reviewed by the undersigned before they were released for the press. He has made no objectionable remark in his speeches nor wrote anything objectionable in the press since my first interview with him in October.

I am confident that Mr. Miller has been made to see his mistake and is now endeavoring to make amends for the same. However, I shall not turn my attention entirely from him, but will give him the benefit of the doubt until we should hear of some new activities.[203]

Though his letter formally relieved Miller's suspicion, he remained on the list of "persons of interest" throughout the duration of the war.[204] In 1918, he published an illustrated book on the war entitled *Kelly Miller's History of the World War for Human Rights*, whose preface read:

… This treatise will set forth the black man's part in the world's war with the logical sequence of facts and the brilliant power of statement for which the author is famous. In this treatise, Professor Miller will trace briefly,

---

[203] March 14, 1918, Walter Loving papers, Box 113-1 folder 10, Military Intelligence Correspondence Jan-Sept. 1918. MSRC.

[204] Theodore Kornweibel, *Investigate Everything: Federal Efforts to Compel Black Loyalty During World War I*, Indiana University Press, IN, Indiana, 2002. Chapter 2 speaks about the incendiary response Miller's "Disgrace of Democracy," open letter to President Woodrow Wilson garnered.

but with consuming interest, the relation of the Negro to the great wars of the past. He will point out the never-failing fount of loyalty and patriotism which characterizes the black man's nature and will show that the Negro has never been a hireling but has always been characterized by that moral energy which actuates all true heroism. The conduct of the Negro in the present struggle will be set forth with a brilliant and pointed pen.

The idea of three hundred thousand American Negroes crossing three thousand miles of sea to fight against autocracy of the German crown constitutes the most interesting chapter in the history of this modern crusade against an unholy cause. The valor and heroism of the Afro-American contingent were second to none according to the unanimous testimony of those who were in command of this high enterprise.

The story of Negro officers in command of troops of their own color will prove the wisdom of a policy entered upon with much distrust and misgiving... The author wisely queries: "When, hereafter, the Negro asks for his rights as an American citizen, where can the American be found with the heart or the hardihood to say to him, Nay.[205]

Miller's *History of the World War for Human Rights* was the only contemporary publication that included the contributions of black women. In his publication he lists the names of all 14 Colored Yeowomen employed by the Navy Department. This radical inclusion contributed to documenting the patriotic agency of black women.

Colored Yeowomen

---

[205] Kelly Miller, " Preface" *Kelly Miller's History of the World War for Human Rights*, Washington, DC: Austin Jenkins Co., 1919.

Accompanying note: "Lead by John T. Risher, a Black seaman, and the active service personnel for the bulk of U.S. involvement in WWI were Black Yeowomen. These first Black yeowomen (Naval member who performs administrative duties) to serve in the U.S. Navy. These fourteen women were first written about by Kelly Miller. There, he provided a listing of their names. These names had some spelling variations that made future research more difficult, but not impossible. Women were not subject to the draft and Black women, therefore, followed the same role limitations as Black men. The WWI active unit consisted of all Black females – the first Black female non-nursing unit of the Navy- and finding any mention of them is hard to come by. They were never at sea due to their race and gender and as such, they did not show up on revolving muster rolls or ship logs to track their movements. Many histories overlook them all together, stating erroneously that WWII was the beginning of Black Naval service as yeomen. Another near miss these women almost all share is initial rejection of service due to a medical disqualification. Those who were initially rejected have notes or memos in their OMPFs recommending them for service specifically to the Muster Roll Division. This fact may support the theory that Risher individually and purposefully built this Division to his specifications. By having women that would otherwise be unfit for service, Risher may have had an easier time convincing the

Navy to let him pool their service together in his command despite their gender and skin color.[206]

The Black Officer's Training Camp

Howard University sent 200 men to the Des Moines, Iowa, Officers Training Camp and documented this momentous event in the *Howard Record*:

> Howard University played its part in this movement consistently and well. In fact, in leading the larger participation of colored youth in the higher forms of war service, she found it necessary to assume a unique role, and to lead off in a campaign for the enlargement of their opportunities for such service. Her efforts were first directed toward securing officer-training facilities for colored men having the proper qualifications.
>
> In reviewing the circumstances which led in May 1917, to the authorization of the United States government for the establishment of an Officers Training Camp for young colored men, one is at the very outset well-nigh overwhelmed by the extraordinary enthusiasm, resourcefulness, confidence, race loyalty and patriotism exhibited by the students at Howard University.

---

[206]https://rediscovering-black-history.blogs.archives.gov/2020/11/09/golden-14/]

> Undoubtedly, much credit for securing the camp for the training of colored officers is due to the activity of many members of the faculties and officers at Howard University many other schools... Though menaced by failure on every hand, the students of Howard University and of other colored colleges throughout the land, in face of almost certain defeat, displayed an enthusiasm and a determination, that has seldom, if ever, been equaled in any single endeavor for the recognition and advancement of the race.[207]

This would be the first time African Americans sought to become officers to oversee segregated troops.

> If everything is considered, the evidence is conclusive that the Negro's response to America's call in the World War will remain a lasting tribute to his patriotism. He furnished his quota cheerfully. The doubts expressed of his Americanism were ill considered and the fears concerning his loyalty were groundless.[208]

Several actions made the idea of deploying African American officers palatable the military. Despite facing racial antagonism, the bravery and valor

---

[207] *Howard University Record* 13:4 ,April 1919, 159-160.
[208] *Kelly Miller's History of the World War for Human Rights*, preface

displayed by Henry Johnson and Needham Roberts during their hand-to-hand combat with German forces while serving in Colonel Hayward's 15th New York regiment in France earned them field honors and helped propel the idea of having Colored officers into the forefront.

Robert Russa Moton influenced President Wilson to move on behalf of blacks. In an address entitled "Robert R. Moton - WHO IS HE!" President Wilson proclaimed that all American citizens were worthy of fair treatment. Miller's *History of the World War* contains a transcript of the President's address in which he embraced the idea of black military service as a direct blow to the behavior of lynch mobs. Miller wrote:

> No man who loves America, no man who really cares for her fame and honour and character, or who is truly loyal to her institutions, can justify mob actions while the courts of justice are open, and the governments of the states and the nation are ready and able to do their duty. We are at this very moment fighting lawless passion. Germany has outlawed herself among the nations because she has disregarded the sacred obligations of law and has made lynchers of her armies. Lynchers emulate her disgraceful example. I, for my part, am anxious to see every community in America rise above that level, with pride and fixed

resolution which no man or act of men can afford to despise... I can never accept any man as a champion of liberty, either for ourselves or for the world, who does not reverence and obey the laws of our own beloved land, whose laws we ourselves have made. He has adopted the standard of the enemies of his country, whom he affects to despise.[209]

As lynching and mob violence against African Americans was a national issue that demanded a solution, Miller penned a letter to Wilson entreating him to acknowledge the threat to the black community's safety, warning that increasing violence irritated the race problem and accusing the government of complicity. He suggested that the problems could be solved by a federal declaration and prosecution of assailants under existing yet unenforced laws. He also cautioned Wilson that his silence was seen as tacit consent:

These periodic outbreaks of lawlessness are but the outgrowth of the disfavor and despite in which the race is held by public opinion. The evil is so widespread that the remedy lies in the hand of the national government... If democracy cannot control lawlessness, then democracy must be pronounced a failure. The nations of the world have a right to demand of us the working of the institutions at home

---

[209] Ibid., 452-454.

before they are promulgated abroad... Reproach is cast upon your contention for the democratization of the world, in face of its lamentable failure at home. Ex-President Roosevelt has openly proclaimed, in dramatic declaration, that these outbreaks make our moral propaganda for the liberation of mankind but a delusion and a snare. Mr. President, can this nation hope to live and grow in favor with God and man based on a lie? A nation with a stultified conscience is a nation with a stunted power. Democracies have frequently shut their eyes to moral inconsistencies... As a student of public questions I have carefully watched your attitude on the race problem. You have preserved a lukewarm aloofness from the tangled issues of this problem. In searching your writings, one finds little or no reference to this troubled phase of American life. You regard it as a regrettable social malady to be treated with cautious and calculated neglect.

Mr. President, ten million of your fellow citizens are looking to you and to the God whom you serve to grant them relief in this hour of their deepest distress. All moral reforms grow out of the people who suffer and stand in need of them. The Negro's helpless position may yet bring America to a realizing sense that righteousness exalteth a nation, but sin is a reproach to any people.[210]

In August 1917, when the War Department finally announced the opening of a training camp for African Americans at Fort Des Moines, Iowa, Spingarn sought educated men to fill the slots. An article entitled "How the Training Camp for Colored Men Happened to be Established" in *The* [Iowa] *Bystander* celebrated the accomplishment with these words:

> The officers training camp at Des Moines, Iowa marks a great epoch in the history of the Negro race. It is a recognition that the black has never received from any country in modern times. The training and commissioning of approximately one thousand Negro officers to lead thirty thousand Negro troops in the titanic war for democracy marks a new era in the history of

---

[210] *Kelly Miller's History of the World War for Human Rights*, 481-495. In this open letter Miller makes mention of Black women who organized prayer vigils to ameliorate the conditions of racial hatred. "Negro women all over the nation have appointed a day of prayer in order that righteousness might be done... The weaker sex of the weaker race is praying that God may use you as the instrument of his will to promote the cause of human freedom at home... They prayed, as their mother's prayed in the darker days gone by, that God would deliver the race...God uses the humbler things of life to confound the mighty. It may be these helpless victims of cruelty and outrage will bring an apostate world back to God." President Wilson a southern by birth offered tepid response to pleas for justice although he publicly denounced lynching he did not offer the federal funding to neither prosecute assailants nor offer remedy to the families of the murdered.

the Negro race throughout the world... [Howard University president], Stephen N. Newman gave every assistance and encouragement to the campaign, and he was one of its foremost workers. Deans Kelly Miller [and others] all gave valiant assistance. The central committee of Negro college men opened regular headquarters at Howard University and labored day and night in the cause.[211]

Spingarn bombarded the Black Press and historically black college campuses for support of the Officers Training Camp. In a letter entitled "Military Training Camp for Colored Men," New York, February 15, 1917. Spingarn wrote:

To the Educated Colored Men of the United States:

It is of the highest importance that the educated colored men of this country should be given opportunities for leadership. You must cease to remain in background in every field of national activity, and must come forward to assume your right places as capacity for leadership must be given an opportunity to test and display it...

---

[211]Thomas M. Gregory papers, Box 37-1 folder 17 clipping *The Bystander*, (Iowa) "How the Training Camp for Colored Men happened to be established," August 31, 1917.

Major General Leonard Wood, of the U.S. Army, commanding the Department of the East, has promised that if two hundred of you apply for admission, he will organize and maintain a military training camp for colored men, with [the right] training to fit you to serve as officers of volunteers in case of war.

Candidates must be between the ages of 20 and 45, in vigorous health, and of good moral character. Men who are graduates and undergraduates of colleges, high schools, normal, agricultural, or industrial schools, or other institutions of learning are preferred; but any man of intelligence, character and ability may join. Previous military experience is not necessary. If you are not a graduate or undergraduate of some institution, it might be advisable to have a letter of recommendation from some person of repute.[212]

Spingarn implored readers to comprehend the long-term investment and critical nature of training black officers would afford, for he noted that,

No one could make a greater mistake than to think that the Army wants colored men to join

---

[212] Joel Spingarn papers, 95-13 folder 534, open letter on Military Training Camp for Colored Men..." 2/15/1917. His papers are labelled JSP in subsequent citations.

this camp. The Army officials want the camp to fail. They refuse to set a time or place until two hundred men apply, because they know that this makes it harder to recruit men for the camp. They merely want to be able to say that they have given the colored people a fair chance and the colored people refused to take advantage of the opportunity...

This project is intended to FIGHT segregation in the Army and not to help it...When war comes, we do not wish to be in the same position. We want to be able to say: Here are colored men fit to be officers, and you have to commission them... A good soldier is a man who has military training; a good officer is a man who has military training, ability to lead, and a GOOD EDUCATION.

Colored men must get officers' training as soon as possible, and there is no other way with the whole Army against them. The South does not want colored men to get any kind of military training; nothing frightens it more than the thought of [Black men numbering in the] millions, [who are] disciplined, organized, and dangerously effective. All pretty talk about volunteering or not volunteering will have to cease; all men will have to go. The choice will no longer be between volunteering and not volunteering, but between CONSCRIPTION and REBELLION.[213]

As men traveled to Des Moines to participate in the effort, the fanfare of victory was overshadowed by the need to train officers for the war. The rigorous daily program began with reveille and flag-raising at 5:30 a.m. and ended with taps at 9:45 p.m. From its May start to the October commissioning, 700 of the 1200 men who entered the training in Des Moines completed it.

The weight of race pride rested on these men who embodied the promises inked during the Civil War. The expectation of victory abroad was expected to bring victory at home and nullify white backlash, position black people as de jure American citizens, liberate them from second-class treatment, and be a beacon for all oppressed and marginalized people. As George H. Woodson pleaded:

> God grant that their efforts and sacrifices may open a brighter and better day for all the down trodden people of the earth and especially the oppressed Colored people in these United States, so as to prevent racial discrimination in public places of accommodation; the denial of the ballot, and the suppression of the vote; the limiting of industrial and civil privileges to

---

[213] JSP, 95-13 folder 535, open letter, "Military Training Camp for Colored Officers...," 1. Woodson was an 1895 Howard University graduate,

menial occupation; the segregation in cities, schools and government departments and public places; the elimination of mob violence and things of the dark past, and give to the country and the world the true principles of the Declaration of Independence and the Constitution of the United States as amended.

With the firm belief that all things must come in the granting of equal rights for every race and people beneath the sun, in a spirit of justice and fair play for all, we sacredly and confidently place the glory of the country and the honor of the flag in the keeping of the first Colored men trained at Fort Des Moines and commissioned to fight in the Black Phalanx with the armies of America for the glory of our God, the honor of our country and the liberty and peace of the world.[214]

On paper, the war ended in November 1918 with the signing of the armistice between the Allied Forces and Germany. However, several faulty stops meant that the actual end came with the signing of the Versailles Peace Treaty on June 28, 1919. While the German government accepted over 440 sections of the treaty without revision, American politicians thought that it deviated from Woodrow Wilson's Fourteen

---

[214] John L. Thompson, *History and Views of the Colored Officers Training Camp of Colored Officers Training Camp for 1917 at Fort Des Moines*, 9.

Points, which sought to direct the country's international policy, and the British politicians thought the measure was too austere. Still, both victors and vanquished faced an uncertain future fraught with the challenges of monetary loss and economic deprivation.

African Americans believed that Germany's defeat promised the long-awaited end to de jure segregation since their military service and show of valor and loyalty would destroy any lingering residue of plantation imagery that littered the theater, movies, and advertisements of the day. Further, amid simmering racial tensions, continued lynchings, and even violence against men in uniform, black people were dedicated to demonstrating their worthiness of inclusion in the American dream. Miller believed with others that a new era would provide a fresh look at African Americans, for he wrote:

> The Negro's actual part in the War provided the basis for his holding his country to its lofty declarations and implied promises…Fully realizing and insisting that the Negro is a man and an unexcelled American and should enjoy and possess every right and privilege of other American workmen… Asking nothing for ourselves which we are unwilling for others to have in rightful proportion. Determined that by seeking nothing but the right to establish and perpetuate in America the principle of right dealing and sane Americanism.[215]

---

[215] *The Negro's Reaction to the World War I*, 8-9.

A piece by Leslie P. Hill, principal of the Cheyney Training School, in the January 1919 issue of the *Howard University Record* addressed the educated African American's role in the post-war world and urged educators to,

> make headway against our vast national indebtedness... to protect and widen the industrial, the moral and the social welfare of the state, always jeopardized by war, we must have the highest intelligence yoked to the active good-will and service of every citizen — a result that can be assured only by unhesitating education of all the people. The nation cannot pass by the other side and leave twelve million of us prostrate in the highway of its progress... Here, then is the aftermath of the war for us, — a wide, hard, upward road with a shining goal at the far end, but beset with severities which no League of Nations, no treaty of Paris, can remove.
>
> These must be removed from within, and by our own hands. The education of our millions for every kind of work, the training of head and heart to understand and feel the duties and responsibilities of democracy, the building of a strong foundation in health and character and competency, the finding of justice and protection by the arm of the law... The school that develops men and women of

this stature must not be permitted to wage a losing battle against. It is our only safe bulwark against the reactionary forces now at work among men. Give us this new world teacher and this new world school and the nation under God shall have her new birth of real freedom.[216]

Miller echoed his contemporaries' hope that their education and patriotism would allow African Americans to enjoy full citizenship. Like them, he felt that the sacrifice and service of black men should mute questions about their "fitness" and asked:

What American will dare stand before any Negro trooper returned from France and thus mock and deride him? Military agency has destroyed the physical concept which the white world had of the Negro in 1914... The Negro has proven his power of moral restraint while guided by leadership of his own color. As a social being he has sacrificed his life for the highest form of social existence, democracy. Who then, is there to call him alien? Today he is no longer Negro, nor Afro-American, nor colored American, nor American of African descent, but he is American - simply this and nothing more.[217]

---

[216] "The Negro Teachers in the Aftermath of the War," *Howard University Record*, 13:3 March 1919 114-117.

[217] *Kelly Miller's History of the World War for Human Rights*, 478.

However, the summer of 1919 snuffed out these hopes when black-and-white tensions flared, and a floundering economy led to the rapid rise of unemployment and inflation. Moreover, the new sense of African American esteem antagonized whites who were not prepared to elevate their fellow citizens socially, culturally, or intellectually. Many whites feared black radicalism and reacted to rumors of subversion and threats of violence.

In six weeks, seventy-six lynchings, including a dozen among still uniformed veterans, were reported. African Americans reacted to such aggression with deliberateness—young black leaders like historian Rayford Logan and labor leader A. Philip Randolph, sociologist E. Franklin Frazier, professor Charles Houston, and diplomat Ralph Bunche used this moment to gauge the level of depravity whites would employ when threatened by real or imagined change. These men reasoned that an accommodationist stance that advocated "being good" would not placate white American society. An article entitled "Riots and Rights," in the October 1919 issue of *The People's Pilot*, articulated the sentiment of young black men who had either served in the war or observed the post-war hostilities.

> If the white man has been thoroughly schooled in the lesson that he must now treat the Negro as a man and fellow citizen, in every way on equal grounds with himself or the white man and the Negro both must die, it is well that the

lesson has been learned in time. There need be no further rioting, unless white people want it. We call tell whether they want to plunge their country into destruction they decide to treat the Negro. Liberty or death is what the white man has taught us.[218]

In March 1919, the *Howard University Record* marked the era with prophetic cynicism, comparing the condition of post-World War I African Americans to the myth about Tantalus, King of Phrygia. In the story, he was tormented by being surrounded by water up to his chin that he could not drink and by trees laden with fruit that the wind continually moved out of his reach. The article remarked on the "striking resemblance between the plight of the American Negro and that of the mythological prototype," asserting that,

> [t]oday the Negro stands chin deep in American freedom and democracy, which recede from him whenever he aspires to taste them. He witnesses just above him the luscious fruits of liberty, but they too prove elusive to his grasp. Nevertheless, history goes on recounting the valor of the black solider, his patriotism, loyalty, and devotion to his country, in every crisis; but when the crisis is passed, and the rewards are measured out, by

---

[218] The Negro's Reaction to World War I, Riots and Rights," *The People's Pilot*. October 1919, p.

some peculiar lapse of logic, the American Negro is not included, though his only demand is that he be permitted to enjoy the rights of a true democracy... The tree of American democracy was bent closer than ever before to the Negro...He was assured that he would necessarily have a share in the world democracy... The modern Tantalus is still chin-deep in freedom. He still reaches for the alluring branches of the tree of liberty, but they continue to mock him. Are there no longer true philanthropists who will essay to stem the receding waters and bend the deceptive branches so low that the American Negro may have taste of real democracy?[219]

Miller and J. Stanley Durkee: 1918-1925

The 1918 arrival of president J. Stanley Durkee promised a new era of student involvement and participation that was quickly dashed on the jagged rock of reality. Durkee's impressive credentials included being educated in New England schools and colleges by liberal-minded men of letters. Yet his relationship with black people was more theoretical than practical, and this lack contributed to his downfall."[220] Earlier presidents had been more directly familiar with the African American community and black culture. As with Andrew Rankin, for example,

---

[219] *Howard University Record,* 13:3 March 1919, 105-106.
[220] Rayford Logan, *Howard University: The First Hundred Years, 1867-1967.* 187.

who had pastored a church with several African American communicants, they appeared to be missionary-minded and respectful.

Nevertheless, in his first year, Durkee made strides comparable to other presidents, and several of his proposals were adopted. For instance, faculty sabbatical leaves were formally approved for the first time, practical graduate work leading to the A.M. degree was established, and a summer school was established.[221]

Durkee assumed the helm of Howard against the background of the prolonged "Red Scare" with its hysteria over the perceived threat posed by Communists and the "Red Summer," when Washington experienced one of its worst race riots up to that time. The early years of his administration coincided with the administration of Warren G. Harding, who some historians consider one of the country's weakest presidents.

To Logan, Durkee's words sometimes directly opposed his actions. Further, he saw him as a compromiser who often yielded to the expediency that made it difficult to attain his goals and who lacked the facility to secure the necessary funding for the institution. Moreover, changing student attitudes would not abide pandering from a paternalistic white president.

The threat of communistic leanings in various sectors of society bristled throughout the federal government, and in January 1920, Senator Reed Smoot

---

[221] Logan, *First Hundred Year*, 192-193.

of Utah threatened that if Howard's library continued to hold Albert Williams' book, *Seventy-Six Questions on Bolsheviks and Soviets,* he would vote against all appropriations for the institution. For him, the volume did not align with American patriotism, so Durkee swiftly removed it and sent a letter that Smoot requested be read into the Senate record. In it, Durkee assured him that,

> I agree with you that such false statements ought not to be circulated and, in my judgment the government should suppress the printing of such pamphlets. I only regret that my attention was not called to the matter before it was necessary to give it to the public.

Durkee's removal of the pamphlet fueled complaints of compromising and muting academic freedom since members of the community felt Howard University was being censured for its political and social ideas. Yet, Logan indicated that Durkee's attempts to engage congressional officials on the issue of academic freedom did not adversely impact the Congressional appropriation.

In attempting to streamline the University administration, Durkee altered the junior college and senior school structures. The junior college enrolled new students and prepared them to enter and graduate from the senior college, which offered professional programs in liberal arts, education, commerce and finance, music, and journalism.

At the time of Durkee's arrival, Miller, who had been at Howard for nearly 15 years, enjoyed the broad alumni and student support. Still, Durkee's creation of a junior college was designed to curb Miller's influence. Prior to the division, Miller had been the sole dean of the College of Arts and Sciences, whose position on the faculty and within the fledgling alum association held great sway. Though Durkee's move was a public offense to Miller and a declaration of war between the two men, Miller remained a popular fixture on the campus.

In Durkee's mind, this move consolidated the faculty. It standardized their curriculums as once sovereign schools and colleges were integrated within a larger structure under his centralized authority, which muted Miller's voice and power. Despite facing hostility from some instructors who had entrenched their positions in various departments, as well as outcries from students, alumni, and faculty, he did not reverse his decision to implement the seemingly progressive idea.

Throughout his administration, Durkee fought with faculty and students over ostensibly progressive moves to secure Howard's place as a Class A university for "colored students." From 1919 to 1925, his report to the Secretary of the Interior remarked that Howard's motive was to "meet a very present and pressing demand for young colored people to gain expert knowledge and practice in commercial and mercantile life…" since "the new curriculum was based on the idea of specialization along business lines... and Howard ha[d] acted wisely in attempting to give opportunity for the colored youth to gain theory and practice along these lines."[222] After incurring heated displeasure from Miller, other faculty, and students, his 1926 report avoided using racial terms to describe Howard's progress

The Howard community was particularly displeased at being dubbed a "class A colored school." It was not created to be a "colored" university, and its first graduating class was made up of four white daughters of faculty members. Its graduation records claim a few domestic and foreign-born white women whose opportunities were limited because of gender. But its patina became increasingly black when Jim Crow laws locked talented students and instructors of color out of other white universities.

Until 1925, the rising displeasure with white administrators simmered in the minds of Howard students. In that year, however, the student strike ignited by a furor over a mandate that they sing Negro spirituals in plantation dialect to entertain white visitors to Chapel services became another issue between the two. Miller defended the students, indicating that Howard had no link to the Deep South or the plantation experience. With his encouragement, students remained stalwart, and these medleys were never included in the repertoire.

Miller's harmonious work with earlier presidents garnered him influence throughout the alumni association and within the African American

---

[222] Logan, *First Hundred Year*. 205.

community. Nevertheless, on June 8, 1925, Miller wrote Emmet Scott,

> [T]he trustees have abolished the junior college I take it for granted that you will be wanting the use of the office. Kindly advise me as to when I must be vacated. I should thank you for as much time as you can conveniently grant, as I must make readjustment for my library and office arrangements.[223]

Still, Miller's displeasure with Durkee resounded throughout the university community. It made its way into a series of articles in Washington's *Afro-American* newspaper co-authored by him and an anonymous colleague whose byline simply read "Alumnus." In these blistering pieces, they turned to their most loyal allies— the African American readership—to paint images of the symbolic struggle between black manhood and emasculation by white power structures.

Alumnus was most probably Neval Hollen Thomas, an outspoken agitator for global civil and economic rights for African people.[224] He held the white autocracy in vitriolic contempt, saw them as agents of exploitation of weaker peoples, and

---

[223] BTWP, Letter to Emmet Scott, June 8, 1925.
[224] Neval Thomas was born in 1874 in Springfield, Ohio. He graduated from Howard University with a Bachelor of Arts degree in 1901 and completed the law degree in 1904; but he never practiced. He began teaching in the M Street High School in 1902 and served in the secondary education until his death in 1930.

denounced "genuflecting Negroes who yielded to race distinctions to enjoy the 'profits of segregation.'" The power of conviction and persuasion of the eloquent, self-confident orator had few equals. He consistently spoke with the superior power of thought, logical consistency, brilliancy of conception, and abundant knowledge.

The president of the Washington branch of the NAACP admired his former instructor and often sought his counsel. His scrapbook at the Moorland-Spingarn Center indicates that he had the making of being an "Alumnus." A small cache of letters between the two shows Thomas' passion for racial justice and determination to right wrongs.

An excerpt from one of their articles provided intricate details:

> One reason for bisecting the college was to eliminate Dean Miller. This did not work. The pension age was a bit too high to catch DM so the thought of making him the publicity agent had some attraction. It looked as though Dean Miller would go on the road, thus ridding the troubled president of his presence. This plan was smashed, so DM has been retained as a dean-professor with the rank of dean. Fraternity Talk: Earlier in Dr. Durkee's career at Howard, he told the combined fraternities that if he were fool enough to try to get rid of Dean Kelly Miller, he would be too big a fool to be president of HU. Well, he has tried to get

> rid of Dean KM, so the reader may expect the rest of the prophecy to be verified. Out of His Class: The point is, that Dr. Durkee was unacquainted with pedagogy and with colored people but accepted a position which required knowledge of both. He was called to Washington to head a colored university... By the assistance of his subordinates, he might learn his job, but his chances of success would be slim; for he would be in an entirely new field, working with a race of people with whom he had not been closely associated.[225]

Another article delved into the little-known details about meetings between Durkee, Miller, and nine other faculty members.

> Miller protested: When the college course was threatened DM was naturally among the ten colored professors who protested. Surely his race would have condemned him bitterly and justly had he sat still when Dr. Durkee was blowing the bubble that just burst. In fact, no colored professor true to his aspirations of the race could have sat silent in those trying days...

---

[225] Kelly Miller, "Alumni Plan to Picket HU unless President Durkee Resigns," *Afro-American* July 18, 1925. KMP, Box 71-3 folder 74 news clippings.

In that memorable meeting between Dr. Durkee and those immortal ten, Dean Miller was made the spokesman. The meeting degenerated into a veritable fuss between the president and the dean with the advantage decidedly the deans. A comparison: If the meeting had no productive value, it at least gave the audience an opportunity to make a comparison between the nimble-witted, resourceful, and erudite colored dean on a salary then of about $2,200 and the narrow-minded hopelessly deficient, and tenaciously obstinate white president, on a salary of about $10,000. It was prophesied that President Durkee could never feel comfortable again in Dean Miller's presence. Machinations: From that day to the present Dr. Durkee has contrived, in every possible way to embarrass Dean Miller. Dr. Durkee's studied means of sidetracking Dean Miller without drawing popular resentment. Step by step, he has been accomplishing his purpose without attracting attention. One reason for bisecting the college was to remove Dean Miller from his position of influence. The removal of Professor Miller from the deanship left him without an office, for the headship of the department of sociology had been filled in time to exclude him from that. There really is not enough work in sociology at Howard for two full-time professors, so the reader may draw his own conclusion as to whether Dr. Durkee had originally intended for Professor Miller work in the college.[226]

The article noted Miller's popularity throughout the university community and suggested that the preaching of his unique gospel of higher education and morality benefitted Howard more than Durkee's token gestures. Alumnus purported that Miller's dismissal from the junior college would adversely affect the students, alumni, and mood of the campus.

> Dean Miller's former students, especially all his graduates, should write Dr. Durkee protesting this treatment given their beloved dean. Letters of sympathy should also be written to DM. Since President D has made him a martyr, he should be treated as one.[227]

The end of the academic year did not impede Alumnus from following the tensions on Howard's campus. On August 29, 1925, he wrote.

> Already Durkee has denied that he ever called Miller any unbecoming name; and now the administration has released the honey-covered statement that "Kelly Miller, for many years, dean of the junior college, will be

---

[226] "HU Alumni Fight on Durkee Makes Necessary Extra Appropriation On" August 1, 1925.

[227] KMP, Box 71-3 folder 74 news clippings, August 1, 1925.

associated with Durkee in this movement." Strange bedfellows have always resulted from politics... After striving industriously to put Miller out of commission, and thus far succeeding in removing him from the post which he has filled with full satisfaction and corresponding distinction... Meanwhile, ALUMNUS will plod on, telling the tragic story of the same institution, real catastrophe of which will not be reached until Durkee is relieved of all the details of internal administration.[228]

By this time, Durkee's popularity was waning, as disappointed students, discouraged alumni, and demoralized faculty saw the "New Negro" rising in art, literature, and public consciousness. Alain Locke, the architect of the movement, asserted that the Negro needed to express himself from a place of cultural familiarity that combined his African past and current life. For him, the myth and folklore had to come from black people and not simply be a colored Eurocentric caricature. This idea bloomed in black communities around the county, including urban centers such as Washington, Chicago, Boston, and most notably, Harlem, where young artists were creating literature, dance, theater, music, and journals that reflected the African Diaspora.

At the same time, black college students and faculty were beginning to see themselves reflected in

---

[228] Ibid., August 29, 1925.

all aspects of their administrations and openly challenging the white power structures of their institutions. In December 1925, Alumnus authored an article detailing the Howard faculty's defense of Miller against Durkee before its Board,"

> The real hero of the meeting was Miller though it is going to be difficult to persuade our readers. Accused of straddling on all former issues and even coaxed into making an alliance last summer with Durkee, Miller laid aside his usual role and hit Durkee such body blows that most referees would have called the bout a knockout. He spared neither president nor trustees. Miller placed a mirror before the eyes of the colored trustees and flayed them unmercifully. He emphasized the gross insult that Durkee hurled at the colored people when he was given permission to run the Curry School which does not admit colored students. He held the colored trustees culpable...These colored trustees, except for Mr. Hawkins and Dr. Wormley, who were not on the board at the time, voted for Durkee [giving him] permission to run a school that insulted their own people... [Durkee publicly] called Miller "pup." In the investigation, Durkee admitted

that he called Miller a "pup" but not a "puppy."[229]

This admission to what he considered a lesser offense meant nothing to alumni and left them, faculty, and students dissatisfied. They felt that any self-respecting black person should feel insulted and concluded that "[a]pparently, the Howard trustees have as much respect for the colored people as they have for dumb animals, and if the colored people stand for this gross insult, may they be showered with more."[230]

In a Trustee Board hearing about the heated argument, Durkee recalled that he defended himself against Miller with hostile actions and foul words, and he had said to him; there is the door, you go. Miller, on the other hand, recalled that Durkee "severely denounced him as being unworthy" And that he felt his manhood had been assaulted."[231]

The Trustees resolved to let the two men agree to disagree, and Miller was granted sabbatical leave from the campus to lecture for Howard and higher education on a cross-country tour. So, while Durkee was rid of Miller's troublesome presence, Alumnus concluded:

---

[229]. Alumnus, "KM Hero as Howard Faculty Testifies Against Durkee Before Board," December 19, 1925. KMP, Box 71-3 folder 75 news clippings, December 19, 1925.
[230] KMP. Box 71-3 folder 74 news clippings, December 19, 1925.
[231] Ibid.

Howard ensnared cheap politics brought to the presidency of Howard University a glaring misfit who has not one qualification for his position that any trustee of Howard University can defend. Cheap political maneuvers have kept this misfit at the head of this institution which he has served by giving his time to the Curry School and by the editing of an encyclopedia of Negro greatness. Cheap political practices have manipulated the appointment of teachers and the dislodgement of teachers... Even when Dr. Durkee resigns, the condition cannot be improved materially, if the same trustees are to elect his successor. They have already demonstrated that they know absolutely nothing about educational matters.[232]

Students subsequently rallied for Durkee's ouster, protesting what they saw as open disrespect of faculty such as Miller by white administrative leadership. Further to them, unlike earlier white educators whose altruism showed a Christian missionary zeal toward formerly enslaved black persons, people like Durkee had paternalistic intentions and were not concerned with providential reconstruction.

After the Miller debacle and severe community disfavor, Durkee returned to his former vocation and sought a position at a Brooklyn, New York church. Howard's alumni dismissed him as "an insignificant

---

[232] KMP. Box 71-3 folder 76 news clippings.

village preacher," but his position as president had elevated him from obscurity.

> The omens are propitious. Dr. Durkee aided and abetted by Dean Brown, President of HU Board of Trustees is not after a job. He is camping at the gate of the fashionable Beecher Church of Brooklyn, N.Y. awaiting a call. This explains his absence from Howard Chapel at the Christmas services... Ordinarily we would complain of such treatment, but no lover of Howard University will begrudge Dr. Durkee any absence which may spell his ultimate removal from Howard University. His catastrophe will not influence them in any way; for, the calling of an outstanding Negro scholar a "pup" and the barring of Negro aspirants from the benefits of an elocutionary training are likely to pass unnoticed in the Christian church of the twentieth century.[233]

At the close of the Durkee era, Miller's loyalty remained to Howard as he described:

> On one occasion an overbearing President summoned me to his office and demanded to know point blank whether I was loyal to him or not. I responded that my loyalty was to the university and not to any individual – which I was loyal to Howard University before he

---
[233] Ibid.

entered the equation and would continue to be after he had left it. This prophecy has been fulfilled.[234]

Negro Sanhedrin All Race Conference

By the 1920s, the pervasive nature of oppression had fostered an intense sense of community among Black Americans. Educated and talented Black people unquestioningly accepted a responsibility to speak on behalf of the masses. In 1923, the 60-year-old educator again turned his attention to the needs of the race. Never one for longstanding conflict and inaction, he believed that the resolute model of leadership was to overcome evil with good. He subscribed to the idea that being a morally upright and informed "social guide" would win over doubters.

This period was dubbed the New Negro era, and black thinkers realized that fighting racial prejudice on a case-by-case basis did not empower the masses to work toward self-sufficiency and self-definition for the entire community. Several events, including the death of Washington, the Red Summer of 1919, the arrival of Marcus Garvey and his Universal Negro Improvement Association (UNIA), and the Great Migration, caused their focus to shift.

Washington's death muted accommodationist thinking. Yet, his Tuskegee Institute laboratory, thrust into public view by the inventions of Dr. George Washington Carver, continued to flourish as the

---

[234] KMP Box 71-3 folder "Full Text Speech"

vanguard of industrial education. The violence of the Red Summer of 1919 enticed tens of thousands of rural black men and women to join in the Great Migration and leave sharecropping, debt peonage, and blatant racism behind as they moved from the deep South to urban centers in the industrialized North for factory, domestic, and railroad work. The composite New Negro who populated these cities included African Americans, West Indians, Afro-Latinos, Afro-Canadians, and indigenous groups who spoke not only English, but French, Spanish, Creole, or Patois.

Marcus Garvey's Universal Negro Improvement Association attracted Caribbean immigrants who encountered not only white supremacy but indifference from American black people. Miller wrote about Garvey on several occasions, including a memorable article on Religion and race published in 1926 in which he presented Garvey as an ardent Black nationalist who desired to paint Christ black, removed the sacredness of divinity, and reduced faith to a tussle between blacks and whites. He was equally bothered by Garvey's use of the color black to identify the Devil. Miller wrote:

> ... some little while ago, [Marcus Garvey] shocked the spiritual sensibilities of the religious world by suggesting that the Negro should paint his God black. The idea was revolting even to the Negro, accustomed as he is to the colour bias of the white race, from

which he has borrowed his ideal conception of all things in heaven and on earth... If Mr. Garvey's ideal should prevail, and celestial beings should be painted black, the change in the colour scheme would be a fatal stumbling block to the white Christian world. Whenever I see Christ and the Angels painted black on the walls of unsophisticated Negro churches, I am reminded of the never-failing tendency of human nature to ennoble and glorify its own type of flesh and blood... The white man always paints the Devil black, although the best examples of the qualities and essence of his Satanic majesty have been clothed in a white skin. Milton's Satan is not satanic at all. Our deities must have our own colour and facial features and must speak our own languages and favour our moral ideals and social aims... [Religion's] double function [is] the salvation of the soul and social salvation.[235]

Miller realized that since black people were not going back to Africa and whites were not returning to Europe, the race problem was an American problem. So he outlined the problem and delineated a solution in a 1923 pamphlet entitled *The Negro Sanhedrin: Call to Conference*. The fifteen subsections explained the history and current condition of African American people:

---

[235] KMP, Box 71-6 folder 160 article "Religion and Race," 3-8.

1. Sanhedrin, the Negro Sanhedrin.
2. The Object of the Conference.
3. The Psychology of the Problem.
4. The Temper of the Conference.
5. A Motto: Is an All-Negro Conference Possible?
6. The Necessity for the Negro Sanhedrin.
7. Why a Negro Conference?
8. The Origins of Race Churches.
9. Early Negro Conventions.
10. Reconstruction Hopes.
11. Recent Organizations.
12. African Movements.
13. Lack of Leadership.
14. Race Aim and Ideal,
15. Inter- and Intra-Race Conference and Politics.

A Big Job for Anybody's Mule

Miller acknowledged the efforts of other organizations that sought to address the race problem and insisted that he was not attempting to create another organization. Rather, he insisted that what he was attempting to do was create a clearinghouse for existing groups not to have to duplicate efforts:

> [There are] innumerable organizations in the racial field operating separately... Each is efficient in its sphere, but no one of them, nor yet all of them combined, can claim to be sufficient as concerns the general welfare of the race... In a nutshell, its object is to make for understanding and unity. It hopes to reach an understanding of the problem as a whole and to promote harmonization of effort of existing agencies to secure the desired end.[236]

The organizations Miller was involved in often floundered under the burden of bureaucracy, internal conflicts, and disagreements over ideology or finances. In searching historical sources about how minority groups overcame injustice, he found that those groups that closed ranks and moved both the conservative and radical forward were the most successful. So Miller sought to unify disparate groups into a coalition that would allow each of them independent sovereignty in their sphere while strengthening their ability to

---

[236] Kelly Miller, *The Negro Sanhedrin: A Call to Conference*, 1923, 1-2.

address the issues confronting African American people.

Miller found his solution in the cultural heritage of Jewish people. Under the direction of Napoleon Bonaparte, Jews, and Gentiles convened a council to voice their concerns to both parties. This was based on the Judaic history of the Sanhedrin, which was an assembly composed of seventy-one members with supreme authority who sat in Jerusalem. These Sanhedrin councils were composed of two parts: The lesser, regional assembly in each province country was composed of twenty-three equal members with limited to local authority. The greater national assembly of seventy-one persons had supreme jurisdiction. Miller envisioned a similar structure for his organization in which the Lesser Sanhedrin, with limited local authority, would address regional concerns and the Greater Sanhedrin functioning at the national level.[237]

The organization, also called the All-Race Council, was to be composed of representatives at large from each national or state organization, with one additional representative for every 50,000 members, and was to be financed by its constituent organizations. A central committee was to be established as a clearinghouse for race-wide interests.

Approximately 300 delegates gathered in Chicago for the first meeting.[238] Mayor William E. Denver

---

[237] Kelly Miller, *The Negro Sanhedrin*, 1.

[238] Some organizations in attendance were delegates from the National Association for the Advancement of Colored People (NAACP), the Equal Rights League, the Race Congress, the Blood Brotherhood, the International Uplift League, and the Friends of the Negro Freedom.

delivered the keynote address. His words and the resolutions adopted during the week-long meeting pleased Miller, who saw it as the beginning of the unification of major civil rights organizations as an essential step in opposing the forces that marginalized black people. During the session, delegates identified seven areas that required intra-racial cooperation:

1. Improvement of public health among Black people.
2. Equal schools.
3. Exploitation of Black labor.
4. Protection of Black franchises.
5. Equal rights for women.
6. The right of protest and public utterance.
7. Interracial relations.

The delegates also recommended seven policies aimed at the internal improvement of the Black community.

1. Building a strong, independent business community.
2. Creation of Black fraternal and charitable organizations.
3. Maintenance of a less partisan and more dignified Black press.

Miller also invited several leading citizens unaffiliated with Black organizations to the initial meeting.

4. The establishment of relationships with black people around the world.
5. The encouragement and support of black youth.
6. Study and promotion of African and African American culture.

According to Miller,

> What was accomplished at the Greater Sanhedrin is a matter of history. The words spoken and the resolutions adopted were such as to give me great pleasure as chairman of the gathering, I appointed an executive committee, officers were elected, and the enterprise appeared to have been successfully launched. Then happened what might have been expected and what had been my one fear while advocating the project. Funds were lacking. We did not have the money with which to pay a competent executive secretary; no money with which to carry forward any of the projects which had been advanced. The good work which we hoped might be done could not be undertaken. That marks the difference between the Jewish and the Negro Sanhedrin's. The Jews had the money with which to push forward, the Negroes had not. The condition emphasized the fact that in other civil rights bodies, such, for instance, the NAACP, the whites who are members furnish

the necessary funds for carrying on. Left to themselves, the Negroes seem powerless.[239]

The delegation approved the initial proposition on February 11, 1924, and issued a press release that touted a new movement aimed at unifying various black organizations. According to the release, the Sanhedrin would focus its attention on the betterment of the whole race. Accordingly, this national clearinghouse would have a significant impact on individual efforts of organizations working for racial betterment, but whose efforts often duplicated and nullified each other.

A meeting was to take place later in the current year to perfect the organization and put the machinery in operation. After that, the sessions were to be held twice a year.

A persistent harmonizer, Miller wanted The Sanhedrin to be a common denominator that did not compete with any existing organization. But he knew that achieving an acceptable scheme amongst the over 100 African American organizations would be hard. These organizations spanned the range of political, religious, educational, economic, benevolent, social, and cultural interest and their only uniting theme was the betterment of the race. In his mind, the Sanhedrin's attempt to integrate these organizations into a social force outweighed individual methods and enriched each.

---

[239] KMP chapter 43 "The Negro Sanhedrin," 2-3.

At the outset, some believed that another group would be needless duplication. However, Miller believed that though they were all aiming at the same objective, without correlation, unity of plan, and harmony of procedure, no existing civic, fraternal, social, and political organization could adequately address the problem of racial inequality. Most of these groups were concerned with a singular aspect, such as education, business, law, or politics, and were devoted to a particular objective exclusive of whole-scale civil rights. In his estimation, the proposed Sanhedrin would unify them without diminishing these individual efforts to bring about racial equality and full citizenship.

For Miller, the American race question was a question of social psychology in that the white race had a fixed attitude towards the Negro in their social scheme. Even after the valiant efforts of World War I and the slaughter of Red Summer, he saw no whole-scale compassion for African Americans. The American president was silent on the issue, while other government officials were indifferent.

Still, many young blacks had developed a new race consciousness that grew in stubbornness and strength. Their fury did not deter Miller, who remained dedicated to his daysman strategy path of education and building morality and considered this higher ground position as the best way to engage injustice. Since he saw speaking truth to power as working in earlier years, he would not abandon what he saw as a proven method, insisting rather that:

Race statesmanship requires that the Negro should study to understand the operation of this outside controlling influence, to withstand it, in so far as it may be hurtful, and with unyielding fortitude, to stand the residue that may not be withstood. The orderly formation or formulated statement of a race consciousness is frustrated by the diversity of blood streams that flow in Negro veins as well as by the many-sided relationship which he sustains to a cultural environment which persists in regarding him as alien to its aims and ideals. Our task is intensified, and our difficulties doubled in that we must wield a multi-blooded race into a one-minded group. For all practical purposes of race statesmanship, we may define a Negro as anyone who would be Jim-crowed in the state of Virginia.[240]

Though Miller maintained that African Americans should be concerned about all black people, he felt that they needed to achieve success at home before attempting to address the global situation. To this end, though Garvey's UNIA and Dubois' Pan-African Congress focused and functioned outside of America, The Sanhedrin's efforts would be limited to this country. Alain Locke concurred that the opportunity for black leadership would lend itself to positive cross-

---

[240] KMP, Box 71-6 folder 155 writing Negro Sanhedrin. Some folders have names and I would include it to remain consistent.

fertilization and viewed the international inroads made by Garvey and Dubois as strident beginnings for African Americans.

Alain Locke

In a 1924 article in the *Christian Science Monitor*, he asserted that:

> Our participation in [global affairs on behalf of other black people] would bring two benefits; for while we American Negroes can bring to the Africans education and the democratic inspiration which we take from our country's institutions, we can at the same time gain a wealth of experience and an outlet for expression from activity in this field, which would be a potent factor in our development here in America. If we do not respond we are

lacking in a sense of opportunity as well as of responsibility.[241]

Though Miller did not travel outside of the country, he corresponded internationally, and his work was read in Brazil and throughout the Caribbean. He was not lost on the concept of the African Diaspora, but his major concern was the possibilities for African Americans. He concluded that,

> internal dissension is [the Negroes] besetting sin. His chief dynamic is derived from dissent. He would a hundred times rather fight his fellow Negro, than an enemy of the white race. Animosity is always intensified by nearness of relationship. Would to the Negro might spend half the energy in combating the common enemy that he wastes in bootless internal strife. How long, O Lord, how long, must these things be? But we must throw off this infirmity, if need be, by sheer calculation and prudence. The Negro leaders must assume the semblance of unity of aim and effort, even though they have it not.[242]

The Negro Sanhedrin incapsulated Miller's hope that black leaders would consolidate forces to echo the concerns and interests of the larger African American

---

[241] KMP Box 71-3 folder 76 "Leaders Say Negro Must Aid Himself," clipping *Christian Science Monitor*, February 14, 1924.
[242] KMP, Box 71-6 folder 155, Writing Negro Sanhedrin.

community. He asserted that they needed to plan an agenda that advanced the whole race, not simply their organization, for he saw the division within the race as allowing subversion of black interest and bankrupting the exiting race as well as unborn generations.

The idea of the Negro Sanhedrin that epitomized Miller's wish to create a movement to implement the platform for progress and monitor its progress was short-lived. External pressure, a lack of executives, and a paid staff also contributed to the ineffectiveness of the organization's demise. [243] Moreover, a rising generation of radicals did not subscribe to the conservative model of intellectually paced dialogue and planning but opted for aggressive confrontation of reality with scientific facts that could be argued in courtrooms and through published media.

Many, including Locke, thought the Sanhedrin failed because it could not incorporate a sense of meaning for black youth whose energy and passion could have sustained it. Ultimately, the Negro Sanhedrin was an influence, not an organization, and its failure marked the end of the popularity of Miller's brand of conservatism. His initial vision of an assembly of wise, intellectually elite, socially positioned counselors ran afoul of the egalitarianism espoused by younger activists. Miller sought to create a world that sought common ground while the Negro

---

[243] C. Alvin Hughes, "The Negro Sanhedrin Movement," *Journal of Negro History*, 69:1 Winter 1984, 11

problem was becoming increasingly more complex, and the landscape was being populated by ideologues who sought solutions with or without coalition building. Born out of a sincere heart but generational inflexibility, the Sanhedrin's desire to strike a unified blow against racial injustice floundered and left Miller lamenting that his seemingly well-planned effort to establish a unified blow at discrimination did not work out.

Stumping for Higher Education at the Capstone

Miller's position at Howard led him to interact with over three generations of students, and his work with The American Negro Academy, The Committee of Twelve, The Bethel Literary Society, The Negro Officers Training Program, and The Negro Sanhedrin jettisoned his influence in importance arenas. Howard Professor George M. Lightfoot saw Miller as,

> [o]ne who won wide acceptance and genuine popularity as a lecturer and speaker throughout the United States. He is known and admired from Canada to Mexico and from coast to coast. His services as a lecturer and speaker have been eagerly sought everywhere by clubs and organizations of both races. As a writer, his style is pleasing, pointed and pithy, carrying with it a logical conviction that is well-nigh irresistible. His views on matters

affecting the race question have been sought by periodicals and newspapers of the highest standards.[244]

The *Afro-Americans* ran a series of articles Miller submitted documenting his travels to the West Coast to promote education. In an article titled "Kelly Miller Makes 10,000 Mile Trip through the West," he reported:

> I have just completed a ten-thousand-mile lecture tour passing through the Middle West, the Inter-Mountain region, the Pacific Slope, and the Southwest. My engagements covered fifty cities along the line of this itinerary. I want, first, to express my thanks to the people everywhere who received with interest and enthusiasm the message of racial progress and promise. This tour was projected on my personal responsibility without the backing of any financial foundation or endowed propaganda. I had no new nostrum or infallible solution to offer, but simply presented principles of universal value which carry their own temporal reward. The people have been so often misled by infallible remedies that they have become suspicious of dogmatic pronouncements. Politics, a certain type of education, the acquisition of wealth,

---

[244] KMP, Box 71-1 folder 10. George M. Lightfoot, "Biographical Sketch of Professor Kelly Miller."

unlicensed radicalism in religion, government, and industry have all been urged as solvents with dogmatic assurance and intolerant emphasis. After testing all these methods, the race problem will undoubtedly exist in all of its intricate perplexities. There is a positive value in each; superlative virtue in none. All are efficient; nonsufficient. We still await the solution that will be solved. In the meantime, we rely upon positive virtues and values of never-failing advantage while feeling after a right solution if haply we may find it.[245]

In city after city, Miller openly embraced his radical form of independent thinking. Still, the perpetual seeker of harmony hoped his travels would engender reconciliation within the black community and noted that:

> My itinerary gave rise to many interesting observations especially in the Inter-Mountain and Pacific States. The colored people are acquiring homes in unprecedented numbers. In some places I have found that home ownership was the badge of respectability. In such places as Salt Lake City, Boise, Butte, Helena and on the Pacific Slope colored people have acquired more homes during the past

---

[245] Kelly Miller, "Kelly Miller Makes 10,000 Mile Trip through the West." *Afro American*, October 1, 1920.

three years than had been accumulated during the previous times... The great need of the race throughout all of this region is an increased number of right-minded Negroes so as to furnish a sufficient and satisfying social life. Seattle, Washington, Portland, Oregon, and Oakland and Los Angeles, California, are rapidly developing a self-sufficiency.[246]

At the conclusion of his 10,000-mile excursion, he was compelled to write:

I find that the aspiration of the people was true to the best racial aims and ideals however widely they may be severed and scattered abroad. The Negro is undoubtedly destined to become one with the American people, but before that time he will become one with himself.[247]

An article entitled "My Lecture Itinerary," in the *Norfolk Journal and Guide* chronicled his travels throughout the Midwest.

I have just completed a lecture itinerary extending as far as the twin cities at the head of the Mississippi River. When one travels over so much territory and looks in upon the habits of so many people, he is apt to indulge

---

[246] Ibid.
[247] Ibid.

his egotism to the extent of supposing that his observations and reflections might interest others.[248]

In each city, he took note of the public school system. In Wheeling, West Virginia, for example, he noticed a comradeship among mountaineers where the color line did not affect human connections. Although there were separate schools for black and white people, they were administered fairly between the races. He asserted that the African American population in Wheeling, West Virginia, was a "model for other states to copy." This agreeable situation came from African American parents refusing to tolerate crowded conditions in inadequate and unsafe buildings.

He called his next stop, Gary, Indiana, "the miracle city which sprung up, as it were overnight," remarking that its schools were not completely segregated. However, he noted that many African American students were assigned a teacher of their own race. Miller saw this locale as a city in the making and an example of a vibrant black community that could plant schools, churches, and businesses that would inspire achievement for other black people.

On the contrary, in Milwaukee, where the Urban League sponsored his visit, he found that:

> The colored contingent of Milwaukee for all the past years has made perhaps as little or less

---

[248] Kelly Miller, "My Lecture Itinerary," *Norfolk* [Virginia] *Journal and Guide*, September 25, 1926, 12.

impression upon the outside world as any like sized group in any of the Northern or Western cities.[249]

However, he was also glad to be able to report that in that same city:

> A new life is being quickened among the population. Negro lawyers, doctors, ministers, and social workers are putting Milwaukee on the map.[250]

One girl was so impressed with his visit that she sent him a letter that he published in the *Norfolk Journal and Guide*.

Dear friend,

> I heard you lecture several years ago in Seattle. On both occasions you spoke in Washington Hall. I shall never forget the subjects from which you spoke. The first one was "Race Construction During the Anti-Slavery Period." The second one was, of "the Negro Problem." The lecture comes back to my mind now just as clearly as if it were only yesterday, I listened to them. I remember you said among other things that we must have a peaceful people if we would have a peaceful country. And as I think on that phrase, over and over

---

[249] Ibid.
[250] Ibid.

again, I am convinced of the truth of it. I was a small girl when you spoke in Seattle, and I remember that as I passed in the reception line and shook your hand, I told you I wanted to be great someday just as you were. And you laughed and replied that anyone could be great who wanted to be. And I thought what a nice, kindly man you must be. I am nineteen years old now, and since that time I have learned that there is nothing in desiring to be just great, but there is everything in giving service. So, I no longer desire to be great, but I earnestly desire to render service.

I remember you as being a tall, heavy set, massively built man with snow white hair and a high forehead. Your eyes are small and have a kindly look in them. The outstanding feature about your appearance is your sideburns which are also snow white and which give you a most dignified bearing. You have a princely carriage and stand gracefully on the platform. You wore on both occasions a black suit with a long tailcoat. Your collar and cuffs and appearance in general were immaculate. In my idea you are not a handsome man at all, but there is something especially nice about you; just what it is I am not able to tell. You made the people laugh when you talked. How does that description fit you? You see I have really seen you, have I not?

In one of your books, you wrote this: "A man who serves his community is great in the positive degree; the man who serves his race is great in the comparative degree; but only the man who serves all humanity regardless of race, color or creed is great in the superlative degree." Mr. Miller, I truly think you are great in the superlative degree, in that you serve all humanity so faithfully and so well.[251]

---

[251] Kelly Miller, "My Lecture Itinerary," *Norfolk Journal and Guide*, (October 9, 1926), 12

Miller's response to his young observer was published within the same column:

> I beg to acknowledge receipt of your favor and to express my appreciation of your generous treatment of the subject of which you selected. I am especially glad to know that you are imbued with the sense of racial enthusiasm,

and service and are anxious to keep informed on racial history, literature, and general life. I am sending you under separate cover a copy of the Negro Yearbook which I am sure will furnish the information you need. It is needless to say that I feel gratified whenever I learn that the seed of duty and service which I have been scattering abroad has fallen on fertile soil, with best wishes. [Please note] I know that reaching a young person interested in learning about the race and practicing social consciousness and race respectability.[252]

Often invited to speak about education or race by former students, Miller hastened to answer any call. These tours increase his recognition among Howard University alumni and other black people. Moreover, his transition from mathematics to sociology placed him at the forefront of the discipline, where his love for analytical, cogent thinking found a voice with black audiences. His publications and groundbreaking work establishing the Department of Sociology at Howard garnered the attention of fellow educators around the country, and colleagues asked his opinion on instructional methods in this infant discipline. In one such letter, Clarence Chase at the University of Southern California, Department of Sociology wrote to Miller:

---

[252] Ibid.

We are not offering a special course in the negro (sic) problem in this department now, but I am sure all concerned would be very favorable to such a course if it can be satisfactorily organized. A text by one of your ability and authority would be invaluable, and I wish to give you all the encouragement in my power to go ahead with your project of preparing a textbook. If your book could be a combined textbook and book of readings, or if you could write a brief text and accompany it with a book of readings, bringing the two within a reasonable compass with respect to price for the students, I think it would be a very valuable work.[253]

In view of this, Miller continued to hold his unique space as the daysman position of a middleman. In an article published by the *Amsterdam News,* on January 12, 1927, titled "The Second Generation of Color Bred Negroes," he wrote:

The first generation is now passing away, I am the middleman, and overlap both. I can therefore look both forward and back. I can stand as a daysman between the two and lay a propitiating hand upon them both. The call is to the surviving educated men and women of the day, whether of the old or the new

---

[253] Letter from Clarence Chase to KM, August 15, 1924. Kelly Miller Papers Box 7 folder 6, MARBL, Emory University

generation. They are challenged to meet the requirements of leadership and direction of the vast estate involved in the possibilities of twelve million of their own race and kin... This is precisely the lesson that the talented tenth must learn. Overall, the Negro press is the greatest voice for righteousness now crying in the wilderness to the American conscience. It is the voice of the masses of the people... It is true that the educated Negro must serve as a middleman between the races. The educated Negro must first make influence and understanding with own race before he can hope to make much impression on the white mind.[254]

Yet the memory of Miller's loggerheads with Durkee remained fixed among Howard presidents and consumed the thoughts of his successor, Mordecai W. Johnson, a Baptist minister who became its first African American president. By the time Johnson arrived on campus in 1926, Miller was no longer a young man. His voice was waning within the Africa American intellectual community, and the graying giant's method for seeking racial reconciliation

---

[254] KMP Box 71-3 folder 78 news articles.

through patient plodding was lost to the rising generation of younger leaders.

Alumni Association of Los Angeles

With Johnson's being selected, Miller's assertion about the ministry as a good beginning point for those who wished to become race leaders seemed ironic. Miller would write that Johnson's religious training appeared to fly in the face of the progress of this academic Eden:

> The Negro preacher will be the spokesman of the people because his support comes directly from them... If the honest, untrammeled voice

of the race, stating its own case and pleading its own cause, is ever to be heard and heeded, it will come from, or be supported by the Negro pulpit. He will be the daysman and peacemaker between the races. The uplift of the race is largely in the hands of the clergy, who will be peacemakers between the races. If the pulpits and bishoprics and other high ecclesiastical stations could be filled by men of the best intelligence, character, and consecration within the race, all its complex problems would be in a fair way toward solution.[255]

Miller retired from Howard in 1934. And though the aging philosopher's influence was shrinking on the national scene, he continued to engage and command the respect of Howard students and alumni. He lived the remainder of his years as an unrepentant daysman, mediator, and harmonizer.

---

[255] Kelly Miller "Ministry: The Field for the Talented Tenth," *Out of the House of Bondage*, 213-214.

Five
My Life: A Yardstick of Progress: 1926-1939

A noble nature strives to become its best self and to contribute to the sum total of human good whatever of worth with which it may be endowed.
"Word to the Twentieth Century Negro,"
Voice of the Negro 1905.

President Durkee's departure left Miller war-weary and demoted from the position of dean to chairman of the Department of Sociology. Initially, he was enthusiastic about the prospect of another Howard University president and potentially the first African American administrator. The Board of Trustees' short list of candidates included Bishop John A. Gregg of the AME church and Baptist minister Mordecai W. Johnson. However, campus speculation also saw George Cook or Miller as possible candidates. Ultimately, Bishop Gregg declined the position, and Booker T. Washington had seemingly endorsed Miller. However, university policy prohibited promoting a faculty person to the presidency because many believed an outsider would garner respect and minimize criticism.

In 1926, Mordecai Johnson was installed as Howard University's eleventh president and the first African American to hold that position. His tenure ran concurrently with international and national events that would mark the period. The rise of Benito

Mussolini and Adolph Hitler captured the minds of people who sensed another world war looming. And America entered the throes of a financial collapse that culminated in its greatest economic fiasco. All sections of society—rich and poor, black and white, Southerner and Northerner—felt the sting of the Great Depression. African Americans employed in the service, domestic, and agricultural sectors suffered its harshest consequences. As unemployment skyrocketed, even their menial jobs were given to white people, and the discriminatory practices used by social relief agencies meant that the needs of the black community were often ignored.

As Johnson navigated the university through the Depression, World War II, and Democratic and Republican politics, he walked a fine line between the macrocosm of Washington and the microcosm of Howard University. Rayford Logan noted that few of those who knew Johnson held neutral views about him; the vast majority of both his fervent admirers and his bitter critics found him to have a messianic personality.

> He used to say on many public occasions: The Lord told me to speak, but He did not tell me when to stop. This statement at times uttered half-facetiously, at other times with deep conviction – symbolized better than anything

else his deep feeling of vocation, of special commitment.[256]

Miller and Johnson

When 36-year-old Johnson came to Howard, his civil and human rights work seemingly provided him with strategies and vision for grooming the next generation of black leaders. However, both Washington, DC, and Howard University proved to be a different environment. The university campus did not adapt to the type of tyrannical rule and demagoguery that Baptist ministers were known for wielding. Both the older established faculty and the highly educated young faculty sought recognition, room to research, and ego massaging. Johnson had to navigate a troubling sea of personalities and influence.

As one of the first African Americans to head the self-proclaimed National Negro University, he stood at the helm of a new brand of leadership. His ability to appease philanthropists, governmental officials, faculty, students, and staff during this tumultuous period surpassed the expectations of both nay-sayers and well-wishers. Though many better-known black colleges and universities, such as Hampton, Morgan, and Spelman, still had white presidents, his success was cited in arguments for the appointment of other black presidents and lesser-known institutions, such as West Virginia State, North Carolina Central

---

[256] Rayford Logan, *Howard University: The First Hundred Years, 1867–1967*. New York: New York University Press, 1969, 249.

University, and Dillard would soon place African American men in leadership. Stephen Wright wrote

> [Johnson] was sui generis - one of a kind. But Howard University is also sui generis. And the two came together at a propitious time in the history of the University for the glory of both.[257]

Miller remained an important figure among Howard students, faculty, and alums and continued to encourage future students to consider matriculating there. But he was among those who were not happy with Johnson. In a series of letters to Harold Ickes, he crusaded for Johnson's removal, citing infractions that included a lack of academic freedom and displacement of senior faculty members. Though Miller's main issue was that Johnson's presidency seemed shrouded in mystery, Howard University archivist Clifford Muse asserts that Miller was embittered by being passed over for a young, Baptist preacher who had not worked in higher education. Miller used the Black Press, such as the *Afro-American,* to release his frustration and vitriol against the Johnson administration. He also used his influence within the various Howard University alumni associations to present his case. In the earliest letter to Ickes in February 1935, Miller opined:

---

[257] Symposium on Johnson, Stephen J. Wright, Reflections on Mordecai W. Johnson as a University President, and His Relationship with Other Presidents. 5-6. Howard University Archives.

> I feel that you are entitled to and would welcome the frank, unbiased opinion representative of the six thousand graduates of Howard University and twelve thousand and some students, concerning the present administration. Having spent fifty-five years as boy and man, student, teacher and official in this Institution, I feel some degree of competency in expressing that judgment which, let me assure you, is fully without animosity or bias but solely in the interest of My Alma Mater.
>
> The gravamen of complaint against President Johnson's administration grows out of the fact that for the past eight years he has kept the Institution in a continual state of turmoil and confusion. There has been perpetual dissatisfaction and strife in the faculty, among the alumni and in the Board of Trustees. This state of strife increases rather than diminishes with time.[258]

Miller's concern for Howard was central to his love and perception of what the university had been and needed to be. Still, his larger issue was the foundational aspects of African American leadership

---

[258] Lucy Slowe papers, Box 90-5 folder 115, administrative material, "In Re: Johnson, Mordecai "The Storm Center, 3/6/1935," MSRC, Howard University. Subsequent reference for Lucy Slowe papers will be LSP.

and administration within higher education. For Miller, Johnson's position as the flagship institution's first African American president was the model against which other black colleges would measure their success or failure. He felt that faculty displeasure and rising alumni anti-Johnson sentiment was not the example of higher education the "Negro Capstone" should present. He asserted that a failure in leadership at Howard would delay the shift in administrative reins from white to black hands at other black institutions:

> It would indeed be a great calamity to the Colored race should the first colored President prove a failure. I had better say that it is a great calamity to the Colored race that the first colored President has proved a failure. The University merely selected the wrong individual with whom to conduct the experiment. The failure of Mordecai W. Johnson is not the failure of the Colored race. Dr. Robert R. Moton of Tuskegee, Dr. John Hope of Atlanta University, and Dr. McCrory of Johnson C. Smith University have conducted these educational trusts with efficiency and satisfaction for a few years. There is no reason why a satisfactory colored man might not be found to succeed President Johnson at Howard University.[259]

---

[259] LSP, Box 90-5 folder 115, administrative material, "In Re: Johnson, Mordecai "The Storm Center, 3/6/1935.

The breach between the two seemed to have involved a personal issue framed by ageism and colorism when its root cause was hurt or jealousy because Miller should have been the first African American president at Howard.[260] Nevertheless, Miller had a dark complexion, while Johnson's complexion was fair.[261] Literary scholar Audrey Kerr studied Washington's interracial strife at elite institutions such as Howard University. She found that there was no written policy restricting darker-complexioned people from leadership positions on faculty. There was an implicit point of divergence in social, religious, and civic arenas where complexion mattered. This dual system was evident throughout the African American community from Chicago to Boston to New York. Miller was aware of this, as was Johnson. Nevertheless, their disagreements transcended complexion and involved Howard's administrative direction. Miller knew Howard from a

---

[260] Ageism was evident in the fight with Durkee. Accounts are replete with references to Miller's "gray head." Conversely, Kerr in *The Paper Bag Principle* examines the issue of colorism within Washington, DC as complexion lore. Charles Parrish in the Journal of Negro Education explores the nomenclature of intra racial categories. Both articles lend credence to the possibilities that colorism between Miller and Johnson might have contributed to antagonisms regarding Howard's administration and direction.

[261] In the African American community, colorism, affected the social migration of people in Washington and other African American communities. The variation of complexion among African Americans is a result of enslavement. There were voluntary and involuntary sexual relationships that resulted in altering the dark complexion enslaved Africans. Recent studies have indicated that the mythological brown paper bag test discouraged and deterred many darker-hued African Americans from social climbing in social and fraternal circle.

visceral, academic, and impassioned experience. Johnson knew Howard as an institution he would shape into a modern university with his imprint visible for everyone to see.

Regardless of its root, however, the dissension between the two remained tense. Miller believed he was vigilantly safeguarding his alma mater and soul mother, the place that stood beside Elizabeth Miller, his natural mother. The institution had nurtured his love for learning, provided employment, and allowed him intellectual latitude to create a sociology department, so he perceived any threat to its future as a threat to him. Though he felt that Johnson might be suited to provide leadership for Howard at another time, he did not deem him fit for this tumultuous political and social era. Rather, in Miller's estimation, Johnson was a dynamic preacher best suited for Christian ministry, not the educational field.[262]

Harold Ickes replied with a succinct response to the February 27 letter informing Miller that university affairs were better managed within the campus community within the chain of command established to air such grievances:

> My dear Professor Miller:
>
> In answer to your letter of 2/27, I should like to say that no investigation of [DePriest]... has

---

[262] Twenty years earlier Miller wrote about the importance of ministry within the African American community and how the talented tenth should serve in pulpits to elevate the race.

shown to my satisfaction that President Mordecai Johnson is guilty of any malfeasance or dishonesty. Whatever turmoil may have been caused at the University or in the press seems to me to me more properly attributed to those who are anxious to remove or Pres[ident] Johnson. I regret very much that some of these people have undertaken to give the press fractions of unfinished investigations. Such biased reports are bound to mislead the reading public and to do Howard University no good. All complaints against the administration of the University should be taken not to me, but to the Board of Trustees. As I have said before, I think real progress has been made at Howard University under the administration of Pres. Mordecai Johnson and I hope very much that it will continue.[263]

Most black reporters and other writers castigated Miller as a man with a bruised ego who missed his opportunity to become president of his alma mater. However, in a March 6, 1935 letter of response to Ickes, Miller explained the depth of his issue with Johnson.

I am now seventy-one years of age and have retired from active service. I am deeply interested in the removal, or rather, the withdrawal of

---

[263] LSP, Box 90-5 folder 115, administrative material letter from Kelly Miller to Harold Ickes.

President Johnson, not by reason of any personal ambition or interest in any person to succeed him. My only concern is my Alma Mater and the welfare of the Colored race. I was among the most ardent admirers and advocates of Pres. Johnson during the early years of his administration. I defended him against the charge of communism which came near wrecking his administration and from which he is not even now wholly exonerate. But I cannot defend the indefensible. The progress which the University has made under the present administration, with which you express satisfaction, is of a material nature. A University is devoted to the inculcation of knowledge and character and not the display of grounds and buildings. These constitute a poor offset to the steady degeneration in character and moral tone. The morale of the faculty and student body is at a lower ebb under the administration of Pres. Johnson than at any time during the history of the Institution.[264]

In public, Miller attempted to muffle his differences with Johnson. However, in a 1934 address to the university's General Alumni Association, he presented his position on Johnson and what he saw as the press's manipulation and misinterpretation of the issue to sell papers. He insisted that his desire to have the president replaced was shared by other older

---

[264] LSP, Box 90-5 folder 115, administrative material letter from Kelly Miller to Ickes, 3.

faculty who equally disapproved of his tactics in dealing with them as well as by younger faculty who were concerned that he lacked a doctorate and understanding of academic discourse.[265] Still, Miller ensured his audience that he and Johnson were amicable, if not polite, toward each other.

> I am, however, a better friend to Howard University than I can be to any individual. The University is greater than the President, the Board of Trustees, the Faculty, or the present-day body of alumni. On one occasion an overbearing President summoned me to his office and demanded to know point blank whether I was loyal to him or not… There is dissension within the Trustee Board, dissension between Trustees and Alumni, dissension between the President, Administrative Deans, and faculty members. This dissension is spread out in public print, is recorded in the Congressional Record, is listed on the calendar of the Courts, and flies from lip to lip among faculty, alumni, student body and the public at large. The internal disturbances at Howard University are read and known throughout all educational circles

---

[265] Lucy Slowe's funeral was a contested place for President Johnson. Logan documents that Johnson was not invited and Slow's executrix upheld that decision. Moreover, Logan and Sterling Brown indicate that the tenure of times on the campus were sour. Issues of pay discrepancies, elitism, and sexism, ageism marred Johnson's presidential infancy. The "Case against Johnson," outlines other grievances.

and have become the scandal of the educational world.[266]

The ever-conscientious Miller explained that Howard had been birthed out of a prayer meeting to inspire young men to Christian principles and character. To him, the internal disturbances within the university reduced this vision to a fallacy and diminished the spirit and energy of both faculty and students. After a nearly five decades relationship with the institution, Miller cast himself as its brick-and-mortar who could chart the university's proper course.

> When 54 years ago I entered Howard University as a boy my spirit leaped within me to the height of hope and expectation that Howard University would be the beacon of light which should lighten the way of the leaders who themselves would stand in the high places of intellectual, moral, social, and cultural authority and would hold out the lamp that should lighten the pathway of a race groping in the darkness. How, retiring at the age of 70, I still entertain the hope and vision of that earlier day. I pledge myself with all that is within me to devote my remaining years to the end that I shall see with mine own eyes the

---

[266] KMP, Box 71-3 folder 84, news article "Full Text of Kelly Miller Speech," June 23, 1934.

fulfillment of that early hope and realization of my dream.[267]

For Miller, Howard needed to be a place of dynamic learning and character building. Thus, the loggerhead between him and Johnson more than a contest about superficial differences such as age, complexion, or curriculum. Rather, it was about a seeming shift in the understanding of what was required to prepare African Americans as leaders and co-laborers for the progress of humankind and the elevation of all oppressed people.

In Miller's era, racial prejudice was seen as the major obstacle to elevating the race, but Johnson's generation was infused with racial pride. He saw the need to incorporate racial accountability into the rising class-stratified American society. And, in his inaugural address, he spoke of a new day in which the Negro problem was of national and world significance. For, he said:

> The urgent question that now confronts the world regarding this republic is: What is going to be the relation to the weaker and disadvantaged peoples of the earth?[268]

---

[267] Ibid.
[268] William Johnson Papers, Box 189-1 folder 9 speech, "Opening Address for Autumn Quarter HU President Mordecai Wyatt Johnson, 1927. 8.

European nations had dominated the international scene, globally subordinating people of color for geopolitical, economic, and pseudoscientific reasons. But, Johnson envisioned a rising black generation whose education, increasing wealth, and professionalism would secure an improved future, as he continued:

> The Negro is now intermixed with all the complex activities of American life. Nothing but the application of intelligence, persistent intelligence in the multitude of complex directions, with one solid good will, can accomplish even in a great length of time the thing which we all desire and which we must have if the destiny of our country is to be fulfilled. Our country, therefore, needs institutions where those studies will be undertaken, in a large and comprehensive way, which will prepare not only the Negro but the nation to understand the Negro is situate, where we want him to go, what the difficulties are in the way, and how, in spite of all the difficulties, but intelligence and persistent application of good will, he can get there.[269]

Johnson promoted the concept of Howard students being responsible for a broader vision of community. He encouraged them to become self-

---

[269] Ibid. 9.

conscious, self-directing, and independent human beings. And while Miller agreed on this goal, they differed on how to reach it.

Johnson's response did not quiet his colleague's voice in the chorus of dissenters. Rising dissatisfaction came from other faculty, students, and alumni. Though all of them had initially been enthusiastic about the appointment of the first African American president, within six years, they no longer viewed him as useful. The Alumni Association assailed him for ignoring the seniority and contribution of older faculty who did not possess a doctorate. In 1932, it issued a pamphlet entitled *The Case against Mordecai W. Johnson, President of Howard University*, demanding that the Board of Trustees review their grievances against the president and call for his immediate removal. The message explained that the worst offense involved prominent faculty, for they contended that,

> Johnson has shown that he is unable to get along with people, and no man, who has violent disagreements with a large number of people, can successfully head a school. Moreover, the alumni believe that Dr. Johnson has used the money appropriated for salaries and salary increases in such an autocratic and unfair way as to create dissension and to impair morale to such an extent that he can never rebuild it.[270]

---

[270] LSP, Box 90-5 folder 115. Dr. Muse noted that most first African American administrators of HBCU's endured struggles between ivy-

Established and younger faculty, Board members, and vocal alumni all claimed to seek what they perceived as best for the university. But, often, their visions and methods clashed with each other.[271]

Johnson's legacy contributed to the golden age of Howard with its scholarship, courses, and innovation firmly cemented within the field of humanities. His expanded curriculum was physical, and he expected some gesture of gratitude from Johnson, for as he saw it, he found Howard "a seedling and left it as a mighty tree." His contributions added to its growth and development. In return, he expected a nod of

---

league educated faculty and mostly white Trustee Boards over their own meager educational backgrounds from liberal art and church colleges. Pressure from the posturing of these faculties was met with equal, yet restrained, pressure from HBCU presidents.

[271] Logan spoke of his own mistreatment by Johnson and others at Howard. In a chapter of his autobiography entitled "My Trials and Tribulations with President Mordecai W. Johnson and Professor Merze Tate; Extra-Curricular Activities, 1953-1955," he reflects on his frustration with his career at Howard. "Mordecai, I am afraid, has less interest in building up an educational institution than… in demonstrating his ability to outwit… all opposition. I could not continue work on the history of Howard University during President Johnson's administration, and I changed my will [so as] to have my diaries deposited in the Library of Congress rather than in Howard University lest some one change what I had written about President Johnson I added in my diary: "I must check with Frazier, Sterling Brown, Dorsey, or some of the other 'Old Timers' to find out what Kelly Miller meant when he called Mordecai a 'murderer [who] killed Lucy Slowe. I later found ou[t] that she had given instructions that President Johnson was not to be permitted to attend her funeral. [He] would be perfectly capable of gloating if I were to die of a heart attack which could be attributed in part to his insulting attack on me. Miller did not dishonor Johnson with open vitriol. He used the Black Press and kept his opinions professional. Rayford Logan Papers, Box 166-34 folder 9.

appreciation as well as a place to practice his teaching method until he decided to end his career. However, in the wake of failing health and at the suggestion of Johnson, his career ended with his retirement in 1934. As Garvey had been deported, and Dubois modulated his platform and embraced Pan-Africanism, Miller drifted to the periphery of black intellectual discourse, leaving the American struggle to another generation.

Johnson's former faculty, students, and contemporaries convened a symposium on his achievements and reflected on the pre-and post-Johnson Howard. Carroll Miller, a faculty member during the waning years of Johnson's administration, remarked:

> Johnson's greatest legacies… was his bold determination to preserve academic freedom… during a period when Howard was beset by internal turmoil and strife; when the outside world seemed indifferent to its status; and when the vitality of the original founders seemed to have been lost with the lack of focus and a positive image. [He] came to Howard with a vision of what Howard could and must become.[272]

---

[272] Symposium on Mordecai W. Johnson, Carroll Miller paper: "Mordecai Wyatt Johnson: The Man and His Vision."13. MSRC, Howard University Archives, Washington, D.C.

Historian Harold Lewis reminded attendees that the relationship between the University and the federal government dated back to the 1860s and that Johnson's era occurred during tumultuous times. The However, each presidential administration could increase or decrease the federal apportionment, which would impact the university's operational budget and projects.

The 1932 election marked a shift in political loyalty for black voters. Democrat Franklin D. Roosevelt ousted Herbert Hoover. Many black people felt neglected by Hoover and other Republicans as his lily-white crusade openly pandered to southern voters.

Further, new faculty members who were accomplished PhDs from Harvard and other prominent institutions resorted to teaching at Howard because racism precluded them from being hired by white universities. Amid this dual tension between the changing federal government and academic realities, Johnson felt the need to establish his authority as President and chief administrator soundly. As Lewis describes the situation:

> One must remember that the crucial era of Mordecai Johnson's administration was the revolutionary era of the New Deal. Mrs. Roosevelt, certainly a personality in the Roosevelt power structure, served on the Howard Board of Trustees. She... consistently approved of Howard University [appropriation] request. Mordecai Johnson's

difficulty, or… Herculean task, was similarly eased by the efforts of Harold Ickes, an extremely sympathetic Secretary of the Interior, whose support made a difference, since Howard was at the time part of the Interior budget. Secondly, one must consider whether "that remarkable group of black scholars," congregated at Howard University presumably because they thought that under President Johnson "intellectual stimulation was supreme.[273]

At the close of his career, Miller retained his dignity and posture on the race problem. Clearly, younger faculty held dyspeptic views of Johnson. Some spoke out, others simmered great distain and others embraced the change. The era of Miller set gracefully as he continued his work addressing the race problem.

Miller and Johnson Portrait Unveiling

---

[273] Symposium on Johnson, Harold Lewis paper: "Total Cultural Setting…Howard University Archive.

Harriet Tubman Society for the Blind

As Miller's beloved campus morphed into Johnson's territory, he increasingly turned his attention to working for black people in other settings. Following his cataract surgery, he became involved with Locke and Charlotte Hunter, founder of the Harriet Tubman Society for the Blind, and his personal experience propelled him to promote that organization. In a document, "Memorandum on the Needs of the Blind in the District of Columbia," the organization stated:

> At the request, this memorandum is submitted on the needs of the handicapped blind, numbering considerably more than half of the thousand odd blind persons residents of the District of Columbia, and divided almost evenly between the white and colored races, with the hope of inspiring a modern, broad, and constructive system for the training, relief of all deserving and promising cases and the decent support of the small fraction of who may remain completely destitute and dependent. Far too little effort in the past has been put upon the instruction, training, and rehabilitation of the blind, with a resulting greater degree and final cost of eventual destitution and dependence. [274]

---

[274] Alain Locke Papers, Box 164-180 folder 2, letter, Harriet Tubman Aid to the Blind, Inc. Subsequent reference will cite Alain Locke papers as ALP.

During the 1920s, when the federal government was indifferent to the needs of the African American community, Miller spoke out against the lily-whitism of the Hoover administration. Yet, during the same era, the spirit of philanthropy emerged within private sector organizations such as the Community Chest, providing resources for projects through strategic fundraising.

Noted fundraiser Elwood Street authored an article entitled "Professional Guidance for the Small-Town Community Chest," that urged communities, businesses, and leaders to help meet social needs within their spheres of influence:

> The advantages... of the community chest method of cooperative finance and planning of social work are so clear, and the instances of almost immeasurable improvement."[275] Street argued that the Community Chest would fund those underfunded initiatives that did not have connections and clout to assure solvency.[276]

While racism limited the reach of the organization, and it did not support black groups, Street insisted that it would only be effective if it helped to alleviate the lack within Washington, DC.

---

[275] Elwood Street, "Professional Guidance for the Small Town Community Chest," *Social Forces*, 5: 4 (June 1927). 639.
[276] Ibid.

This must be a united effort of the entire city, not of white Washington working apart from colored Washington; representatives of both races must meet and participate as equals.[277]

At its initial meeting, white and black Washingtonians laid out a plan for the fledgling initiative. Frederic A. Delano, the uncle of President Franklin D. Roosevelt, was elevated to the presidency, and Miller was appointed vice president. Their interracial leadership brought white Washingtonians closer to the living conditions of black Washington while "self-protective" black people learned about the city's intra-racial issues. At the initial gala dinner, Street and other whites observed the Jim Crow laws and dined separately. On this occasion, Miller attended dressed in tails and white tie accompanied by Mrs. Street. The Chest "scored its chief triumph in pricking the conscience of white people and arousing deeper charitable interest among black people, but had only slight effect on interracial collaboration was slight."[278]

Miller's concern for the poor was amplified by his temporary loss of vision in 1934. In an undated article from the *Boston Chronicle*, Miller writes:

I was compelled to undergo an operation for cataract last June. For several months my

---

[277] Constance Green, *Secret City*. 215.
[278] Ibid.

eyesight was in a state of total eclipse which caused suspension of my releases for several months. Since my first operation I have not been able to read one word of a printed page, and have not been compelled to rely upon the radio and audible reading of others...The loss of sight may intensify the power of reflection...When one loses his sight, he becomes illiterate; that is he can neither read nor write. After passing thru the actual experience, I am fully able to appreciate the value of literacy and the disadvantage of losing it when once attained.

But illiterate people are not necessarily ignorant, nor are they more deficient in thought power than their more fortunate literate fellows. Visual symbols of knowledge are a wonderful aid in facilitating the thought process, but they cannot originate it. I can repeat with keener understanding the Methodist hymn which I sang as a boy in South Carolina: I once was lost but now I'm found, was blind but now I see.

The Depression resulted in limited resources for the disabled, poor, and African Americans. Nevertheless, the Tubman Society realized that the black people who were blind in Washington needed adequate resources for immediate and long-term survival. There were four areas of importance for the Tubman Society.

1. Proper common school education of blind young adults and minors. Proper education would ensure that they were suitably fitted for a career in a trade or vocational work, allowing them to take part in society as productive and self-supporting citizens.

2. Promote vocational education for blind adults who incurred after childhood or failed to meet constructively the needs and handicaps of the blind child.

3. Seek adequate provisions for the needs of the indigent blind during their period of training until they are economically stabilized.

4. Provide a space for "recreational and wholesome community" activity.[279]

The Society sought to be listed with the local Community Chest, but the Washington Board of Trade did not accept new registrations in 1931. Hunter struggled to conduct the business without compensation, soliciting aid from friends, churches, and organizations. In March 1933, the Washington branch of the Federal Board for Vocational Education provided salaries for two teachers in handcrafts for the

---

[279] ALP, Box 164-180 folder 2 memorandum.

society. The Society conducted a campaign in 1933-1934 for funds to purchase property and a salary for the director, who had worked without compensation for over two years. They used the Black Press to convey their appeal for funding. Miller's involvement with the black press was advantageous, and in public appeal, he published an open letter which read in part:

Dear Sir or Madam:

> Will you not join the group of friends who already through the campaign of the Merchants and Manufacturer's Association and the Daily News have lent encouragement to this worthy public service by sending your check or donation to the Institution's headquarters, 1416 Eleventh Street, N.W. for use toward the pressing current items of rent, fuel and maintenance of the shelter and workshop located there. Checks should be made to the Harriet Tubman Aid to the Blind, Inc...We thank you for any contributions and help, however small, you may be moved to make.[280]

In 1934, Hunter listed the trustees as Locke, H.C. Corpening, a supervisor for the Federal Board for Vocational Education, Ralph Campbell, Executive Secretary of the Columbia Polytechnic Institute for the

---

[280] ALP, Box 164-180 folder 2.

Blind, Hattie L. Maddux, John Meshaw, and herself.[281] In reporting the activities from 1931 to 1934, the Statement recounts the Tubman Society's history.

> On May 11, 1931, the first workshop for the colored blind was opened at 1416 Eleventh Street, Northwest Washington D.C. by the efforts of a Negro woman, Miss Charlotte E. Hunter whose goal was to establish a means whereby the self-respecting colored blind might be saved from paupery... On October 3, 1931, she organized the Harriet Tubman Aid to the Blind, and the institution was incorporated, and began its operations with headquarters in the same location.[282]

In an undated article, the Society was dubbed "Washington's first institution for the vocational rehabilitation of blind Negroes of the city." Unfortunately, however, efforts to raise funds fell short, Miller's involvement with the Community Chest did not alleviate the Society's financial burden, and Hunter's efforts floundered. Presumably, by 1934, its activity ended.

> For more than three years Charlotte Hunter has attempted to operate the Tubman home,

---

[281] ALP, Box 164-180 folder 2. Charolette Hunter "Statement of Aims and Activities of the Harriet Tubman Aid to the Blind, Inc." December 10, 1934.
[282] Ibid.

but ineffective support coupled with the financial stress of the times has reduced the institution to poverty and today the rent is long overdue. The Harriet Tubman Aid to the Blind is on the verge of being moved out into the street. The $340 rent bill [is due]. The Community Chest has refused its support. So has the Federal Government... The real victims of this apathy are the physically able but blind Negro folk of the city who might be taught a vocation to make them self-supporting and save them from lives of dependence upon friends and relatives.[283]

Roosevelt's New or Raw Deal (1930-1938)

The coalescing of political parties drove Miller to author a flurry of articles with insightful analysis of national politics. Franklin Roosevelt's 1932 presidential election signaled the beginning of the departure of African Americans from the Republican Party. Four years earlier, Miller had written about "Negro disillusionment" with regard to the nature of American politics. In his "Kelly Miller Says" column, he wrote:

It required 40 years to disillusion the Negro concerning his political status. A whole generation has had to pass before this disillusionment became complete. In a spasm

---
[283] ALP, Box 164-180 folder 2.

of moral delirium, the nation gave the Negro potential political equality. The reconstruction enactments were adopted to put this purpose into effect... The reconstruction regime was not overthrown by the deviltry of the South nor yet by the bartering of Rutherford B. Hayes, but by the slowly sinking thermometer of the national passion.[284]

The article traced the derailing of the GOP to 1884, when African American interests were muted by materialistic politicians who opted to transition the party's heart from enthusiastic devotion to practical interests. Throughout 1928, African Americans were in a quandary over political parties and allegiances. Herbert Hoover made no secret about his desire to restore the lily-white face of the GOP, regardless of African American allegiance. In Miller's eyes, he had ignored their contributions and determined that the party would not complicate its campaign with race issues.

In 1931, Miller had joined others under the leadership of black Illinois Congressman Oscar DePriest to convene the National Non-Partisan Negro Conference and League to find a political solution for black people. The original Non-Partisan League (NPL) emerged in 1915 as a political organization under former Socialist party organizer Arthur Charles (A.C.) Townley. However, this group of disgruntled farmers that once challenged corporate political interest in the

---

[284] KMP, Box 71-3 folder 79 news article.

mid-and far-western United States evolved into an office-seeking political party. In 1931, African Americans on the East Coast adopted its spirit and organized the Non-Partisan Negro Conference in Washington. In calling the conference, DePriest declared:

> In my extensive travel over this country, I have studied the political status of the Negro. I have had many personal contacts and conferences in various centers. I have sensed a serious and deep-seated dissatisfaction among all classes of Negroes in every section of the country. The time seems now ripe for concerted action. Furthermore, the masses are expecting the leaders to appeal for justice and definite relief.[285]

One hundred seventy-nine delegates representing institutions and groups throughout 25 states and the District of Columbia gathered at this historic meeting. Churches, fraternities, Masonic lodges, university and college presidents, politicians, judges, and women's club leaders were represented. Miller chaired the Findings Committee, which generated twenty areas of interest.

Miller's concern centered particularly around five specific areas:

1. Our Americanism;

---

[285] Omni Gatherum, Item 786, pamphlet. MSRC. Manuscript Division.

2. Patriotism and Loyalty Made Difficult;
3. Parties as a Tool;
4. Howard University; and
5. The Future Outlook.

But there were also findings related to Communism, Non-Partisanism, The Negro in the North, Political Units, Colored Women Disfranchisement in the Southern States, Eligible Voters in the South, Vote for the Best Southern Whites, The NAACP, Restrictions Short Lived, Civil Service, Lynching, National Aid to Negro Education, Negro Population Statistics, and Economics and Industry.

The section of findings on Our Americanism sought to demonstrate loyalty to the country, insisting that,

> we wish to reaffirm our undeviating devotion to the principles of American institutions, as set forth in the Declaration of Independence and the Constitution of the United States, believing that no other foundation can be laid than that which has been laid.[286]

---

[286] In an undated article, the Society was dubbed "Washington's first institution for the vocational rehabilitation of blind Negroes of the city." Unfortunately, however, efforts to raise funds fell short. Miller's involvement with the Community Chest did not alleviate the Society's financial burden, and Hunter's efforts floundered. Presumably, by 1934, its activity ended. ALP, Box 164-180 folder 2.

Delegates affirmed that black people's loyalty to America had withstood every test to which they had been subjected. Yet, they lamented the oppressive nature of American society expressed through white supremacy and de jure and de facto discrimination.

The NPL appealed to the fair judgment of the American people and warned that this patriotism and devotion could be displaced by harsh and unjust treatment. The delegates were aware of Hoover's desire to restore the Republican party to a lily-white political group. Thus, they realized that

To the NPL, politics was a gamble since political parties were useful instruments rather than deities to be worshiped. The organization asserted that, as tools wear out and grow blunt, they need to be sharpened or replaced. It asserted that the black community did not embrace any deep-seated political conviction but sought to ensure their full legal rights and saw the ballot as a defensive weapon to effect change potentially.

On the cusp of his retirement, Miller sought to provide for Howard University through his work with The Non-Partisan League. He and other leaders proposed establishing a national educational fund to provide grants to black institutions and the creation of a Division of Negro Education to replace the National Advisory Commission on Negro Education within the Department of Education. As envisioned, this body would conduct studies and recommend how the federal government could aid existing institutions.

They identified Howard as the National Negro University because of its location and special congressional support. They urged Congress to provide for the maintenance of the University since it was historically attached to the federal government and received special financial assistance. According to archivist Clifford L. Muse, Jr., however, Howard's funding had waned under Democratic presidencies, and,

> The Roosevelt administration did not provide critical funds needed for the improvement of the educational programs of the university. Throughout the New Deal era, the Congress and the Roosevelt administration adhered to a policy of providing only the minimum of funding to the university for its basic educational needs... [Failing] to render more assistance to Howard, in essence, was also a failure to render more assistance to a major black private institution of higher education during a critical period both in the history of American higher education and the nation. Ironically, while Howard was "losing ground:" there was some improvement in the condition of state-supported "land grant" institutions.[287]

---

[287] Clifford L. Muse, Jr., "Howard University and the Federal Government," *The Journal of African American History*, *New Perspectives on African American Educational History* 87 (Autumn, 2002). 403-415.

Lastly, conference delegates concluded the equality, employment, and equal legal protection promised in the Civil War amendments had been successfully legislated but were toothless. They realized that it was incumbent upon them to chart a path for coming generations, and League delegates concluded in their final statement that they wrote,

> … we would encourage the race to face the future, with optimism and hope. It is a far cry from the starting point of a human chattel to the fullness of the status of American citizenship, although, we have not yet reached the mark of the high calling, yet our progress has been marvelous. We may gain encouragement and hope by looking back upon the path already trod as well as by regarding the uncompleted journey which lies before us. In the accomplishment of this goal, we must rely upon the innate sense of justice and fair play of the American people and upon the gracious favor of almighty God.[288]

The 1932 election proved to be a watershed moment in African American political history since this was the first time that many voted in total for Franklin D. Roosevelt, a Western Democrat. Many hailed the victory as the dawning of a new era in America that signaled hope and progress.

---

[288] Omni Gatherum, Item 786, pamphlet.

The self-proclaimed iconoclast believed that Roosevelt's platform was the better choice for African American progress in general and Howard University in particular. Still, as a realist regarding the impact presidential powers could exert over society, the self-proclaimed iconoclast knew that all presidents had limitations and political ambitions. In an article entitled "The Blue Eagle and the Jim Crow," he compared the two birds to the African American experience during the Great Depression. For him, the eagle, a noble bird, symbolized strength, while Jim Crow was a stereotype created during enslavement.

> Jim Crow and eagle are mortal enemies. They cannot thrive in the same atmosphere. The eagle must destroy Jim Crow or have his dominion polluted with cowardice, injustice, and the slavish spirit. The two are so deeply contrasted in nature and spirit that they cannot exercise joint dominion. The spirit of these emblematic birds finds concrete illustration in the NRA [National Recovery Act] which the present administration has set up to promote recovery and lift the nation out of the depression... The blue eagle well characterizes the spirit of Franklin D. Roosevelt—equal opportunity for all - but Jim Crow is an ugly fact whose existence cannot be ignored. According to the Roosevelt intention, the NRA must be operated without regard to race, creed or color - but when the blue eagle meets Jim

> Crow it stands athwart... all those who are in any way charged with NRA administration have been instructed, we prefer to believe, that Jim crow must be pushed aside, and his former dominion reduced to a minimum, while the blue eagle asserts his imperial right of way.[289]

The Blue Eagle initiative sought to standardize wages and employment practices. Still, Miller explained that the Jim Crow provided the immoral loophole many private and state agencies used to undercut African American workers. He concluded that watching and trusting was not a passive act, and Roosevelt would have to answer for any lack of progress. Unfortunately, the legislation did not overcome the racism. White workers displaced African American workers, while domestic work and other service industries were not included as occupations worthy of financial relief.

Miller inferred that the New Deal was not a square deal for African Americans. For to him, while, on paper, the NRA sought to alleviate the dire straits of the poorest citizens by offering middle-class benefits, the pervasive beast of white supremacy impeded the realization of economic stability. Further, most black workers were employed in agricultural and domestic jobs that were not given financial assistance or covered by social security.

---

[289] KMP, Box 71-3 folder 82 news clipping.

If the New Deal is to be a square deal, the Blue Eagle must take the Negro under his wings along with the rest. Usually, the Negro is not considered as an integral part of general equation but must be dealt with by a special formula... Special dispensation must be made for him, or he will be left out of the picture. He is in truth and deed the forgotten man and must ever remind the nation of his existence and presence as a factor which must be reckoned with... The [New Deal] codes do not cover agriculture and domestic service, the two pursuits in which three-fifths of the race find a livelihood. This is because the individual character of these occupations is such that they cannot be easily regimented.[290]

Black American citizens had trusted Roosevelt to institute the New Deal changes needed to alleviate the inequalities between the races. Yet, Miller asserted that its financial recovery efforts only offered them a placebo that failed to address preexisting poverty, underemployment, and job security.

"Weaving in My Own Life Incidents."

The close of the 1930s was a somber time for Miller. The nation was burdened under the weight of the Great Depression. His decade-bright hopes for Howard dimmed under Johnson's austere

---

[290] KMP, Box 71-3 folder 82 news clipping *Chicago Bee* September 22, 1933.

administration, and his career ended abruptly with his retirement. Still, Miller continued to use the Black Press to engage social issues with an exquisite vocabulary and stinging pen.

Miller never returned to South Carolina. The occasion of his father's death was the last time he traveled home. The first visit was in 1886 to purchase the farm for his parents. Miller did not retain close relationships with his siblings or their children. A cache of letters between him and his brother Robert reveals only a thin layer of brotherly affection. The six years of correspondence between the two offer a glimpse into the esteem the family held for him. On May 7, 1933, Robert wrote:

> Dear bro,
>
> I have just telegraphed you of the death of my son Kelly. He had insurance enough to bury him, but I am having some trouble [collecting] money so I am at a loss as to know what to do…I don't want you to pay it unless you so desire that but give him your signature please do that right now so we can bury the boy.

Miller in his Garden

The Depression severely affected the financial condition of the Southern farming community, and in October 1933, Robert made another appeal for financial assistance to make repairs on the farm. Three years later, the Robert grew weaker and informed his brother that he intended to sell his current home and move into a smaller house where he could live and manage better.

Miller with Family Dog

In July 1938, the issue of money prompted another letter from Robert, whose financial need and limited mobility led to the sale of some parts of the family farm.

Dear bro,

July 1938

It has certainly been a long time since I heard from you. I wrote to you several times, but you have not any letters. I am at a loss as to why. I hope you will see how it is down here as you know this South Carolina a poor small country and the chance for living is hard... As I have told you that am not in a shape to do very much work, so I have to live on it. I need 10.00 to begin the job now can you please spare me that much if I can get that I will begin immediately please let me know yours truly, Robert.[291]

By the time Robert wrote his final letter to his brother in November 1939, his health was waning and the payments and physical upkeep were beyond his ability so he informed Kelly had he had sold the remaining acres of the Miller farm since:

My dear bro,

I will write you a few lines to inform you of my health this let you know that I am not doing very well as to health for I not were but I am still trying hold up as best I can I hope you are doing the same when I sold the farm I reserved

---

[291] Letter from Robert Miller to KM, Kelly Miller papers Box 15 folder 4, MARBL, Emory University

the largest part of the money by taking a mortgage on the farm for 5 years at paying 100 per year or with interest on the dollar per year.[292]

We don't know how Miller felt about the sale of his graduation gift to his parents. The earnest farmer at heart had maintained his Washington garden, but he was not able to return to full-time farm life.

By 1936, the 73-year-old's health was failing, and his eyesight was weakened from cataracts, yet he continued to write his weekly syndicated column for tens of black newspapers across the country. Aging did not dim his passion for gardening, politics, or Howard University.

During this time, he was writing his memoirs and reliving his life through pen and paper. Migration and the advent of World War II had changed the city Miller knew during the Depression. As he conceded in his autobiography, he preferred the simpler Washington of the 1880s, and the noise of honking horns and jazz music sullied its peaceful elements of living:

> Many of my readers will be interested in a description of the Washington into which I found myself projected more than a half century ago. Everything is so different than I often pause and wonder at the metamorphosis. In that day, no airplanes pierced the clouds or were seen in silhouette

---

[292] Letter from Robert Miller, November 23, 1939

against the blue sky; and no drone of motors came from above. No motor driven vehicle was in the streets and the clatter of horses' hoofs was sweet music as compared with the roar of exhausts, the detonations of backfire... No red, yellow, and green lights at corners to warn pedestrians when it would be safe to cross a street. At rare intervals, a runaway horse might do some damage to a person or property, which event would be chronicled in the newspapers as among the great events of the day.[293]

On December 9, 1939, he wrote, "I have assumed the role, not of a leader but as an analyst, not of an agitator, but an expositor. I shall hope during the next ten years to be of still more efficient service in guiding the race in the way it should go." He expected to live into his 90s like his father, but he suffered a heart attack and died ten days later.

The residue of the conflicts with Johnson lingered after Miller's death. Their long-standing antagonism made it unlikely that Johnson would accept petitions from faculty, students, and alumni to name a building for him.[294] Though they vehemently protested his decision, Johnson weathered the criticism.

---

[293] KMP, chapter 13 "Washington in the year 1880." 101.

[294] Logan, *The First Hundred Year.* 348. As late as 2008, Gloria Miller Clark, continued to advocate for recognition denied her grandfather. The member of the Class of 1946 refused to make additional donations the University until something would be done for her grandfather.

Miller's funeral was held on January 2, 1940, in Howard's Andrew Rankin Chapel at the University. Bishop Monroe H. Davis conducted the invocation, and Reverend W.A.C. Hughes delivered the Bible message. Reverend J. Francis Gregory delivered the eulogy, and Walter H. Brooks delivered the benediction. The University Glee Club performed two selections, and Music Professor Louia Vaughn Jones performed a solo.

Hughes was among several former students and colleagues who eulogized Miller in these words:

> For some weeks I have noticed the earthly house, in which Mr. Miller lived, gradually giving way. The roof ragged, the sides bulged, the foundation crumbled the other day and the structure collapsed. But when it fell, Mr. Miller was not caught in it; he escaped unhurt. With his mental and spiritual faculties intact, he was gone to a life unhampered by human frailties in a sphere as wide as eternity.[295]

He opened by quoting the Apostle Paul's letter to the church at Philippi. Then, stating of Miller, offered:

> The man who knows God has the best that the world can give. Kelly Miller knew GOD. He was not a church man. Domination, organization, ritual, creed, or formal acts of

---

[295] KMP, Box 71-7, scrapbook. The source contains several clippings arranged possibly by May or her Kelly junior. Many of the statements are in undated clippings.

worship seemed not [to] engage him but he impressed all of us with his simple obedience to the great ethical imperatives of our religious faith... He was kinder than most people. Something made him see truth a little more clearly...Something exalted his vision, broadened his outlook, and stimulated his enthusiasm for that which was good and righteous. Something made him humble enough to be the friend and companion of children. Something made him love his home and his endearing, affectionate "Mamma" will be a precious memory forever...I loved the simplicity of Kelly Miller. I think this was his greatest charm... He loved the countryside, country people, their ways, their homes, their gardens, and their simplicity. Nothing delighted him more than to hear these people tell their Christian experiences and sing songs they loved.[296]

D.O.W. Holmes, another former student and President of Morgan State College, offered remarks on Miller, the Educator:

His golden tongue, so effective in debate, so keen in criticism, so powerful in defense, is silent. His facile pen is put aside, the pen which wrote so much with success, so little in vain. His eager heart so kindly and so

---

[296] KMP, Box 71-7, scrapbook.

courageous is still. These things are true. But to those of us who knew him well, who studied under him, who worked with him and who fought battles in his company or against him, to us the idea of Kelly Miller dead is unthinkable. As long as we remember the struggle of its advocates for the higher education for Negroes, so long will the memory of this man remain green. And while there is a Howard University or a Howard Alumnus, Kelly Miller will live here at this place and throughout the world wherever the name is known... A great college teacher must be to his students a rich source of knowledge or a drill master or a great inspiration or some combination of these. Kelly was all three; but to me, as to a great majority of his discipline, he was first of all the inspirer who opened our eyes and fired our ambitions. He was at first a teacher of mathematics and as such was very exacting... I consider that his lecture tours, as a missionary of higher education for Negroes, constitute his most important and permanent contribution to education. When the esteem for the Negro college was at its lowest point, due largely to the dramatization of the then new industrial education movement, Kelly Miller took to the road every summer for over ten years and, living as it were on the country and from one end of this land to the other, he preached the gospel of college education in city and town and crossroads, in churches and lodge halls and schoolhouses... It is easy to underestimate the power of example. Kelly Miller taught Negro youth by example the importance of decent living, of high thinking, and of publishing their thoughts... To those of us who were his pupils either in the narrow sense of the classroom or in the broad sense of the world's arena, Kelly Miller was the teacher, the Dean, the sage, the scholar, the like of which seldom passes this way... Of such stuff is immortality made.[297]

Leaders such as Mary Church Terrell, Mary McLeod Bethune, Nannie Helen Burroughs, Ambrose Caliver, St. Elmo Brady, Albert Cassell, Carl Murphy, and Congressman Arthur Mitchell attended the service. Active pallbearers included Charles Thompson, James Herring, Major Campbell Johnson, James A. Scott, Merrill H. Curtis, and Frederick D. Wilkinson. Members of Alpha Phi Alpha Fraternity, to which Miller belonged, were honorary pallbearers. There were additional honorary pallbearers from the Epsilon Chapter of Sigma Pi Phi and Howard notables such as Emmett J. Scott, Alain Locke, Charles Wesley, and others such as Judge James Cobb, L.M. Hershaw, Howard H. Long.

The *Journal of Negro History* published an obituary by Carter G. Woodson that read in part:

---

[297] Ibid.

His life touched so many ramifications of that of his race and country, however, that he may be truthfully designated as one of the important men of the entire country. He represented in a great measure that generation of enterprising Negroes who were inspired by the missionary teachers from the North to prepared for service among their lowly people... His analytical mind, then, centered on the race problem. He ceased to teach mathematics and took up sociology. On every important public question concerning the Negro he delivered a lecture or wrote a pamphlet. His style was highly literary. Because of his commanding position at Howard, what he produced was widely read. He lectured more extensively probably than any Negro who has ever lived, and he thus demonstrated the capacity of the Negro to profit by higher education at the time when others sought to restrict the race to the study of fundamentals and practical pursuits.[298]

The Alpha Phi Alpha Fraternity ran a memorial tribute in the February 1940 issue of their magazine, *The Sphinx*,

Tribute to Brother Dr. Kelly Miller...A powerful pen is dry. Kelly Miller's life spans

---

[298] Carter G. Woodson, "Kelly Miller (1863-1939)" *Journal of Negro History* Volume 25, number 1, January 1940, 137.

the Negro's struggle for integration into the American ideal. An uncompromising warrior against the barrier of race he was the astute social philosopher who found the good in every disadvantage. Countless men and women gained their inspiration from Kelly Miller... His wit smoothed out many of the idealistic entanglements of the youthful architects. His wisdom was sealed in the cornerst[one] of the General Organization of Alpha Phi Alpha Fraternity.[299]

The Black Press ran numerous death announcements and dedicated pages for notable people to write tributes to Miller. A front-page headline read: 'Kelly Miller Dead, The Silver Pen Silenced." One paper dedicated an entire page to famous African Americans under the banner heading "Nation's Leaders Pay Tribute to Kelly Miller." Colleagues, friends, and former students, including Dr. Channing Tobias Nannie Helen Burroughs, memorialized him. Dr. Eugene Kinckle Jones, who wrote on behalf of the National Urban League.

> His service to his fellow has been such as to merit lasting respect and devotion. Our sorrow is merged with that of his host of friends and admirers who sympathize with you and your family in your loss.

---

[299] KMP, Box 71-7, scrapbook.

Burroughs saw Miller as "the Sage of the Potomac."

And one of the educational rocks, in a weary land, upon which the colored race has been building for over fifty years - has gone to his reward. Soon after the nation laid down the sword that won our physical emancipation, he dedicated himself and took up his pen in the cause of intellectual freedom and fundamental human liberties. He was gifted with a perspicacious mind. He dedicated it to freedom, justice, and goodwill. He walked with Kings but lost not the common touch. He was a Crusader. He died with his armor on.[300]

Longtime friend and Black Press colleague Carl Murphy of the *Afro-American* spoke well of Miller in his memorial.

In the years when Howard's preparatory school students outnumbered those in the college, it was Dean Miller who carried the message by way of the lecture platform, to hundreds of communities. Most beloved professor - he persuaded more college students to enroll than any other living man, and today is the most beloved Howard professor. They loved him for his never-failing good nature, his insight into common

---

[300] KMP, Box 71-7, scrapbook.

problems his love of learning the simplicity of his reasoning, his personal interest in his students, his frequent visits to their dormitory rooms, where, he was always welcome, and his constant insistence upon the relation of scholarship to public problems... He was a prince in private morals and personal integrity, frugal and a hard worker. Simple in dress and habit, he never wore a watch or a ring his clear, yet forceful. He occupied a place midway between the conservatism of Washington and the radicalness of DuBois. The former argued for industrial education, the latter for college education. Miller saw both as necessary, and the world has come to see that he was right. [301]

Educator and journalist, William Pickens referred to Miller as a balanced man who sought to understand the world and contribute to its betterment such that,

Kelly Miller's life was so outstandingly full of good...He was a prolific writer...Many of those who respected and admired him, did not always agree with his philosophy – often disagreed with it... For an elderly man, he was much attracted to the new and unusual – and yet was never "radical." The spirit of compromise breathed through his style... He has a definite and permanent place in the

---

[301] Ibid.

history of his race and his country. He will long be remembered. His death is the closing scene in a colorful and unique career.[302]

Congressman Arthur Mitchell introduced a note in the Congressional Record in which he sought to memorialize Miller's influence on the nation.

> His life was purely unselfish, and he lived primarily for the good he could do mankind. His contribution in the building of substantial citizenship among Negroes and in lessening race prejudice... During my tenure in office as Congressman, it was my custom to call him in consultation about every important question involving the interest of the race. He was always enthusiastically anxious to do what he could to lessen race friction and to put the case of the Negro squarely before the country on its merit. In his passing I sustained a great personal loss for it was upon his shoulders that I leaned more heavily than upon the shoulders of any other leader in the country. Although he was weak [toward] the end. Being a great patriot, in his illness, as in his days of health, he thought of others and his country before he thought of himself... The largest contribution made by this unselfish and untiring patriot is bound to live and express itself in the fruit

---

[302] William Pickens, Kelly Miller, *Chicago Sunday Bee* [1940] that KMP, Box 71-7, scrapbook.

borne out in the lives of those who are to live after him. His passing is a distinct loss to the Nation.[303]

Miller participated in numerous events that placed him in the public eye.[304] Yet, he lived to improve the conditions of African American people. His influence resonated throughout the halls of Congress, and he would find himself involved in numerous causes that advanced that end.[305]

George Lightfoot summed up Miller as representing the spirit and highest ideals of his alma

---

[303] KMP, Box 71-7, scrapbook.

[304] Such as the Hearing before the House Judiciary Committee, June 18, 1935; Committee of 12; Community Chest; Conference on American Relations with China; Conference on Negro Education in North Carolina; Shaw University 1923 Consumer's Conference on Farm Problems, Washington, D.C. January 25, 1936; Council of Negro Women; Democratic National Campaign Headquarters; Epsilon Boule, Family Services Association; Friends of Charlotte Hunter; Hampton-Howard University Alumni Association; Instructive Visiting Nurse Society; National Association for the Advancement of Colored People; the NAACP Press Service; National Conference on Colored Work; National Negro Congress; National Negro Non-Partisan League; National Urban League; National Youth Administration; Negro Sanhedrin; Non-Partisan Conference; Peabody School; Phelps-Stokes Fund Program for the Improvement of Race Relations Presented to the Governor's Conference; South Sociological Congress, 1919; Public School of the District of Columbia Report of Committee on Coordination of the Work of State and Independent Schools, 1923; Sigma Pi Phi, Zeta Boule, 1925; Urban League; Washington Conference on the Racial Question, 1924; Works Progress Administration; the Phyllis Wheatley YWCA.

[305] For example, he belonged to organizations such as the All-Race Conference; Alpha Phi Alpha; American Negro Academy; Bethel Historical and Literary Society; Central Union Mission; Citizens Committee on Race Segregation; and the Commission on Negro Affairs.

mater's motto, "veritas et utilitas de et Rei publicae" — truth and service for God and the Republic. He lived the life of an unrepentant daysman who taught, lectured, published, and aligned himself with men and women who sought to lift the race out of ignorance, second-class citizenship, and strife.

Epilogue

My Father

With springtime my father comes alive
In the lilac bush he planted
At the kitchen door that we
Might hear the plain voice
Of Walt Whitman burst
Through the bloom
In the season's green-tipped
Hedge, he lives again.

The Clearing and Beyond, May Miller,

The egregious omission of Miller from the canon of African American scholarship is not mysterious. His daysman philosophy consigned him to the unappreciated middle ground between radicals and conservatives. Moreover, the schism between him and Johnson muted his influence during the golden age of Howard University, where his deepest roots were planted. The marginalization and lack of analysis of this private, public, and polemic thinker further relegated knowledge of his contributions to the periphery, For as Edward Robinson has noted:

> In a fundamentally racist culture that could tolerate only a limited number of black exemplars, portrayals of America's past commonly ignore these black citizens who failed to capture the limelight, and the nation thereby loses the thread of continuity that ties

an effective present gone. This neglect shrouds those who contributed significantly to the republic's progress even as it foreshortens our understanding... With these narrow perspectives and limited consequences, black Americans who inhabited the less lofty reaches of American society fall into historical oblivion, and their contributions to the national culture remain unexamined and uncelebrated.[306]

After the failure of the Negro Sanhedrin and ideological differences with rising thinkers, Miller's popularity waned though he continued to influence the topics of his day. His hesitancy to pen his autobiography highlights the fact that he never intended to become immortal. Still, his omission from the academic canon represents benign neglect.

Still, Miller's influence on the city of Washington is evident. In the 1940s, The Washington Alley Dwelling Authority started construction on the 169-unit Kelly Miller dwellings. The complex is situated at the convergence of Fourth, Fifth, V, W, and Oakdale Streets in the city's northwest quadrant, within feet of his campus housing in the shadow of Howard University. In 1950, the city named a junior high school in his honor. When the school was dedicated, Mary Church Terrell offered:

---

[306] Edward Robinson, *To Lift Up My Race: The Essential Writings of Samuel Robert Cassius.* Knoxville: University of Tennessee Press, 2008, xiv.

> I shall refer to Professor Miller only as a friend of many years standing... I shall refer to [him] as a friend which whom I used to often joke... [he] was aware of the faults and defects of both the government and the human beings in it. But in commenting upon those faults and defects he did not plunge us precipitately into the abyss of despair. It was his habit to present the conditions under which we were then living in such a way that we felt in looking toward the future we had a good reason and a perfect right to hope in spite of the obstacles which confronted us.[307]

Though the remain fixtures of the city's landscape, few students or residents know anything about their namesake.

In a 1904 article about Frederick Douglass, Miller laid out what he considered the mark of o a great leader:

> [The] highest function of a great name is to serve as an example and as a perpetual source of inspiration to the young who are to come after him.... [Douglass] built no institution and laid no material foundation. True, he left us no showy tabernacles of clay. He did not aspire to be the pontifex maximus, or boss mechanic of the colored race. The greatest things this of this

---

[307] Mary Church Terrell papers, Box 102-3 folder 102 speech "Remarks at the Dedication of Kelly Miller Junior High School".

world are not made with hands but reside in truth, righteousness, and love.[308]

He never desired greatness for himself, but viewed himself in line with men like Douglass, who lived to encourage and inspire the youth. He effectively used his talents where they were most needed.

Throughout his life, Miller garnered several titles, among them World's Greatest Unknown Negro, Straddler, Belated Rationalist, Contemptible Cur, Old Turk, Sage of the Potomac, and Lighting Calculator. Regardless of these labels, he strove to communicate truth grounded in moral accountability. He believed that education made men wiser and more efficient, but that intellect should not exert sovereignty over morality. For him, though education could afford upward progression, it did not make a whole person. Being an ideological and spiritual daysman by birth order and generation, he believed that the intangible aspects of spirit, character, and purpose were essential in forming a productive member of society and race. He preached his unique doctrine of education and morality wherever one or one hundred African American children could be inspired.

Theologian Reinhold Niebuhr asserted that "the final wisdom of life requires not the annulment of incongruity but the achievement of serenity within and

---

[308] Kelly Miller, "Fredrick Douglass," *Voice of the Negro* 1:10 October 1904.

above it."[309] Miller's life as a delicate balance of a daysman dedicated to racial uplift through mediating and harmonizing disparate ideas is worthy of recognition and mining.

---

[309] Reinhold Niebuhr, "Happiness, Prosperity and Virtue" in *The Irony of American History*, University of Chicago, IL. 1952, 63.

Chronology of Miller's Life

July 18, 1863	Born in Winnsboro, South Carolina, the sixth child of Kelly Elizabeth Roberts Miller.
1878	Admitted to the Fairfield Institute at the age of 15.
1880	Awarded a scholarship to Howard University's Normal Department.
November 2, 1880	Registered as a student at Howard University.
1882-1884	Worked a variety of jobs to supplement his tuition.
1882	Completed the Howard University's Normal Department.
1884-1889	Appointed a clerkship in the U.S. Pension Office earned $900.00 a year.
1886	Received a B.A. degree in liberal studies from Howard University.

1886	Purchased a 200-acre farm for his parents as a graduation gift for the family.
1886-1890	Met Frederick Douglass, John Mercer Langston, and Blanche K. Bruce.
1886-1889	First African American admitted to Johns Hopkins University where he did post-graduate work in mathematics and physics toward a Ph.D.
1886-1913	Started corresponding with Booker T. Washington on racial uplift, industrial education, Howard University, and other topics.
1889	Attended Johns Hopkins University, but financial support from family in South Carolina forced him to leave.
1889-1890	Taught mathematics at the M Street High School in Washington, D.C.

1890	Appointed first alumni professor of mathematics at Howard University.
July 17, 1894	Married Annie Mae Butler with whom he fathered five children: Kelly Jr., Isaac Newton, May, Irene, Paul Butler.
1895-1925	Earned national reputation for lecturing and writing about race relations and promoting higher education and emerged a notable race man.
1896	Often spoke in meetings of the Bethel Literary and Historical Society.
December 18, 1896	Miller, John Cromwell, Paul Laurence Dunbar, and Walter Hayson accepted Alexander Crummell invitation to form the society which would be formally named the American Negro Academy.
1898	Openly criticized Washington's Atlanta Exposition speech and accommodationist ideology.

1901	Contributed a chapter entitled "The Education of the Negro" to the *Report of the United States Bureau of Education*.
	Received an A.M. degree from Howard University.
1903	Wrote an article in response to the schism between Washington and Dubois that derided both for being too narrow and established Miller as harmonizer, later a straddler, regarding the means of solving the race problem.
	Received an LL. D degree from Howard University.
1904	Served as secretary for the "Committee of 12," the direct forerunner to the NAACP.
1906-1912	Recruited heavily for Howard University traveling cross country lecturing in high schools and churches about the value of higher education.
1907	Appointed interim Dean of the College of Arts and Sciences at Howard.

January 21, 1908	Appointed Dean of College of Arts and Sciences. Inducted in Alpha Phi Alpha, Beta Chapter during their first national meeting on Howard's campus.
1908	His first book *Race Adjustment* a collection of essays that examined education, religion, gender, and the race problem was published.
1914	The Moorland Foundation was established at Howard University as the first step towards the dream of the National Negro Museum and Library. Miller's second book, *Out of the House of Bondage.* published.
1917	Authored *Progress and Achievements of the Colored People: Containing the Story of the Wonderful Advancement of the Colored Americans: A Handbook for Self-Improvement Which Leads to Greater Success.*
1918	Wrote his fourth book *An Appeal to Conscience; America's. Code of Caste a Disgrace to Democracy.* His questioning the American system

	of democracy that discriminated against African Americans. impugned the President and led to investigation by the Military Intelligence branch of the Army.
1919	Wrote his fifth book *Kelly Miller's History of the World War for Human Rights, Being an Intensely Human and Brilliant Account of the World War, and Why and for What Purpose America and the Allies Are Fighting, and the Important Part Taken by the Negro, Including the Horrors and Wonders of Modern Warfare, the New and Strange Devices, Etc.*
1924	Organized the Sanhedrin/All Race Conference in Chicago that was attended by over 300 delegates from over 50 African American organizations. Wrote his sixth book *The Everlasting Stain*.
1925	President Durkee abolishes the junior college and bisects the College of Arts and Sciences, demoting Miller from dean to professor.

1932-1933	Joined the Harriet Tubman Society for the Blind with Alain Locke.
1934	Retired from Howard University.
1935-1937	Started to collect information and funding for the writing of his autobiography.
December 19, 1939	Miller has a heart attack.
December 29, 1939	Miller died at age 76.
January 2, 1940	Funeralized at Andrew Rankin Memorial Chapel, Howard University. Interred at Lincoln Memorial Cemetery in Washington.
1947	Howard University purchased the former private Miller home as the Kelly Miller House to use as off-campus housing for women students.
1949	Kelly Miller Middle School opens in Washington, DC.

1985	Dedication of the Fairfield Institute, Kelly Miller historical marker by the Fairfield County Historical Society.
1993	Miller posthumously inducted into South Carolina Academy of Authors.
2009	An issue of the *Journal of Blacks in Higher Education* was dedicated to Miller.

Bibliography

Sixth Triennial Meeting of the College Alumni Association of Howard University. Washington, DC: Howard University Press, 1892.

Banks, William M. *Black Intellectuals: Race and Responsibility in American Life.* New York: W. W. Norton & Company, 1999.

Blackwell, James E. *Black Sociologists: Historical and Contemporary Perspectives.* Chicago: University of Chicago Press, 1974.

Bond, Horace Mann. *Black American Scholars: A Study of Their Beginnings.* Detroit: Balamp Publishing, 1972.

Bracey, John H., Jr., August Meier and Elliott Rudwick, eds. *The Black Sociologists: The First Half Century.* Belmont, CA: Wadsworth Publishing, 1971.

Coulibaly, Sylvie. "Kelly Miller, 1895–1939: Portrait of an African American Intellectual." PhD diss., Emory University, 2006.

Cromwell, Adelaide M. *Unveiled Voices, Unvarnished Memories: The Cromwell Family in Slavery and Segregation, 1692–1972.* Columbia, MO: University of Missouri, 2007.

Cruse, Harold. *The Crisis of the Negro Intellectual: A Historical Analysis of the Failure of Black Leadership.* New York: William Morrow, 1967.

Cruse, Harold. *Plural but Equal: A Critical Study of Blacks and Minorities and America's Plural Society.* New York: William Morrow, 1987.

Davis, John P. "A Survey of the Problems of the Negro Under the New Deal." *The Journal of Negro Education* 5:1 (January 1936), 3–12.

Diner, Steven J. *A Very Different Age: Americans of the Progressive Era*. New York: Hill and Wang, 1998.

Dyson, Walter. *Howard University: The Capstone of Negro Education. A History: 1867–1940*. Washington, DC: The Graduate School, 1941.

Eisenberg, Bernard. "Kelly Miller: The Negro Leader as a Marginal Man." *The Journal of Negro History* 45:3 (July 1960), 182–197.

Foner, Philip S. and James S. Allen, eds. *American Communism and Black Americans: A Documentary History, 1919–1929*. Philadelphia: Temple University Press, 1987.

Fossett, Judith Jackson and Jeffrey A. Tucker, eds. *Race Consciousness: African-American Studies for the New Century*. New York: New York University Press, 1997.

Franklin, John Hope. *Mirror to America: The Autobiography of John Hope Franklin*. New York: Farrar, Straus, Giroux, 2005.

Franklin, John Hope and Alfred A. Moss, Jr. *From Slavery to Freedom: A History of African Americans*, eighth edition. Boston: McGraw Hill, 2000.

Franklin, John Hope and August Meier, eds. *Black Leaders of the Twentieth Century*. Urbana, IL: University of Illinois Press, 1982.

Franklin, V.P. *Living Our Stories, Telling Our Truths: Autobiography and the Making of the African-American Intellectual Tradition*. New York: Scribner, 1995.

Franklin, V. P. and Bettye Collier-Thomas. "Biography, Race Vindication, and African American Intellectuals." *The Journal of African American History* 87, (Winter 2002), 160–174.

Fredrickson, George M. *The Black Image in the White Mind: The Debate on Afro-American Character and Destiny, 1817–1914*. New York: Harper & Row, 1971.

———. *Black Liberation: A Comparative History of Black Ideologies in the United States and South Africa*. New York: Oxford University Press, 1995.

Garrett, Romeo B. *The Presidents and the Negro*. Washington, DC: Associated Publishers, 1982.

Gatewood, Willard B. *Aristocrats of Color: The Black Elite, 1880–1920*. Bloomington, IN: Indiana University Press, 1990.

Gilman, Charlotte Perkins. "The Duty of Surplus Women" *Woman's Journal*, May 12, 1900.

Grandison, Kenrick Ian. "Negotiated Space: The Black College Campus as a Cultural Record of Postbellum America." *American Quarterly* 5 3 (September 1999), 529–579.

Green, Constance McLaughlin. *The Secret City: A History of Race Relations in the Nation's Capital*. Princeton, NJ: Princeton University Press, 1967.

Harlan, Louis R. *Booker T. Washington: The Making of a Black Leader, 1856–1901*. New York: Oxford University Press, 1972.

———. *Booker T. Washington: The Wizard of Tuskegee, 1901–1915*. New York: Oxford University Press, 1983.

———, ed. *The Booker T. Washington Papers*. Urbana, IL: University of Illinois Press, 1972.

Harrell, James A. "Negro Leadership in the Election Year 1936." *The Journal of Southern History* 34:4 (November 1968), 546–564.

Hawkins, Hugh, *Booker T. Washington and His Critics: The Problem of Negro Leadership.* Boston: D. C. Heath and Company, 1962.

Hughes, C. Alvin. "The Negro Sanhedrin Movement." *The Journal of Negro History* 69:1 (Winter 1984), 1–13.

Kerlin, Robert T. *The Voice Of The Negro, 1919 (1920).* New York: E. P. Dutton & Company, 1920.

Keith, Verna M. and Cedric Herring. "Skin Tone and Stratification in the Black Community." *American Journal of Sociology,* Vol. 97, No. 3 (Nov., 1991), pp. 760-778

Lewis, David Levering. *W.E.B. DuBois: Biography of a Race, 1868–1919.* New York: Henry Holt and Co., 1993.

_____. *W.E.B. DuBois: The Fight for Equality and the American Century, 1919–1963.* New York: Henry Holt and Co., 2000.

Logan, Rayford W. *Howard University: The First Hundred Years, 1867–1967.* New York: New York University Press, 1969.

_____. *The Negro in American Life and Thought.* New York: Da Capo Press, 1997.

Logan, Rayford W., and Michael R. Winston, eds. *Dictionary of American Negro Biography.* New York: Norton, 1982.

Luker, Ralph E. *The Social Gospel in Black and White: American Racial Reform, 1885–1912.* Chapel Hill, NC: University of North Carolina Press, 1991.

Marks, Carole. *Farewell—We're Good and Gone: The Great Black Migration.* Bloomington, IN: University Indiana Press, 1989.

McGruder, Larry. "Kelly Miller: The Life and Thoughts of a Black Intellectual, 1863–1939." PhD dissertation, Miami University, 1984.

McKinney, Richard I. *Mordecai, the Man and His Message: The Story of Mordecai Wyatt Johnson.* Washington, DC: Howard University Press, 1997.

———. "Mordecai, the Man and His Message: The Story of Mordecai Wyatt Johnson." PhD dissertation, Howard University, 1997.

McKinstry, Jessie M. "The Role of the Presbyterian Church in Providing a System of Education for Negroes in Winnsboro, South Carolina (Fairfield County) After the Civil War." Unpublished manuscript. Inez Parker Moore papers.

McMaster, Fitz Hugh. *History of Fairfield County, South Carolina, from Before the White Man Came to 1942.* Spartanburg, SC: The Reprint Company Publishers, 2007.

Megginson, W. J. *African American Life in South Carolina's Upper Piedmont, 1780–1900.* Columbia, SC: University of South Carolina Press, 2006.

Meier, August. *Negro Thought in America, 1880–1915.* Ann Arbor, MI: University of Michigan Press, 1967.

———. "The Racial and Educational Philosophy of Kelly Miller, 1895–1915." *The Journal of Negro Education* 29:2 (Spring 1960), 121–127.

Miller, Kelly. *An Appeal to Conscience; America's. Code of Caste a Disgrace to Democracy,* Berkeley, CA: University of California Libraries, 1920.

———. "The Choice of a Profession." *Howard University Record* 15:1 (January 1921), 152–155.

———. "The Choice of a Profession." *Howard University Record* 15:2 (March 1921), 322–326.

_____. "Education for Manhood." *Kelly Miller's Monographic Magazine*, Vol. 1. Washington, DC: Kelly Miller, 1913.

_____. *From Servitude to Service: Being the Old South Lectures on the History and Work of Southern Institutions for the Education of the Negro.* Boston: American Unitarian Association, 1905.

_____. "Howard: The National Negro University" in Alain Locke, ed., *The New Negro: An Interpretation*, New York: Albert & Charles Boni, 1925, 312–322.

_____. "Is the American Negro to Remain Black or Become Bleached?" *South Atlantic Quarterly* 25:3 (July 1926).

_____. "Moral Pedagogy." *Education*, (November 1913).

_____. *The Negro Sanhedrin: A Call to Conference.* Washington, DC: Kelly Miller, 1923.

_____ "An Oblique Prayer." *The Voice of the Negro*, 2 (November 1905).

_____. *Out of the House of Bondage.* New York: The Neale Publishing Company, 1914.

_____. "The Political Plight of the Negro." *Kelly Miller's Monographic Magazine*, 1 (1913).

_____. "The Primary Needs of the Negro Race: An Address Delivered Before the Alumni Association of the Hampton Normal and Agriculture Institute." Washington, DC: Howard University Press, 1899.

_____. *Race Adjustment: The Everlasting Stain.* New York: Neale Publishing Company, 1908.

_____. "Religion and Race." S.l.: s.n. 1926.

_____. "The Reorganization of the Higher Education of the Negro in Light of Changing Conditions." *The Journal of Negro Education* 5:3 (July 1936), 484–494.

_____. "A Reply to Tom Watson—Is the Negro Inherently Inferior?" *The Voice of the Negro*, 2 (August 1905).

_____. "Roosevelt and the Negro." *The Voice of the Negro*, 1 (September 1904).

_____. "Segregation: The Caste System and the Civil Service." Washington, DC: Howard University Press, s.d.

_____. "A Word to the Twentieth Century Negro." *The Voice of the Negro* 2: (January 1905).

Miller, Kelly and Joseph R. Gay. *Progress and Achievements of the Colored People: Containing the Story of the Wonderful Advancement of the Colored Americans: A Handbook for Self-Improvement Which Leads to Greater Success*. Washington, DC: Austin Jenkins, 1917.

Moore, Jacqueline M. *Leading the Race: The Transformation of the Black Elite in the Nation's Capital, 1880–1920*. Charlottesville, VA: University of Virginia Press, 1999.

Morgan, Julia Boublitz. "Son of a Slave." *Johns Hopkins Magazine*, (June 1981), 20–26.

Moses, Wilson Jeremiah. *Alexander Crummell: A Study of Civilization and Discontent*. New York: Oxford University Press, 1989.

_____. *The Golden Age of Black Nationalism, 1850–1925*. New York: Oxford University Press, 1988.

Moss, Alfred A., Jr. *The American Negro Academy: Voice of the Talented Tenth*. Baton Rouge, LA: Louisiana State University Press, 1981.

Muse, Clifford L., Jr. "Howard University and the Federal Government During the Presidential Administrations of Herbert Hoover and Franklin D. Roosevelt, 1928–1945." *The Journal of Negro History* 76:1/4 (Winter–Autumn 1991), 1–20.

Nelson, H. Viscount. *The Rise and Fall of Modern Black Leadership: Chronicle of a Twentieth Century Tragedy.* Lanham, MD: University Press of America, 2003.

Newby, I.A. *Jim Crow's Defense: Anti-Negro Thought in America, 1900–1930.* Baton Rouge: Louisiana State University Press, 1965.

Nieman, Donald G. *The African American Family in the South, 1861–1900.* New York: Garland Publishing Inc., 1994.

Obear, Katharine Theus. *Through the Years in Old Winnsboro.* Spartanburg, SC: The Reprint Company Publishers, 1980.

Parrish, Charles H. "Color Names and Color Notions." *The Journal of Negro Education* 15:1 (Winter 1946), 13–20.

Record, Wilson. "Negro Intellectuals and Negro Movements; Some Methodological Notes." *The Journal of Negro Education* 24:2 (Spring 1955), 106–112.

Roberts, Samuel K. "Kelly Miller and Thomas Dixon, Jr. on Blacks in American Civilization." *Phylon* 41:2 (1980), 202–209.

Robinson, Edward J., ed. *To Lift Up My Race: The Essential Writings of Samuel Robert Cassius.* Knoxville, TN: University of Tennessee Press, 2008.

Rudwick, Elliott M. "Race Leadership Struggle: Background of the Boston Riot of 1903." *The Journal of Negro Education* 31:1 (Winter 1962), 16–24.

Salzman, Jack, David Lionel Smith, and Cornel West, eds. *Encyclopedia of African-American Culture and History*. New York: Simon & Schuster, 1996.

Sernett, Milton C. *Bound for the Promised Land: African American Religion and the Great Migration*. Durham, NC: Duke University Press, 1997.

Smith, Alfred E. "America's Greatest Unknown Negro." *Negro Digest* 8 (April 1950), 42–46.

Smith, Billy. "The Late Dean – Kelly." *Silhouette Pictorial* (March 1940).

Span, Christopher M. "'I Must Learn Now or Not at All:' Social and Cultural Capital in the Educational Initiatives of Formerly Enslaved African Americans in Mississippi, 1862–1869." *The Journal of African American History* 87:2 (Spring 2002), 196–205.

Spencer, Thomas T. "The Good Neighbor League Colored Committee and the 1936 Democratic Presidential Campaign." *The Journal of Negro History* 63:4 (October 1978), 307–316.

Stanfield, John H., II. "A Neglected Chapter in the History of the Scholarship of Teaching Sociology." *Teaching Sociology* 31:4 (October 2003), 361–365.

Stokes, Richard T. "An Historical Analysis of Afro-American Higher Education with Special Emphasis on the Educational Ideas of Kelly Miller." MA thesis, Howard University, 1974.

Thomas, William B. "Black Intellectuals' Critique of Early Mental Testing: A Little-Known Saga of the 1920s." *American Journal of Education* 90:3 (May 1982), 258–292.

Thompson, John L. *History and Views of Colored Officers Training Camp: for 1917 at Fort Des Moines, Iowa*. Des Moines, IA: The Bystander, 1917.

Thorpe, Earl E. *The Mind of the Negro: An Intellectual History of Afro-Americans*. Westport, CT: Negro Universities Press, 1970.

Tindall, George Brown. *South Carolina Negroes, 1877–1900*. Columbia, SC: University of South Carolina Press, 1952.

Toll, William. "Free Men, Freedmen, and Race: Black Social Theory in the Gilded Age." *The Journal of Southern History* 44:4 (November 1978), 571–596.

Turner, James and C. Steven McGann. "Black Studies as an Integral Tradition in African-American Intellectual History." *The Journal of Negro Education* 49:1 (Winter 1980), 52–59.

Verharen, Charles C. "A Core Curriculum at Historically Black Colleges and Universities: An Immodest Proposal." *The Journal of Negro Education* 62:2 (Spring 1993), 190–203.

Watkins, William H. *The White Architects of Black Education: Ideology and Power in America, 1865–1954*. New York: The Teachers College Press, 2001.

Weiss, Nancy J. *The National Urban League, 1910–1940*. New York: Oxford University Press, 1974.

Williams, Charles H. *Negro Soldiers in World War I: The Human Side*. New York: AMS Press, 1970.

Williams, Heather Andrea. "'Clothing Themselves in Intelligence': The Freedpeople, Schooling, and Northern Teachers, 1861–1871." *The Journal of African American History* 87, 'New Perspectives on African American Educational History' (Autumn 2002), 372–389.

Winston, Michael. *Education for Freedom: The Leadership of Mordecai Wyatt Johnson, Howard University, 1926-1960: A Documentary Tribute to Celebrate the Fiftieth Anniversary of the Election of Mordecai W. Johnson as President of Howard University.* Washington, DC: Howard University Archives, Moorland-Spingarn Research Center, 1976.

Wish, Harvey. "Negro Education and the Progressive Movement." *The Journal of Negro History* 49:3 (July 1964), 184–200.

Wright, W. D. "The Thought and Leadership of Kelly Miller." *Phylon* 39:2 (1978), 180–192.

Zaluda, Scott. "Lost Voices of the Harlem Renaissance: Writing Assigned at Howard University, 1919–31." *College Composition and Communication* 50 2 (December 1998), 232–257.

Archival Sources

Emory University, Manuscript, Archives and Rare Book Library
    Kelly Miller papers
    May Miller Sullivan papers

Howard University, Moorland Spingarn Research Center
    Kelly Miller papers
    Rayford Logan papers
    Lucy Slowe papers
    Walter Loving papers
    Joel Spingarn papers
    Thomas Montgomery Gregory papers
    Ralph Bunche oral history collection

The Johns Hopkins University Hamburger Archives
    Record Group 13.010, Office of the Registrar, subgroup 1, series 2. Student file of Kelly Miller

Johnson C. Smith, Inez Parker Moore Archives
    President H. L. McCrorey Collection

Newspapers

African American, Baltimore edition

African American, Washington edition

Bystander Iowa

Norfolk New Journal and Guide

Philadelphia Tribune

Index

Alumni Association, iii, 18, 88, 230, 241, 246
American Negro Academy, ii, 98, 108-112, 218, 283, 292
Archduke Franz Ferdinand, 161

Baker, Newton D., 164, 167
Bethune, Mary McLeod, 4, 92, 124, 128n., 129, 139, 140n., 160, 277
Biddle University, 37, 38, 54, 65
Black Officer's Training Camp, 173-189
Brawley, Benjamin, 156, 158, 159
Brown, Charlotte Hawkins, ii, 139, 140
Bunche, Ralph, 187, 309
Burroughs, Nannie Helen, ii, 4, 92, 137, 138, 139, 160, 277, 279, 280

Cardoza, Francis, 85, 86, 111
Carver, George Washington, 204
Churchill, Winston, 165n.
Cleveland, Grover, 13, 78, 79
Colored Yeowomen, iii, 171, 172-173
Community Chest, the, 252, 255, 257, 258, 261n., 283n.

Crummell, Alexander, i., 21, 92, 108, 109, 110, 111, 160, 292

Darwin, Charles, 2, 164
DePriest, Oscar, 239, 259, 260
DuBois, William Edward Burghardt (W. E. B.), viii, x, xiii, 4, 5, 6, 14, 92, 93-103, 214, 215, 248, 281, 293
Dunbar, Paul Lawrence, i, 92, 108, 109, 110, 292
Durkee, J. Stanley, 18, 189-203, 229, 232, 238n., 295

Edison, Thomas Alva, 2
Emancipation, xii, 19, 22, 23, 29, 58, 64, 80, 81, 105, 128, 130, 280
Epsilon Boule Sigma Pi Phi Fraternity, 129

Fairfield Institute, 61-72, 290
Frazier, E. Franklin, 175

Garvey, Marcus, 6, 205, 206, 214, 215, 248
Gilman, Charlotte Perkins, 132
Great Depression, 12, 233, 265 267
Great Migration, 12, 204, 205
Griffith, D.W., 2

Grimke, Francis, i, 101, 102, 103n., 143
Harding, Warren G., 12, 127, 190
Harriet Tubman Society for the Blind, 251-258, 296
Hoover, Herbert, 249, 252, 259, 262
Houston, Charles Hamilton, 187
Howard University Board of Trustees, 154
Hughes, Langston, 131, 156n.
Hunter, Charlotte, 251, 255, 256, 257, 283n.

Ickes, Harold, 235, 239, 240, 241n., 250

Jim Crow era, 11, 79, 97, 164, 193, 253, 265, 266,
Johns Hopkins University, 60, 83n., 84, 85n., 291, 309
Johnson, Henry, 175
Johnson, Mordecai, iii, 18, 159n., 229, 232, 235n., 237, 240, 244n., 246, 247, 248, 249, 250

Langston, John Mercer, 92, 98, 131, 143n., 144, 291
Library of Congress, 157, 247n.
Lightfoot, George M., 112, 218, 219n., 283
Lincoln, Abraham, 21, 22, 23, 38
Locke, Alain, iii, 156, 193, 199, 215, 217, 251, 256, 277, 296

Logan, Rayford, 156n., 160, 187, 189n., 191, 233, 234n., 242n., 247n., 273
Loving, Walter Howard, 165, 166, 168, 169n., 309
M Street High School, 86, 87, 111, 165n., 194n., 291
McCurdy, L. M., 36, 37, 38, 39
Military Intelligence Section, 164, 165
Miller, Adam, 52, 53, 68
Miller, Elizabeth, 25, 29, 31, 34, 45, 50, 70, 239, 290
Miller, Kelly Sr. (Big Kelly), 25, 31, 34, 46, 47, 70
Miller, Isaac, Sr., vi, 145, 146, 147, 292
Miller, Isaac, Jr., 25, 35, 53, 73
Miller, Irene, 31, 153, 292
Miller, May, vi, xii, 31, 147, 148, 149, 150, 152n., 285, 309
Miller, Millie, 41, 42
Miller, Paul Butler, 153, 292
Miller, Robert, 268, 269, 270, 271, 272n.
Moorland, Jesse, ii, 3, 157, 159n., 160n.
Moorland Spingarn Research Center, ii, iv, v, 3, 5n., 159, 195, 309
Moton, Robert Russa, 175, 237

National Association for the Advancement of Colored People (NAACP), 164n., 195, 209n., 211, 261, 283n., 293

National Negro Library and Museum, 3, 156, 157, 158, 159
National Non-Partisan Negro Conference and League, 259, 260
National Training School for Women and Girls, 137
Negro Sanhedrin, iii, 4, 18, 204-207, 208n., 209n., 211, 214n., 216, 217, 283n., 286
New Deal, the, 13, 249, 263, 266, 267
New Negro, the, 156n., 199
New Negro era, 204
Newman, Stephan M., 107, 179
Non-Partisan League (NPL), 259, 262, 283n.

Pan-African Congress, 214
Presbyterian Church, 22, 24, 54, 61, 62n., 68, 73, 87n., 302
Prillerman, Byrd, iii, 149, 150n., 152
Putman, Herbert, 157

Randolph, A. Philip, 187
Rankin, Andrew, 189, 274, 296
Rankin, Jeremiah, 88, 129
Reconstruction, xii, 2n., 3, 24, 25, 31, 38, 46, 58, 89, 132, 162, 202, 259
Red Scare, 190
Red Summer, 190, 204, 205, 213
Richardson, Willard, 5, 17, 52, 60, 61, 62n., 63, 64, 66, 68, 69
Roberts, Needham, 175

Roosevelt, Franklin D., 13, 103, 104, 127, 177, 249, 253, 258-267
Schomburg Research Center, i, ii, iii, 160
Schomburg, Arthur, 160
Smoot, Reed, 190, 191
Spingarn, Joel Elias, 164, 178, 179, 180, 181, 309

Terrell, Mary Church, v, 4, 92, 111, 134, 135, 136, 137n., 139, 277, 286, 287n.
Thirkeld, Wilbur, 105, 106
Thomas, Neval Hollen, 194, 195
Townley, Arthur Charles (A.C.), 259
Tuskegee Institute, iii, 5, 6, 14, 100, 204

Universal Negro Improvement Association (UNIA), 6, 204, 214
Urban League, 222, 278, 282n.

Washington, Booker T., iii, viii, x, 4, 6, 14, 92, 93-107, 148, 150n., 232, 291
Wesley, Charles H., 158, 159, 277
Wilson, Woodrow, 2, 3n., 13, 128, 169n., 175, 176, 178n., 183
Wood, Leonard, 180
Woodson, Carter G., 4, 87n., 92, 111, 128, 129n., 182n., 277

World War I, xii, 4, 17, 133n., 145, 161, 164n., 169n., 184n., 188, 213

www.ingramcontent.com/pod-product-compliance
Lightning Source LLC
Chambersburg PA
CBHW070047080526
44586CB00013B/950